HUMAN ACTION
IN THOMAS AQUINAS,
JOHN DUNS SCOTUS &
WILLIAM OF OCKHAM

HUMAN ACTION

IN THOMAS AQUINAS,

JOHN DUNS SCOTUS &

WILLIAM OF OCKHAM

THOMAS M. OSBORNE JR.

The Catholic University of America Press
Washington, D.C.

Cataloging-in-Publication Data
available from the Library of Congress
CLOTH ISBN: 978-0-8132-2178-6
PAPER ISBN: 978-0-8132-2874-7

In piam memoriam

REVERENDI EDUARDI PATRICII MAHONEY

CONTENTS

Acknowledgments   ix

A Note on the Texts   xi

Introduction   xiii

1. CAUSES OF THE ACT   1

Thomas Aquinas   5

John Duns Scotus   19

William of Ockham   44

Trajectory of the Positions   56

2. PRACTICAL REASON   61

Thomas Aquinas   64

John Duns Scotus   80

William of Ockham   91

Practical Knowledge, Prudence, and
the Practical Syllogism   103

3. THE STAGES OF THE ACT   109

The Aristotelian Background   110

Thomas Aquinas   113

John Duns Scotus and William of Ockham   132

Additions and Changes to Aristotle   145

4. EVALUATION AND SPECIFICATION OF THE ACT 149

Thomas Aquinas   154

John Duns Scotus   166

William of Ockham   175

Object, End, Circumstances   182

5. INDIFFERENT, GOOD, AND MERITORIOUS ACTS 185

Natural and Moral Goodness   186

Morally Good, Bad, and Indifferent   192

Merit, Demerit, and Indifference to Merit   200

The Shift to the Interior Act   218

CONCLUSION 221

Bibliography   229

Index   247

ACKNOWLEDGMENTS

This book has its proximate origin during a 2009–2010 sabbatical at the Thomas-Institut, University of Cologne, which was funded by an Alexander von Humboldt Fellowship for Experienced Researchers. I owe special gratitude to Andreas Speer, the director of the Thomas-Institut, and to the Alexander von Humboldt Foundation. I profited from my interaction with the many fine scholars at the Thomas-Institut, including but not limited to Guy Guldentops, Thomas Jeschke, Smilen Markov, Maxime Mauriège, and Ubaldo Villani-Lubelli. Wolfram Klatt, the librarian, was extraordinarily generous to me.

Timothy Noone, Peter Eardley, Jeffrey Brouwer, and Tobias Hoffmann were generous with their advice. Many colleagues at the Center of Thomistic Studies at the University of St. Thomas, including especially Steven Jensen and Rollen Edward Houser, gave encouragement and correction. Steven Jensen assisted me both through discussion and by making remarks on the entire text. Two students, Charles Robertson and John Macias, provided much-needed help with the manuscript. The anonymous readers caught several mistakes and infelicities and gave many suggestions for improvement.

A Note on the Texts

For Thomas Aquinas, when possible I cite the incomplete Leonine edition of his *Opera Omnia* (Rome: Commisio Leonina, 1884–). The reader will see in the notes "Leonine," with the volume and page numbers. Since the Leonine edition of Thomas Aquinas's *Summa Theologiae* has been reprinted and sometimes improved in a variety of editions, I follow scholarly convention by merely citing the text divisions, and abbreviate the title as "S.T." The current edition of his Sentence Commentary is the *Scriptum super libros sententiarum*, edited by Pierre Mandonnet and M. F. Moos, 4 vols. (Paris: Lethielleux, 1927–1947). I cite vols. 1–2 as "Mandonnet" and vols. 3–4 as "Moos."

The critical edition of John Duns Scotus's philosophical works is complete, in *Opera Philosophica*, edited by Girard Etzkorn et al., 5 vols. (St. Bonaventure, N.Y.: Franciscan Institute, 1997–2006). I abbreviate this edition as "OPh." For his theological works, when available I cite the incomplete Vatican edition of his *Opera Omnia*, edited by the Scotistic Commission (Vatican City: Typis Polyglottis Vaticanis, 1950–). I abbreviate this edition as "Vat." For his unedited theological works, I use *Opera Omnia*, edited by Luke Wadding (Lyons: Laurentius Durandus, 1639; repr. Georg Olms: Hildesheim, 1968). This edition is abbreviated as "Wadding ed."

There is an excellent critical edition of both Ockham's' philosophical and theological works: *Guillelmi de Ockham opera philosophica et theologica*, edited by Gedeon Gál et al. (St. Bonaventure, N.Y.: Franciscan Institute); *Opera philosophica*, 7 vols. (1974–1986); *Opera theologica*, 10 vols. (1967–1986). I abbreviate "*Opera philosophica*" as "OPh" and "*Opera theologica*" as "OTh."

Some readers may wish to consult translations of the texts that are cited in the footnotes. The many English translations of Thomas Aquinas are listed in Gilles Emery, "A Brief Catalogue of the Works of Thomas Aquinas," in Jean-Pierre Torrell, *Saint Thomas Aquinas: The Person and His Work*, rev. ed. (Washington, D.C.: The Catholic University of America Press, 2005), 330–61, 424–38. I cite many texts from Scotus and Ockham that have not been published in translation. But important texts from Scotus in Latin and English can be found in Allan Wolter, trans., *Duns Scotus on the Will and Morality* (Washington, D.C.: The Catholic University of America Press, 1986). William A. Frank slightly revised this book as an English-only edition, which was republished by the same press in 1997. Unfortunately, neither edition has a comprehensive list of the included texts. A list of Scotus's texts in English translation can be found in Thomas Williams, ed., *The Cambridge Companion to Scotus* (Cambridge: Cambridge University Press, 2003), xv–xvi. Some of Ockham's texts can be found in William of Ockham, *Quodlibetal Questions*, 2 vols., trans. Alfred J. Freddoso and Francis E. Kelley (New Haven, Conn.: Yale University Press, 1991); Rega Wood, ed. and trans., *Ockham on the Virtues* (West Lafayette, Ind.: Purdue University Press, 1997). Wood translates Ockham's *Quaestiones Variae*, q. 7 *"De connexione virtutum"* (OTh 8, 321–407).

INTRODUCTION

This book covers the basic theories of actions that are developed by Thomas Aquinas, John Duns Scotus, and William of Ockham. These three figures are arguably the three most significant philosophers and theologians of the central period in the development of Scholastic thought. Thomas Aquinas, along with his teacher Albert the Great, was instrumental in the reception of Aristotle's *Nicomachean Ethics*, which had been introduced to the Latin West in the early thirteenth century. Scotus and Ockham were part of a later theological tradition that accepted the authority of Aristotle's *corpus* as unproblematic. At about the same time as Aristotle's works began to be introduced, the Latin Church placed a new emphasis on the Sacrament of Penance and the importance of training priests to be confessors. Thomas, Scotus, and Ockham worked in the context of a new moral theology that placed an emphasis on the description and evaluation of particular acts. The thirteenth and fourteenth centuries were pivotal for the development of new philosophies of action that could be used in this context.

Later theological schools transmitted these developments to the later medieval and early modern thinkers. Even if Aquinas, Scotus, and Ockham were not the most significant thinkers of the Middle Ages, they would still be the most influential Scholastic thinkers on account of the later importance of Thomism, Scotism, and even a kind of Ockhamist or Nominalistic theology. Thomism was probably the school with the earliest development and greatest coherence.[1] Although Thomas was important within and without the Domini-

1. Romanus Cessario, *A Short History of Thomism* (Washington, D.C.: The Catholic University of America Press, 2005).

can Order even from the time of his death, from the fifteenth century through the late eighteenth century his writings were expounded and defended by a host of commentators.

Similarly, Scotus had great influence early on and eventually became the most important theologian for Franciscans as a whole. Scotus's influence can be seen in the establishment of Scotistic chairs in medieval universities and in the decrees of the sixteenth-century Council of Trent.[2] The influence of Polish Scotists led to the rise of Scotism even in Lithuania.[3] Scotism was developed into a system by the seventeenth- and eighteenth-century Scotists in France, Spain, and Italy.[4] During this later period, it has been suggested that Scotists might have been more numerous and important than the Thomists. Some scholars even think that Scotus and Scotism greatly influenced Reformed theologians.[5]

2. Maarten J. F. M. Hoenen, "Scotus and the Scotist School: The Tradition of Scotist Thought in the Medieval and Early Modern Period," in *John Duns Scotus: Renewal of Philosophy*, Acts of the Third Symposium Organized by the Dutch Society for Medieval Philosophy Medium Aevum, May 23 and 24, 1996, ed. E. P. Bos, *Elementa* 72 (1998): 197–210; Isaac Vazquez, "La Enseña del Escotismo en España," in *De doctrina Ioannis Duns Scoti*, Acta Congressus Scotistici Internationalis 11–17 Sept. 1966, Studia Scholastico-Scotistica 4, vol. 4: *Scotismus de cursu saeculorum* (Rome, Societas Internationalis Scotistica,1968), 191–220; Valens Heynck, "Der Einfluss des Skotismus auf dem Konzil von Trient (Bonaventura Pio da Constacciaro, OFM Conv., Der Führer der Skotischen Gruppe in der Ersten Tagungsperiode, 1535–1547)," in *De doctrina Ioannis Scoti*, 4.259–90; Heiko Augustinus Oberman, "Duns Scotus, Nominalism, and the Council of Trent," in *John Duns Scotus, 1265–1965*, ed. John K. Ryan and Bernardine M. Bonansea, Studies in Philosophy and the History of Philosophy 3 (Washington, D.C.: The Catholic University of America Press, 1965), 311–44.

3. Viktoras Gidziunas, "Scotism and Scotists in Lithuania," in *De doctrina Ioannis Scoti*, 4.239–48.

4. Vazquez, "La Enseña"; Benignus Millett, "Irish Scotists at St. Isidore's College, Rome, in the Seventeenth Century," in *De doctrina Ioannis Duns Scoti*, 4.399–419; Jacob Schmutz, "Le petit scotisme du Grand Siècle: Étude doctrinale et documentaire sur la philosophie au Grand Couvent des Cordeliers de Paris, 1517–1771," *Quaestio* 8 (2008): 365–472.

5. See the discussion and texts menioned in J. Beck and A. Vos, "Conceptual Patterns Related to Reformed Scholasticism," *Tijdschrift* 57 (2003): 224–33, as well as a dissenting view in Richard Muller, "The 'Reception of Calvin' in Later Reformed Theology: Concluding Thoughts," *Church History and Religious Culture* 91 (2011): 257–60.

As a general rule, in many periods and locations, Dominicans would learn Thomism and Franciscans would learn Scotism. By the sixteenth century, however, there were also important Thomists who belonged to no religious order or to other orders, such as the Augustinians, Benedictines, Carmelites, Mercedarians, and Jesuits.[6] Official Scotism did not spread as much in this way outside its original home among the Franciscans, but the Scotistic influence was also present through the influence of Scotistic philosophical terms and theses on the wider philosophical and theological community.[7]

There is less evidence for an Ockhamist school with a similar devotion to its founder's writings.[8] Nevertheless, in the fourteenth century Ockham's views at least were a principal influence behind a "Nominalist" via moderna alternative to the via antiqua that was represented by earlier thinkers such as Thomas and Scotus. By the fifteenth century a distinctive Ockhamist school developed, which included many influential theologians such as Gabriel Biel.[9] Much Reformation theology developed as a result of and in reaction to these theologians.[10] Even though Ockham's influence on the early modern period cannot always be easily tracked by looking for self-described Ockhamists, his

6. Leonard Kennedy, *A Catalogue of Thomists, 1270–1900* (Houston, Texas: Center for Thomistic Studies, 1987).

7. Jakob Schmutz, "L'héritage des subtils cartographie du Scotisme du l'Âge Classique," *Les Études philosophiques* 1 (2002): 51–81.

8. William J. Courtenay, *Ockham and Ockhamism: Studies in the Dissemination and Impact of His Thought*, Studien und Texte zur Geistesgeschichte des Mittelalters 99 (Leiden/Boston: Brill, 2008); Idem, "The Academic and Intellectual Worlds of Ockham," in *The Cambridge Companion to Ockham*, ed. Paul Vincent Spade (Cambridge: Cambridge University Press, 1999), 28–29; Zenon Kaluza, *Les querelles doctrinales à Paris: Nominalistes et réalistes aux confins du xive et du xve siècles* (Bergamo: Lubrina, 1988). The importance of Ockam is emphasized in Rega Wood, "Introduction" to Eadem, trans., *Ockham on the Virtues* (West Lafayette, Ind.: Purdue University Press, 1997), 12–18.

9. Heiko Augustinus Oberman, *The Harvest of Medieval Theology: Gabriel Biel and Late Medieval Nominalism* (Cambridge, Mass.: Harvard University Press, 1963).

10. Thomas M. Osborne Jr., "Faith, Philosophy, and Nominalism in Luther's Defense of the Real Presence," *Journal of the History of Ideas* 64 (2002): 63–82; Graham White, *Luther as Nominalist: A Study of the Logical Methods Used in Martin Luther's Disputations in the Light of Their Medieval Background* (Helsinki: Luther-Agricola-Society, 1994).

influence on late medieval theology was so fundamental that in one way or another Ockhamist views made a mark on early modern philosophy.

Consequently, Thomas, Scotus, and Ockham are each important, both for their own philosophical work and for their influence on Western thought. Each thinker's moral psychology has been subject to extended scholarly scrutiny with respect to its internal coherence or structure and immediate historical context. Without neglecting the contributions of now more obscure medieval theologians, it seems to me appropriate to consider the moral psychology of these three major thinkers in comparison to each other. Although some notice is taken of contemporary scholarship and philosophy, this book's focus is on the medieval issues. The topics include the causation of the act by the intellect and the will, the nature of practical reason, the stages of human act, its specification, and its evaluation. Its contents roughly follow the order of Thomas Aquinas's discussion of human action in the *Prima Secundae* of his *Summa Theologiae,* qq. 6–21, which is the only systematic full treatment of human action given by any of the three thinkers. The footnotes include references to the most recent scholarly literature and to the most valuable scholarship from the middle of the twentieth century. This book should be valuable to those who wish to have an overview of the various medieval issues and those who wish to understand better the historical background to Reformation theology and early modern philosophy. Apart from its historical importance, a comparison of the different medieval figures with each other sheds light on the important philosophical issues that are developed by each figure.

The differences between Thomas, Scotus, and Ockham are embedded in the context of a wider agreement over the nature of rationality, the existence of the will, and versions of Christian Aristotelianism. In many respects, they share certain beliefs that distinguish them from both ancient and contemporary philosophers. For instance, their understanding of reasons for action sets them apart from many later philosophers and their concept of the will sets them apart from many ancient philosophers. With respect to practical rationality, like many

ancient philosophers and unlike many contemporary philos
all three think that good actions are rational and that it is irratic
sin. Moreover, they think that good reasons are sufficient to mou
human action, given that the intellect is always accompanied by an
intellectual appetite, namely the will. Although nonrational desires
can influence human action, they are often unnecessary and always
at least insufficient explanations of distinctively human acts. They
do not consider the modern view that humans can be moved to action only on account of some further nonrational desire or passion.[11]
Moreover, all three quote Aristotle as an authority in ethics. More importantly, all of them agree on the inerrancy of biblical revelation and
the importance of Church Fathers such as Augustine.

The belief that the will as a faculty or power plays an explanatory
role perhaps sets medieval thinkers apart from most if not all ancient
philosophers.[12] Whereas many ancient thinkers held that reason and
passion are alternative sources for action, medieval thinkers hold that
the agent has an underlying rational faculty that chooses between
different alternatives. Although Scotus, Thomas, and Ockham disagree about the will's nature and how it causes acts, they agree that
there is such a faculty. Even though this focus on the will at least on
the surface distinguishes these thinkers from Aristotle, they generally
do not recognize the possible extent of their difference from Aristotle
and other ancient philosophers.

Unlike contemporary consequentialists, Thomas, Scotus, and Ockham all think that some actions are intrinsically wrong, and they generally agree on which actions are so. For them this view is unproblem-

11. Philippa Foot, "Locke, Hume, and Modern Moral Theory: A Legacy of Seven-
teenth- and Eighteenth-Century Philosophies of Mind," in *Moral Dilemmas* (Oxford:
Clarendon Press, 2002), 116–43.

12. Albrecht Dihle, *The Theory of the Will in Classical Antiquity* (Berkeley and Los
Angeles: University of California Press, 1982). For discussions of Dihle's treatment of
this point, see Charles Kahn, "Discovering the Will: From Aristotle to Augustine," in
The Question of Eclecticism: Studies in Later Greek Philosophy, ed. John M. Dillon and
A. A. Long (Berkeley and Los Angeles: University of California Press, 1988), 236–38;
Alasdair MacIntyre, review of *The Theory of the Will in Classical Antiquity*, by Albrecht
Dihle, in *Ancient Philosophy* 6 (1986): 242–45.

atic, since, as shall be shown, this belief is reflected in Aristotle and in the Bible, as well as in earlier medieval theology. Consequently, there are often only minor differences between them concerning what should or should not be done. For instance, all of them agree that it is impossible to rightly murder, commit adultery, lie, fornicate, or hate God. This agreement means that there is less of an appeal to particular cases in order to settle philosophical disputes. Contemporary Kantians and Consequentialists might argue over which moral intuitions should prevail in a particular case in which someone needs to shoot an innocent person to save the lives of others. The particular instance is used to illustrate the wider differences. In contrast, such an example does nothing to explain the differences between Thomas, Scotus, and Ockham. All of them agree that such an instance is murder and consequently unjustifiable. The real difference is in such issues as how it can be known to be bad, how this knowledge affects action, why the successful murder is worse than the unsuccessful one, and whether God could make such an act morally good or even meritorious. But none disagree about the act's badness.

Despite their many shared assumptions, significant differences between their historical contexts make it difficult to compare them with each other. They each belonged to a different generation of Scholastic theologians, and Thomas belonged to a different religious order. Each generation and order had its own distinct sets of issues and its own understanding of which theologians were most significant. Thomas wrote and taught during the period in which Aristotle was being fully incorporated into Latin theology. His concern was with the incorporation of the Aristotelian corpus into an already existing early Scholastic tradition, based in part on Augustine's Latin writings, as well as on some more newly introduced Greek theologians such as John Damascene. In contrast, Scotus and Ockham worked in the context of a more fully developed Franciscan Scholastic tradition. This tradition was aware of Thomas's thought and often critical of it, but its targets and concerns were often developed by its own theologians and important secular theologians such as Henry of Ghent. In Scotus's mind, Henry seems to be more important than Thomas Aquinas.

In the context of human action, the Franciscans were generally sympathetic to the bishop of Paris's 1277 condemnation of some views held by members of the Arts Faculty and perhaps even by theologians such as Thomas Aquinas. But in this area as well as others Scotus is more concerned to criticize other figures than to correct Thomas. Similarly, although Ockham is a Franciscan and often discusses Scotus's views, he is also concerned with Thomas Aquinas, Henry of Ghent, and his own contemporaries. These different historical contexts make it difficult to relate the views of the different figures. Scotus usually does not compare his own views with those of Thomas, and Ockham was not primarily concerned with either Thomas or Scotus. Although many recent scholars have considered Thomas and Scotus as figures who tower above their contemporaries, many or most thinkers at the time did not have this perspective. Even if it were desirable to do so, it would be impossible to compare the views of Scotus and Ockham with Thomas by always looking at their own accounts of their disagreements with him.

The various kinds of text also make it problematic to consider the differences between Thomas, Scotus, and Ockham. Thomas wrote a lot, and much of his work was on moral psychology and moral theory. Thomas was the only one of the three figures to write a commentary on Aristotle's *Nicomachean Ethics*. One of the *Summa Theologiae*'s primary purposes seems to be instruction in moral theology. Consequently, Thomas gives a full discussion of every area of moral psychology that was important at the time, and his discussions vary depending on the genre and period in which he writes. I have tried to mention possible developments and differences between Thomas's texts, but my main attempt is to give a more systematic account of his views.

Scotus did not write as much on moral psychology. Moreover, his discussions of it are less systematic, often arising in connection with particular problems. The main sources are at least three different *Sentence* commentaries and his Quodlibetal Questions.[13] He seems to have

13. Allan B. Wolter, "Reflections on the Life and Works of Scotus," *American Catholic Philosophical Quarterly* 67 (1993): 1–36; Thomas Williams, "Introduction" to *The*

lectured on the *Sentences* at least twice, once at Oxford and later at Paris. His earliest Oxford *Lectura* on the *Sentences* is now in a critical edition but does not include the commentary on Book IV of the *Sentences*. His *Ordinatio* is his incomplete revision of these early lectures, and may reflect his most mature opinion. At this present moment there is a critical edition up through the beginning of Book IV. There are several later *Reportationes* of his Paris lectures.[14] The current scholarly view is that these "Reportationes" are based on students' records of lectures. They generally provide a good indication of what was taught, and some were even looked over *(examinata)* by the teacher before publication. In the seventeenth century, Luke Wadding published particular *Reportationes* for Books III and IV. Some scholars now believe that for Books I and II he mistakenly printed William of Alnwick's *Additiones Magnae,* which are believed to express Scotus's thought even though they may not be verbatim reports of Scotus's teaching. The attribution of "authorship" to William is far from certain. These different records of the Paris lectures often contain views that are at odds with those expressed in the *Ordinatio,* and they may express Scotus's more mature thought. It is fairly certain that when the Scotistic Commission, which edits Scotus's *Opera theologica,* publishes the *Reportationes,* there will be new and different opinions about these works. When discussing Scotus's views, it is often necessary to consider a variety of his texts, some of which are have not been published in critical editions. Moreover, some seem to be in conflict with each other. I address these problems when necessary.

There is a complete critical edition of William of Ockham's theological and philosophical works. Unfortunately, many of these works survived only as *Reportationes,* and his *Sentence* Commentary is incomplete. But he also discusses moral psychology in many of his Quodlibetal Questions, as well as in some "miscellaneous notes" that

---

Cambridge Companion to Scotus, ed. Thomas Williams (Cambridge: Cambridge University Press, 2003), 1–14.

14. The best recently published discussion is Barnaba Hechich, "Il Problema delle 'Reportationes' nell' Eredità Dottrina del B. Giovanni Duns Scotus, OFM," in *Giovani Duns Scoto: Studi e ricerche nel VII Centenario della sua morte,* ed. Marin Carbajo Nunez (Rome: Antonianum, 2008), 59–129. But scholarly opinion continues to evolve.

have been preserved.[15] Ockham does address some moral issues in his later political works, but the relationship between the academic and political works is unclear, and Ockham's intention in the later works can also be obscure.[16] Consequently, I cite the academic works.

These textual differences should be kept in mind. Thomas develops his views at length in often more than one text. In context, Scotus's texts are often slightly different variations on the same theme, and his discussions can seem ad hoc. Since Ockham wrote much less, it can be hard to determine the exact nature of his contribution to some issues. This problem clearly affects chapter 3's discussion of the act's stages. Thomas's *Prima Secundae* includes an extended discussion of many acts of the will, including intention, consent, and choice. In contrast, Scotus's discussion of these issues occurs as an ad hoc discussion in several *Sentence* commentaries that belong to different periods. Most of Ockham's discussions are very brief, although there is one somewhat lengthy aside in his commentary on the *Sentences*'s prologue. Chapter 3 would look very different if Thomas had not written the *Prima Secundae,* or if Scotus or Ockham had written sustained discussions of an act's stages. Nevertheless, I have attempted to provide a more equal account of the three figures, even though there is such disparity in the length and number of relevant texts.

The scholarly literature is also unequal. The amount of scholarly literature on Thomas far exceeds that on Scotus and Ockham together. In contrast, there are a limited number of monographs on Scotus's moral psychology, and only a few monographs that touch on Ockham's moral psychology. Similarly, there are far fewer articles on Scotus and Ockham. Moreover, the scholarly literature more evenly covers Thomas's entire moral psychology. Scholarly literature on Scotus focuses mostly on the will, synchronic contingency, and happiness, although there are also discussions of the connection of the virtues, the Decalogue, and merit. But there is little material on Scotus's positions concerning practical reasoning, the relationship between choice

15. Paul Vincent Spade, "Introduction" to *The Cambridge Companion to Ockham,* 6–7.

16. Courtenay, "Academic and Intellectual Worlds," 26–28.

and deliberation, or his understanding of the moral object. Although I address the secondary literature, this book is organized more according to the issues than to previous scholarly discussions. Some views that are emphasized in the scholarly literature will be mentioned only in passing, and some issues discussed at length are almost absent from this literature.

The book develops thematically. Chapter 1 is on the causation of the act. It focuses on the way in which both the known object and the will cause an act. According to Thomas, the known object is a final cause and the will is an efficient cause of the act. This attribution of different roles to the intellect and will shows that for Thomas each faculty has its own role in each stage of the act. Scotus usually describes the known object as a partial efficient cause of the act, and Ockham more carefully states that the act of understanding plays the same causal role. Ockham agrees with one presentation of Scotus's position that the known object is a partial cause, but he disagrees with Scotus's belief that the known object's subordinate role explains how the volitions can be free. For Ockham, freedom includes the ability to will for or against the same known object.

Chapter 2 is on practical reasoning. Its focus is on the nature of practical knowledge and the role of the practical syllogism in human action. Thomas thinks that there are degrees of practical knowledge. Prudence differs from moral science because it immediately directs action. A fully practical syllogism's conclusion is the judgment of choice, which is the cognitive element accompanying the will's act of choice. Scotus thinks that choice occurs after an action has been presented to the will by the intellect. Prudence is closer to action simply because it is less universal. Ockham thinks that directive knowledge is distinct from speculative knowledge because its conclusions dictate action. The practical syllogism of prudence concludes in a statement such as "This house should be built." The agent is free to accept or reject the conclusion.

Chapter 3 discusses the act's stages. Thomas draws on a variety of sources to analyze the act into many stages. The principal stages are simple willing and choice. Although they produce different acts, the intellect and will always work together. For Scotus, there are fewer acts of the will, although he thinks that there are two kinds of choice. One follows deliberation whereas the other occurs without it. The will and the intellect have more independence from each other. Like Thomas, Ockham gives a schema of the act's stages. But he lists fewer stages. He also seems to think that these stages are discrete acts. In many respects, his account of the act's stages resembles Scotus's account of those acts that follow from deliberation.

Chapter 4 considers the act's object and morally relevant circumstances, including the end. Thomas gives the most sophisticated account, according to which the proximate end is the object, and the same matter can be considered either as the object of the exterior act or as the end of the interior act. Scotus thinks that the distinction between the object and the end is sharper, and he even thinks that some acts can be willed apart from any morally relevant end. Ockham gives a new account of the interior act, according to which morally relevant features belong to the object. Ockham transforms the circumstances that are separated from the object in the earlier tradition into either (1) morally relevant features of a merely physical act, or (2) secondary partial objects.

Chapter 5 is on the act's evaluation. Thomas thinks that there are no morally indifferent acts. Acts are indifferent to merit only if they are morally good and performed by someone who lacks charity and is consequently unable to merit. For Thomas, merit results from God's free decision to make some acts meritorious, but the grace that he gives somehow makes the act intrinsically worthy of merit. For Scotus, some acts are morally indifferent because they are directed to no morally worthy end. Similarly, anyone can perform good acts that are indifferent to merit, since these acts can be performed without being directed to God. Scotus thinks that merit consists in the relation whereby the act is acceptable to God and involves an order to eternal happiness. Ockham seems merely to assume that acts can be morally indifferent and indifferent to merit. Ockham defends Scotus's view that merit is forensic, and he makes the stronger claim that God could grant merit even to normally sinful acts.

The conclusion shows that although the different philosophies of action cannot be explained in terms of any one major difference or principle, there are some common themes that run through each chapter. These most notable themes are (1) a developing separation between nature and the will, (2) an increased emphasis on the will's activity, and (3) a changing view of mental causation. Although these three themes should become clearer after reading the book, a brief overview at this point might be helpful.

Thomas thinks that the natural perfection of the human being is obtained through acting in accordance with natural inclination. The will's indeterminacy makes it distinct from determined natures, but even it has a natural ordering to happiness. In his description of action, he delineates carefully the different contributions of the intellect and the will in the production of one free human act. They are different kinds of causes. The intellect is involved with formal and final causality, whereas the will efficiently causes the act. Similarly, the act has stages in which the activities of the will and intellect are often necessarily connected. Thomas thinks that the "exterior" or willed act forms one act with the interior act of the will and intellect, and has its value mostly insofar as it is united to the will's act. Thomas incorporates the medieval notion of the will into a more explicitly Aristotelian framework that is based on the cooperation of appetition and knowledge, and places great value on natural teleology.

Scotus separates the ability to choose the just from the natural inclination of the will, which like other natural inclinations is directed to the individual's own advantage. He focuses much more on the role of the will in human action, and provides a less complicated account of how the will and the intellect interact. Scotus frequently but not always states that both the known object and the will are efficient causes of the human act. He tries to ensure the primacy of the will by subordinating the known object's efficient causality to that of the will. For Scotus, although the source of moral worth is the will, the exterior act produced by the will has its own goodness or badness. He holds that the interior act of the will causes a separate exterior act.

In many ways Ockham's view of human action separates him from his predecessors, but especially in his understanding of free will and the structure of the act. Unlike Scotus and Thomas, Ockham does not give a role to the will's natural tendencies. Although Ockham agrees with his predecessors that it is easier for the will to go along with the passions, he states that the will can will for or against anything. Ockham's account of human action separates practical reasoning from willing. They are distinct activities that contribute to or form part of the human act. Even though Ockham rejects Scotus's view that the exterior act has its own moral worth, but he does this because he severs the exterior or commanded act from the act of the will. Ockham's focus is almost entirely on interior will acts. This focus on the interior act of an unlimited free will foreshadows some elements in modern moral philosophy.

Even though the differences are rooted and more understandable in the detailed arguments and positions, these broader themes should be kept in mind, both for signifying the general approach of each author and for understanding the influence of these authors on later thought.

HUMAN ACTION
IN THOMAS AQUINAS,
JOHN DUNS SCOTUS &
WILLIAM OF OCKHAM

1

Causes of the Act

Thomas Aquinas, John Duns Scotus, and William of Ockham all discuss the relationship between cognition and willing in the context of how a human act is caused. In this context, a *cause* is something that plays an explanatory role in the effect's production and is in some sense a source of the effect's existence. They use the term "cause" in a variety of ways, although each way indicates an explanation for why the effect exists in a particular manner or even at all. It is important to recognize that the medieval understanding of causality differs greatly from many accounts in contemporary philosophy, according to which causal events are analyzed in terms of causal properties, laws, and relations.[1] Medieval accounts of human action also differ from other contemporary accounts that are concerned primarily with mental states that are necessary or sufficient for a production of an action.[2] Medieval thinkers generally understand causation in terms of

1. There are some exceptions. See Thomas M. Osborne Jr., "Rethinking Anscombe on Causation," *American Catholic Philosophical Quarterly* 81 (2007): 89–107. For relevant medieval views on causation, see especially Marilyn Adams, *William Ockham*, 2 vols. (Notre Dame, Ind.: University of Notre Dame Press, 1987), 741–98; Stephen L. Brock, "Causality and Necessity in Thomas Aquinas," *Quaestio* 2 (2002): 217–40; Aurélien Robert, "L'explication causale selon Guillaume d'Ockham," *Quaestio* 2 (2002): 241–65.

2. For discussions in the context of Thomas Aquinas, see especially Stephen L.

the capacities and activities of agents, and they are not preoccupied with causal laws. In many respects, their understanding of causation is closer to that found in our everyday use of causal language, as opposed to contemporary philosophical and scientific use.

Although the three thinkers differ in their description of causation, they more or less follow a broadly Aristotelian model with a schema of four causes, which can be briefly illustrated in the case of a statue. Two causes are internal, namely the formal and the material. The formal cause is the statue's shape, whereas the material cause is the material of the statue, such as bronze. Two causes are external, namely the efficient and the final. The sculptor is the efficient cause, whereas the completed statue and further purposes of the sculptor are final causes. Medieval debates over the causation of human action primarily address the action's efficient and final causes, and the relationships between these two causes.

Since human acts are contingent, they cannot be necessitated by their causes. All three thinkers agree that human acts are free and contingent, and that it is easy to know that human acts are so.[3] The main difference between the thinkers rests in the explanation of how human acts are free and contingent. There is a disagreement among the authors concerning the extent or at least the explanation of contingency in nonrational creatures. According to Scotus, contingency in created beings is ultimately explainable by the freedom of God's will.[4] Ockham agrees with Scotus that contingency is rooted in free

---

Brock, *Action and Conduct: Thomas Aquinas and the Theory of Action* (Edinburgh: T & T Clark, 1998), 49–196; Anthony Kenny, *Aquinas on Mind* (London: New York: Routledge, 1993), 59–88, esp. 84–88. For the relevant problems in the contemporary context, see P. M. S. Hacker, *Mind and Will, Volume 4 of an Analytical Commentary on the Philosophical Investigations*, part 1 (Oxford: Blackwell, 1996), 191–259; Rosalind Hursthouse, "Intention," in *Logic, Cause and Action: Essays in Honour of Elizabeth Anscombe*, ed. Roger Teichmann (Cambridge: Cambridge University Press, 2000), 83–105.

3. Among many passages, see Thomas, *De Malo*, q. 6, resp. (Leonine, 23.141–42); Scotus, *Quaestiones super libros metaphysicorum Aristotelis*, lib. 9, q. 15 (OPh, 4.682–83); William of Ockham, Quod 1, q. 16 (OTh, 1.88).

4. Scotus, *Ord.* 1, d. 2, p. 1, qq. 1–2, nn. 79–87 (Vat., 2.176–79); Idem, *Ord.* 1, d. 8, p. 2, q. un., nn. 281–82 (Vat., 4.313–14); Idem, *Lect.* 1, d. 39, qq. 1–5, nn. 32–61 (Vat., 17.488–500).

will, although he stresses the created will.[5] Consequently, for both Scotus and Ockham, a contingent effect or act is either a free voluntary act or ultimately traced back to a free will. In contrast, Thomas thinks that there is much contingency in our world of generable and corruptible material things on account of their very matter.[6] For Thomas, free voluntary acts are only one kind of contingent act, and they do not explain all contingency. Thomas admits that all created causes and effects, including contingent causes and effects, can ultimately be traced back to God's free act of creation, conservation, and motion. However, according to Thomas, the contingent character of God's will does not serve to distinguish between necessary and contingent created causes and effects, or necessary and contingent creatures. They are all effects of God's free choice. Nevertheless, even though these three figures disagree over whether all contingency is explained by willing, they agree that there are contingent acts of the will.

Although many causes influence human action, the two necessary proximate causes are the human intellect and the will. If an act is not caused by the intellect and will, then it is not fully human. Although the three philosophers differ in their description of the intellect and will, they each distinguish the intellect and will in some way not only from each other, but also from those cognitive and appetitive powers that are shared with other animals. Cognitive powers differ according to the way in which the object is presented to the knower, and the appetitive powers differ according to the way in which the appetites follow a particular kind of cognition. For instance, just as dogs and cows can desire food when they have sense cognition concerning it, so can humans desire food when they see or smell it. Nevertheless, humans can also grasp goods such as food intellectually. Sense cognition and intellectual cognition differ in the way that the food is known as good. Similarly, humans have a rational appetite, according to which they desire what they recognize as good through intellectual cognition. This distinctive rational appetite is the power of the will (noun), by which humans will (verb) or choose to eat the food.

---

5. Ockham, Quod 2, q. 2 (OTh, 9.116); Idem, Quod 1, q. 17 (OTh, 9.90–93).

6. Thomas, *S T.*, I, q. 115, art. 6; Idem, *Summa contra gentiles*, 3, cap. 86 (Leonine, 14.261–62).

Humans are distinctive in that they have intellects whose activity is connected to that of a human body. Animals do not have intellects. God and angels are pure intellects who are incapable of sensation. The distinctively human intellect is sometimes called "reason." Similarly, humans have an intellectual appetite that differs from that of animals in that it is intellectual, but differs from that of angels and God, who are purely intellectual. In general, will is intellectual appetite, or, as Scotus thinks, it necessarily includes the intellectual appetite. The distinctively human will is a "rational appetite," which is not only joined to the distinctive cognitive abilities of humans, but is also influenced by the various appetites that belong to or in some way accompany human sense powers, namely the sensitive passions.

The influence of these sensitive passions on the human intellect and will indicates that human action is not merely a product of a noncorporeal understanding and willing. Why is it important to focus more narrowly on certain acts of the intellect and will? Although the bodily passions and even passions of the will generally influence human action, they are not themselves direct causes of the human action, but only insofar as they in some way influence an act of willing.[7] Medieval philosophers and theologians also think that the stars influence humans through bodily changes, and consequently they affect human actions, but only indirectly through the will.[8] Moreover, they agree that habits influence and perfect actions, although they dis-

7. For the sensitive appetite, see especially Thomas, *S.T.*, I-II, q. 10, art. 3; Ibid., q. 77, art. 7; Ockham, *Q.V.*, q. 8 (OTh, 8.446–48). See also the passages and discussions in Richard Russell Baker, *The Thomistic Theory of the Passions and Their Influence upon the Will* (Notre Dame, Ind.: University of Notre Dame Press, 1941); Taina M. Holopainen, *William of Ockham's Theory of the Foundations of Ethics* (Helsinki: Luther-Agricola-Society, 1991), 26–38; Vesa Hirvonen, *Passions in William of Ockham's Philosophical Psychology*, Studies in the History and Philosophy of Mind 2 (Dordrecht/Boston/London: Kluwer, 2004), 107–40; Thomas M. Osborne Jr., "William of Ockham on the Freedom of the Will and Happiness," *American Catholic Philosophical Quarterly* 86 (2012): 443–46. For a treatment of the sensitive appetite along with the influence of habits on the will, see Scotus, *Lect.* 3, d. 33 (Vat., 21.267–96, passim); Idem, *Ord.* 3, d. 33 (Vat., 10.141–75, passim); Ockham, Quod 3, q. 22 (OTh, 9.291).

8. Thomas, *De Veritate*, q. 5, art. 9 (Leonine, 22.161–68); Idem, *S.T.*, I-II, q. 95, art. 5; John Duns Scotus, *Quaestiones super secundum et tertium De Anima* (OPh, 5.89–96); Idem, *Lect.* 2, d. 14, q. 14, n. 36 (Vat., 19.126).

agree over how habits depend on and are developed through the intellect and will.[9] Although the controversy over the production of human action centers on the intellect and will, it should not be thought that the activity of these two powers occurs in isolation from passions or habits of the will, other human powers, or even external events. But every created causal influence on a distinctively human action other than the intellect and will has causal force only indirectly through the relevant acts of the intellect and will.

THOMAS AQUINAS

According to Thomas Aquinas, the will and the intellect are two distinct powers or capacities *(potentiae)* that are distinct from each other and from the soul.[10] He gives a variety of arguments against the then common position that the soul's powers *(potentiae)* are identical with its essence.[11] For instance, he argues that since all created substances are merely in potency to various acts, there must be some other principle of operation, namely the power, in order to explain the movement from potency to act. Moreover, because the human soul is in potency to a variety of activities, it follows that there must be distinct principles for these distinct activities. For our purposes, perhaps the most interesting argument is based on the connection between the soul's powers and the body. Some powers belong to the human

9. In addition to the texts cited above, see Bonnie Kent, *Virtues of the Will: The Transformation of Ethics in the Late Thirteenth Century* (Washington, D.C.: The Catholic University of America Press, 1995).

10. For a philosophical discussion and defense, see Robert Pasnau, *Thomas Aquinas on Human Nature: A Philosophical Study of Ia 75–89* (Cambridge: Cambridge University Press, 2002), 143–70. For an attempt to coordinate Thomas's different discussions, see Lawrence Dewan, "The Real Distinction between Intellect and Will," *Angelicum* 57 (1980): 557–93, reprinted in Lawrence Dewan, *Wisdom, Law, and Virtue: Essays in Thomistic Ethics* (New York: Fordham University Press, 2008), 125–50.

11. My discussion here follows closely Thomas, *De spiritualibus creaturis*, art. 11 (Leonine, 24.2.114–23). But see also Idem, *S.T.*, I, q. 77, art. 1; Idem, *Quaestiones disputatae de anima*, q. 12 (Leonine, 24.1.105–12). For more texts and a detailed exposition, see John F. Wippel, *The Metaphysical Thought of Thomas Aquinas: From Finite Being to Uncreated Being*, Monographs of the Society for Medieval and Renaissance Philosophy 1 (Washington, D.C.: The Catholic University of America Press, 2000), 275–94.

body, such as nutrition, growth, generation, and sensation. But the intellect and will, since they do not belong to the body, must be distinct from these other powers. The distinction between the intellect and will can also be shown by the fact that they are ordered to each other. Since the will chooses an object that is shown to it by the intellect, it follows that in some way the intellect moves the will and as a mover is distinct from it. Thomas does not think that these powers are substances, or distinct "things" that can exist on their own. Nor are they ordinary accidents that exist in a substance but can be changed or taken away, as a particular color or size might be. He writes, "The powers of the soul are a medium between the essence of the soul and accidents just as natural or essential properties are; that is, they naturally follow the soul's essence."[12]

Thomas thinks that we know the powers of the soul through their operations, and the essence of the soul, or "what it is," through the powers. The metaphysical priority is reverse, as the operations belong to the powers, and the powers to the essence. The operations or acts themselves are distinguished by their objects, or what they are about.[13] For example, the act of seeing has color as its proper object, whereas sound is the proper object of hearing. For Thomas, the important distinction between intellect and sense is that sense is concerned with particular material objects, whereas intellect is concerned with objects that are immaterial at least in the sense that they are abstracted from sense.[14] For example, with sight I can see the horse "Seabiscuit." But the intellect is not concerned with Seabiscuit himself, but rather with "horseness," or what it is to be a horse. Thomas also de-

12. "potentie anime sunt medium inter essentiam anime et accidens quasi proprietates naturales uel essentiales, id est essentiam anime naturaliter consequentes"; *De spiritualibus creaturis,* art. 11, resp. (Leonine, 24.1.120).

13. Lawrence Dewan, "'Obiectum': Notes on the Invention of a Word," *Archives d'histoire doctrinale et littéraire du moyen âge* 48 (1981): 37–96, reprinted in Dewan, *Wisdom, Law, and Virtue,* 403–43.

14. Thomas, *S.T.,* I, q. 78, art. 1. See Edward P. Mahoney, "Sense, Intellect, and Imagination in Albert, Thomas, and Siger," in *The Cambridge History of Later Medieval Philosophy: From the Rediscovery of Aristotle to the Disintegration of Scholasticism: 1100–1600,* ed. Norman Kretzmann, Anthony Kenny, and Jan Pinborg (Cambridge: Cambridge University Press), 605–11; Kenny, *Aquinas on Mind,* 89–110.

scribes certain "interior" powers as senses. For instance, I can imagine the particular horse "Seabiscuit" when he is not present.

Another important distinction is between the appetitive and the cognitive powers.[15] "Cognitive" here takes a broad meaning in that it applies both to intellectual knowledge and also to the information that is grasped through sensation. For example, smelling is the cognitive power by which I obtain the sense information that enables me to judge whether a piece of bacon is rancid or not. My sense appetite reacts to the information with desire or aversion. Even nonhuman animals can know whether food is edible or not through their senses. Humans have sense appetites just as other animals do. But, since humans have intellects, they also have the intellectual appetite, which follows on the knowledge presented by the intellect.[16] This intellectual appetite is the will, and is common even to nonbodily creatures such as angels. The distinction between the will and the intellect is a distinction between an appetitive and a cognitive power. The distinction between the will and the sense appetites is a distinction between the desire or aversion for particular objects of sense, and that for objects that are apprehended by the intellect. Even when humans will some particular good, they will it insofar as it falls under some more universal aspect of goodness.[17]

Thomas's understanding of the causation of human acts rests in the mutual interaction between this appetite and the intellect.[18] Although the two powers are distinct, Thomas does not think that it is possible to have one power without the other. Every creature with an intellect can grasp the good and also will it, whether the will be the purely intellectual appetite of the angels or the intellectual but rational appetite of human beings. Every nature has a natural inclination, and the natural inclination of an intellectual substance is toward the good in general.[19]

15. Thomas, *S.T.*, I, q. 78, art. 2; Ibid., q. 79, art. 1, ad 2.

16. Thomas, *S.T.*, I, q. 80, art. 2.

17. See especially Thomas, *S.T.*, I, q. 80, art. 2, ad 2.

18. "Et pro tanto necesse est quod homo sit liberi arbitrii, ex hoc ipso quod rationalis est"; Thomas, *S.T.*, I, q. 83, art. 1.

19. Thomas, *S.T.*, I, q. 60, art. 1; *Summa contra gentiles*, 2, 46–47 (Leonine, 13.376–80).

In his early *Commentary on the Sentences,* Thomas explains how the intellect makes free choice possible in a way that includes points that are significant throughout his career.[20] He argues that only intellectual creatures are able to know the nature *(ratio)* of the end and how actions can be ordered to this end. This ability to recognize this order makes it possible to choose different acts that are within the agent's power. This ability to choose in turn explains why an intellectual creature is able to exercise control over its own acts. In this early passage are contained three themes that have been shown by David Gallagher to be present throughout Thomas's many discussions of free choice.[21] First, the indetermination of free choice results from the intellectual agent's ability to know different goods in a way that is not determined by material conditions. Second, this indetermination allows for reflection on how ends are instantiated in or achieved by means of different acts. Third, the movement to the good is controlled by the will, which moves not only the intellect but also the other powers of the soul. Nevertheless, as Thomas writes in another early work, the *De Veritate,* the "root of all liberty is constituted in reason."[22] In his much later *Prima Pars* of the *Summa Theologiae,* Thomas makes a similar statement: "Only that which has an intellect is able to act by free judgment, insofar as it knows the universal nature [*ratio*] of the good, from which it is able to judge this or that to be good."[23]

The will is free precisely because the intellect can present it with a variety of objects. This freedom is not a mere freedom from external coercion, but belongs to the will as such. Thomas does admit that the will is necessitated with respect to the ultimate end, which is happiness.[24] By its very nature the will is determined not to any particular

20. Thomas, 2 *Sent.,* d. 25, q. 1, art. 1, sol. (Mandonnet ed., 2.645).

21. David Gallagher, "Thomas Aquinas on the Will as Rational Appetite," *Journal of the History of Philosophy* 29 (1991): 559–84.

22. "totius libertatis radix est in ratione constituta"; Thomas, *De Veritate,* q. 24, art. 2 (Leonine, 22.3.685).

23. "solum id quod habet intellectum, potest agere iudicio libero, inquantum cognoscit universalem rationem boni, ex qua potest iudicare hoc vel illud esse bonum"; Thomas, *S.T.,* I, q. 59, art. 3.

24. Thomas, *De Veritate,* q. 22, art. 5–6 (Leonine, 22.3.692–96); Idem, *S.T.,* I, q. 19,

good, but to the good in general. No particular good that we k
this life is identical with happiness or with the good in genera
sequently, the agent is free with respect to choosing this or that particular good. The will's necessary desire for happiness does not ex-
clude the freedom to choose between different alternatives, especially
in this life.

In the *De Veritate*, Thomas explains three ways in which the will
is free from determination.[25] First, it is free with respect to willing
or not willing an act. The intellect may present the will with a cake
to be eaten or alms to be given, and the will can simply not choose
those particular goods that are presented to it. Nonrational creatures
lack the ability to refrain from acting. Second, the will can choose between different means or instances of happiness or the good in general.[26] Thomas often uses the phrase "ea quae sunt ad finem" to indicate such goods.[27] Often this phrase is translated as "means," but in
Thomas it is used not only to describe useful goods such as money,
but also good acts that are themselves instantiations of happiness,
such as almsgiving. This kind of indetermination is not between different bad acts, but between different truly good acts. For instance,
someone might choose to give alms to one person rather than another, or he might decide to join one religious order rather than another.
These different goods are true goods, even though these goods are
incompatible with each other. The notion of good is so general that
in our present life we are not always constrained to choose one particular good or instantiation of happiness rather than another. A third

art. 10; Idem, *S.T.*, I, q. 82, art. 1–2; Idem, *S.T.*, I-II, q. 10, art. 2. For Thomas's under-
standing of happiness, see Georg Wieland, "Happiness (IaIIae, qq. 1–5)," trans. Grant
Kaplan, in *The Ethics of Aquinas*, ed. Stephen Pope (Washington, D.C.: Georgetown
University Press, 2002), 57–68.

25. *De Veritate*, art. 6, resp. (Leonine, 22.3.627–28).

26. For a development of Thomas's point, see Colleen McCluskey, "Intellective Appetite and the Freedom of Human Action," *The Thomist* 66 (2002): 434–42. She uses
this point to partly reply to Scotus in Eadem, "Happiness and Freedom in Aquinas's
Theory of Action," *Medieval Philosophy and Theology* 9 (2000): 69–90.

27. Paul Morriset, "Prudence et fin selon saint Thomas," *Sciences ecclésiastiques*
15 (1963): 77–83.

kind of indetermination is the ability to choose goods that are merely apparent goods. This is the ability to choose evil acts. Such acts are always willed under the formality *(ratio)* of goodness, although they are not themselves good. Thomas explains that this kind of indetermination is proper to the present life. The blessed in heaven are not free to perform evil actions because they cannot choose a merely apparent and unreal good that is inconsistent with happiness. They can choose to pray for a particular person, or some other such work.

This passage shows that the indeterminacy of the will with respect to good or bad actions is not the only and most important aspect of freedom according to Thomas. There is also indeterminacy with respect to different but incompatible good actions. The important point is that insofar as the will is determined, it is not determined by the intellect but rather by its own nature, which is to will happiness and the good in general. The intellect presents the will not only with the alternative between true and false goods, but also between different and incompatible true goods. No particular good in this life completely exhausts what it means to be good, and consequently the will is indeterminate with respect to any such good. In the *Prima Pars,* Thomas explains, "Since the good is manifold, on account of this [the will] is not by necessity determined to one thing."[28]

In both the *Prima Secundae* of the *Summa Theologiae* and the *De Malo,* q. 6, Thomas carefully gives an overview of the different ways in which the will is free in eliciting an act by distinguishing between the act's exercise and specification.[29] The distinction is described more concisely in the *Prima Secundae,* q. 10, art. 2, which concerns "Whether the will is moved by its object out of necessity." Thomas writes:

The will is moved in two ways: in one way with respect to the act's exercise, in another way with respect to the act's specification, which is from the ob-

28. "Sed quia bonum est multiplex, propter hoc non ex necessitate determinatur ad unum"; Thomas, *S.T.,* I, q. 82, art. 2, ad 1.

29. "Utrum voluntas moveatur de necessitate a suo obiecto"; Thomas, *S.T.,* I-II, q. 10, art. 2. "utrum homo habeat liberam electionem suorum actuum aut ex necessitate eligat"; *De Malo,* q. 6 (Leonine, 23.145–53). See also *S.T.,* I-II, q. 9, art. 1, resp. and ad 3; *S.T.,* I-II, q. 9, art. 3, ad 3.

ject. Accordingly, in the first way the will is moved out of necessity by no object, for someone has in his power not to think about whatever the object is, and consequently not to will it actually.[30]

The act's exercise involves the will's ability to act or not to act. The freedom of exercise to will or not to will rests in the ability of the will to not think about the object. For example, if I do not will to think about eating ice cream, then I can "not will" *(non velle)* to eat the ice cream. This freedom extends to any object whatsoever.

Freedom consists not only in this ability to "not will," but also in the ability to will something else. Whereas the freedom to will or not is based on the subject of willing, namely the will itself, this other kind of freedom, namely the freedom of specification, is based on the objects that are presented to the will by the intellect. For instance, instead of thinking about ice cream, I might will to think about my figure, or even a mathematical problem. The ability to think about another object brings into view the freedom of specification, which directly involves the intellect's ability to think about alternative objects. In the same article 2, Thomas explains:

If some object that is good universally and from every point of view is proposed to the will, out of necessity the will tends to it, if it wills anything, for it cannot will the opposite. If however some object is presented to it that is not good from every point of view, the will does not respond to it out of necessity.... All other particular goods [aside from the perfect good], insofar as they are lacking some good, can be regarded as not good, and from this point of view they can be assented to or rejected by the will, which can respond to the same thing according to diverse points of view.[31]

30. "voluntas movetur dupliciter: uno modo quantum ad exercitium actus; alio modo, quantum ad specificationem actus, quod est ex objecto. Primo ergo modo, voluntas a nullo obiecto ex necessitate movetur: potest enim aliquis de quocumque obiecto non cogitare, et per consequens neque actu velle illud"; Thomas, *S.T.*, I-II, q. 10, art. 2, resp.

31. "si proponatur aliquod obiectum voluntati quod sit universaliter bonum et secundum omnem considerationem, ex necessitate voluntas in illud tendet, si aliquid vellet : non enim poterit velle oppositum. Si autem proponatur sibi aliquod obiectum quod non secundum quamlibet considerationem sit bonum, non ex necessitate fertur in illud.... Alia autem quaelibet particularia bonam, inquantum deficiunt ab aliquo bono, possunt accipi ut non bona: et secundum hanc considerationem, possunt repu-

The act's specification comes from different objects that are apprehended as good. Short of the perfect happiness of the beatific vision, no particular good is good in every respect. Consequently, this freedom extends to every possible good object that is not happiness. Consequently, there is a sense in which the will's motion is necessitated, but only with respect to (1) specification rather than exercise, and (2) an entirely good object, such as is known in the beatific vision.

A difficulty remains. Is the will free with respect to the exercise of the act in loving God in the beatific vision? This question is not concerned with the sense in which God is implicitly willed. There is a way in which, since every created good is good by some similitude of God as the first good, willing a created good is implicitly willing God.[32] Similarly, since every truth is in some way a similitude of divine truth, there is a way in which knowing a created truth is implicitly knowing God. Even every sinner implicitly wills God insofar as he is willing the good. The choice is not between implicitly loving God or not, but between different real or merely apparent created goods. This implicit willing does not present the same problem for freedom that is presented by the willing that follows on the explicit vision of God, the complete good, in the beatific vision. Nevertheless, Thomas's position on the implicit willing has an effect on his understanding of explicitly willing God. If every created good is willed insofar as it is in some way ordered to or a similitude of God, then there is something supremely desirable about God. In the beatific vision God is known in such a way that he cannot be thought of as deficient or bad.

Although we have seen that in the *Summa Theologiae*'s *Prima Secundae* Thomas claims that the will is always free with respect to exercise, regardless of the object, in the earlier *Prima Pars* of the same work Thomas had denied that someone with the beatific vision can turn his attention away from God to another object.[33] Did he mean to

---

diari vel approbari a voluntate, quae potest in idem ferri secundum diversas considerationes"; Thomas, *S.T.*, I-II, q. 10, art. 2, resp. I am indebted particularly to the translation in St. Thomas Aquinas, *Summa Theologiae*, vol. 17: *The Psychology of Human Acts*, trans. Thomas Gilby (Cambridge: Cambridge University Press, 1964), 89.

32. Thomas, *De Veritate*, q. 22, art. 2 (Leonine, 22.3.616–17).

33. Thomas, *S.T.*, I, q. 82, art. 2.

say that such a person only lacks the freedom of specification, or was he making the apparently stronger claim that for such a person there is no freedom of exercise to love God or not elicit an act of loving? Since such a person cannot turn his attention from God, it seems that he cannot refuse to love God. If he cannot refuse to love God, then in what sense is he really free? It seems to me that the important point here is that God in the beatific vision is not an object that replaces the will's self-motion. The will is moved efficiently to its exercise by its natural inclination and is not necessitated by the object except insofar as the object, namely God, is the giver of the natural inclination.[34]

With respect to the specification of the act, the will can in a sense be determined in this one special case, because the intellect presents to it an object that is completely good in every way and is in itself the universal good. The only such good is God, and we know God in this way only in heaven. In this case the will's natural inclination to happiness and the good in general corresponds to the complete good that is presented to it by the intellect. Short of heaven, the intellect is incapable of presenting the will with any one complete good. This ability of the intellect to present different goods causes the freedom of specification, which is the ability to choose between one act and another.

There are two problems concerning Thomas's use of the distinction between exercise and specification. First, in early texts, Thomas does not so clearly discuss the two kinds of freedom, but rather focuses on the distinction between the known object as a final cause and the will as an efficient cause. Thomas moves from more causal language to language concerning the two kinds of freedom, although there is no scholarly agreement concerning the nature and importance of this development, and the dating of a relevant text is unclear. Although the earlier and later discussions are otherwise similar in many respects, some scholars have thought that the later texts reflect a shift to a more voluntaristic view.[35]

34. See Cajetan, In S.T., I-II, q. 10, art. 2, n. 2 (Leonine, 6.86). A more contemporary treatment can be found in Simon Francis Gaine, Will There Be Free Will in Heaven?: Freedom, Impeccability and Beatitude (London/New York: T & T Clark, 2003), 126–35.

35. For the different discussions, see especially David Gallagher, "Free Choice and Free Judgment in Aquinas," Archiv für Geschichte der Philosophie 76 (1994): 261–62,

It seems to me that Thomas consistently states that the known object specifies in that it is a formal and final cause, whereas the will is an efficient cause in that it causes the act's exercise. In the *Summa contra gentiles*, Thomas writes:

The will applies every power to its [the power's] own act; for we understand because we will, and we imagine because we will, and so it is with other things. And this is the case because its object is the end; although the intellect, not according to the mode of an efficient or moving cause, but according to the mode of a final cause, moves the will, in presenting to it its object, which is the end.[36]

In this passage the will is the efficient cause and the intellect moves the will because it presents the end to the will. The intellect's causal influence belongs to final causality. This same use of the distinction between the efficient and final cause is just as explicit in two passages

---

esp. nn. 40–42; Michael Sherwin, *By Knowledge and by Love: Charity and Knowledge in the Moral Theology of St. Thomas Aquinas* (Washington, D.C.: The Catholic University of America Press, 2005), 49–53. The question is related to whether *De Malo*, q. 6, is an early or late text. For various problems with the dating, see especially the introduction to the Leonine, 23.3–5; Jeanne-Pierre Torrell, *Initiation à saint Thomas d'Aquin: Sa personne et son oeuvre*, 2nd ed. (Fribourg: Editions Universitaires de Fribourg, 2002¹), 293–301; Flannery, *Acts Amid Precepts: The Aristotelian Structure of Thomas Aquinas's Moral Theory* (Washington, D.C.: The Catholic University of America Press, 2001), Appendix C, 247–49. A history and criticism of the position that Thomas changes his views can be found in Flannery, *Acts Amid Precepts*, 111–43; Yul Kim, "A Change in Thomas Aquinas's Theory of the Will: Solutions to a Long-Standing Problem," *American Catholic Philosophical Quarterly* 82 (2008): 221–36; Daniel Westberg, "Did Aquinas Change His Mind about the Will?" *The Thomist* 58 (1994): 41–60. For the thesis that Thomas changes, see originally Odon Lottin, *Psychologie et morale aux xiie et xiiie siècles*, 2nd ed., 6 vols. (Louvain: Abbeye du Mont César; Gembloux: Ducolot, 1942–1960), 1.226–43, 252–62, and recently James Keenan, *Goodness and Rightness in Thomas Aquinas's Summa Theologiae* (Washington, D.C.: The Catholic University of America Press, 1992). For a convincing case that the development is one of pedagogical efficacy and not of doctrine, see Lawrence Dewan, "St. Thomas, James Kennan, and the Will," *Science et Ésprit* 47 (1995): 157–71, reprinted in *Wisdom, Law, and Virtue*, 151–74.

36. Thomas, *Summa contra gentiles*, 1, 72: "voluntas omnem potentiam applicat ad suum actum; intelligimus enim quia volumus, et imaginamur quia volumus, et sic de aliis. Et hoc habet quia obiectum eius est finis:—quamvis intellectus non secundum modum causae efficientis et moventis, sed secundum modum causae finalis, moveat voluntatem, propenendo sibi suum obiectum, quod est finis" (Leonine, 13.210).

from Thomas's earlier *De Veritate*.[37] It is not difficult to see how this causal distinction applies to the distinction between the freedom of specification and the freedom of exercise. The freedom of specification is rooted in the partial character of the goods presented by the intellect. The intellect provides the principle of specification, because the known object gives the formal character to the act, that is, the intellect presents a good that has one set of characteristics rather than another. The freedom of exercise involves the will's control over deliberation, which is reasoning about the means toward attaining these goods, and the choice of the good itself. These points seem to be consistent throughout his career.

The second and perhaps more interesting problem, which is related to concerns over the causal role of the intellect, is that some Thomists, such as Cajetan, argue that the known object is an efficient cause of the will's movement.[38] This argument occurs in the context of later debates with Scotists and other Scholastics. Although this interpretation conflicts with the words of Thomas, it has had some success. But other Thomists stick more carefully to Thomas's texts.[39] Why would some Thomists wish to describe the known object as an efficient cause? Thomas does at times discuss the intellect as a kind of efficient cause of the will's motion.[40] For instance, in the *Prima Secundae*, Thomas argues that ignorance can be a cause of sin insofar as it removes an impediment to sin, namely knowledge. [41] This kind

37. Thomas, *De Veritate*, q. 22, art. 9, resp. (Leonine, 22.3.632); Idem, *De Veritate*, q. 22, art. 13 (Leonine, 22.3.642).

38. See Cajetan, *In S.T.*, I, q. 80, art. 2 (Leonine, 5.284–87). For the different Thomistic commentators and the relevant texts of Thomas, see Jacobus Ramirez, *De actibus humanis: In I-II Summae Theologiae Divi Thomae Expositio (QQ. VI–XXI)*, ed. Victorino Rodriguez, Edicion de las Obras Completas de Santiago Ramirez 4 (Madrid: Instiuto de Filosofia "Luis Vives," 1972), 107–26.

39. For example, see John Capreolus, 2 *Sent.*, d. 25, art. 1, prima conclusio, et ad argumenta contra primam conclusionem, in *Defensiones Theologiae Divi Thomae Aquinatis*, 7 vols., ed. C. Paban and T. Pègues (Tours: Cattier, 1900–1908; reprint, Frankfurt am Main: Minerva, 1967), 4.230, 239–50.

40. For an interesting attempt to revise and defend some aspects of Cajetan's view, see Ramirez, *De actibus humanis*, 126–32.

41. Thomas, *S.T.*, I-II, q. 76, art. 1.

15

of cause, namely a cause "*remotio prohibentis*," is in technical terms a "per accidens efficient cause." More generally, Thomas thinks that final causality can in some way be reduced to efficient causality. In his late commentary on the *Liber de Causis*, although he is not discussing human action, Thomas states that "the end in such is the cause insofar as it moves the efficient cause to act, and thus, insofar as it has the aspect [*ratio*] of a mover, it pertains in some way to the genus of efficient cause."[42] I would make two points. First, Thomas is discussing the final cause as "in some way" *(quodammodo)* belonging to an efficient cause only insofar as it moves the efficient cause. The end does not take away from the agent's efficient causality. Second, in his many explicit discussions, Thomas is consistently clear that the known object is only a final or formal cause, and that the will is an efficient cause. Any attempt to describe the known object as an efficient cause in Thomistic terms requires a lot more exposition and explanation than we find in the texts of Thomas.

Thomas's denial that the known object is an efficient cause brings out one of the many problems with Robert Pasnau's influential claim that Thomas seems to be a compatibilist in the sense that his view allows for the determination of action by an agent's own beliefs and values. Pasnau writes that "if we are determined, we are determined by our own beliefs and values, not simply by the brute design of nature and the happenstance of events. This difference, for Aquinas, makes all the difference."[43] What does Pasnau mean by "value"? If

42. "nam finis in tantum est causa in quantum movet efficientem ad agendum, et sic, prout habet rationem moventis, pertinet quodammodo ad causae efficientis genus"; Thomas Aquinas, *Super librum de Causis*, lib. 1, prop. 1a, in *Sancti Thomae de Aquino super Librum de causis expositio*, ed. G. D. Saffrey, Texts Philosophici Fribugenses (Fribourg: Société Philosophique; Louvain: Nauwelaerts, 1954), 9.

43. Pasnau, *Thomas Aquinas on Human Nature*, 233. For a somewhat similar view, see Jeffrey Hause, "Thomas Aquinas and the Voluntarists," *Medieval Philosophy and Theology* 6 (1997): 167–82, and to a lesser extent Terence Irwin, *The Development of Ethics: A Historical and Critical Study*, vol. 1: *From Socrates to the Reformation* (Oxford: Oxford University Press, 2007), 488–91, 677–78. For the alternative view that Thomas in contemporary terms might be a kind of "libertarian," see Scott MacDonald, "Aquinas's Libertarian Account of Free Choice," *Revue Internationale de Philosophie* 2 (1998): 309–28; Eleanor Stump, *Aquinas* (London/New York: Routledge, 2003), 277–

a value is an act of the will, then by definition it cannot be causally determined, and it is part of an undetermined human action. If a value is simply our orientation to the good, then it is not subject to choice, but it also does not suffice for the determination of any particular act. Beliefs do not exercise direct efficient causality over the act. Moreover, we have seen that for Thomas beliefs about goods are undetermined with respect to real and merely apparent goods, as well as different real goods. With respect to the particular goods known in this life, the will's acts cannot be causally necessitated by any causal influence, including their specification by the intellect.

Thomas is clear that there are only two immediate created causes of the will's movement, one that is final or formal, the other that is efficient. Is the will a self-mover? The known object is a final cause of the act as its goal, and it is formal insofar as it gives specification to the act. This final causality in no way determines the will when the object presented is a particular good such as we find in the present life. The efficient cause of the will is the will itself. There is no other created immediate mover. Not even the passions of the sense appetite can force the will to act.[44] If the passions do efficiently cause the act, then the act is not a free human act. How is this self-motion compatible with the principle that "everything that at some time is in an agent in act and sometimes is in potency, needs to be moved by another thing in motion"?[45] Thomas thinks that this principle also applies to the will, because no created being is the first principle of its own motion. Thomas writes, "The will with respect to one thing sufficiently moves itself, and in its own order, as a proximate agent: but it cannot move itself with respect to everything.... Therefore it must be moved by another just as by a first mover."[46] Nevertheless, he states

---

306, which incorporates much of her earlier "Aquinas's Account of Freedom: Intellect and Will," *The Monist* 80 (1997): 576–97.

44. Thomas, *S.T.*, I, q. 10, art. 3.

45. "Omne enim quod quandoque est agens in actu et quandoque in potentia, indiget moveri an aliquo movente"; Thomas, *S.T.*, I-II, q. 9, art. 4. For the history and use of this principle, see Roy R. Effler, *John Duns Scotus and the Principle "Omne quod movetur ab alio movetur"* (St. Bonaventure, N.Y.: Franciscan Institute, 1962), 1–15.

46. "voluntas quantum ad aliquid sufficienter se movet, et in suo ordine, scilicet

that the will is distinctive in that its motion comes directly from God. This point has not been recognized by some recent scholars, who seem to think that the first mover must either be the known object or the will itself.[47] In contrast, Thomas explicitly states that the will can be a self-mover in its own order, although God is the ultimate cause of this and every created motion.[48]

How is the efficacious movement of the will by God compatible with the will's indeterminacy?[49] According to Thomas, necessary and contingent motion properly belongs to secondary, created causes. Both necessary and contingent effects are efficaciously caused by God, who is apart from this secondary order. Consequently, although in its own order the will is contingent insofar as it is self-determining and self-moving, this self-determination and self-motion must be caused by a cause of another order, and this cause can only be God. Any other efficacious cause would conflict with the freedom of human free choice. Thomas's discussion of astrology illustrates this point.[50] In Thomas's cosmology, natural movers are moved by God through

---

agens proximum: sed non potest seipsam movere quantum ad omnia.... Unde indiget moveri ab alio sicut a primo movente"; Thomas, *S.T.*, I-II, q. 9, art. 5, ad 3. Among the many such statements, see especially *De Veritate*, q. 22, art. 9, resp. (Leonine, 22.3.632); *De Malo*, q. 6, resp. (Leonine, 23.149).

47. Gallagher, "Free Choice and Free Judgment," does not mention the importance of seeking a mover outside of the agent. See the critique by Lawrence Dewan, "St. Thomas and the Causes of Free Choice," *Acta Philosophica* 8 (1999): 87–96, reprinted in *Wisdom, Law, and Virtue*, 175–85. See also Peter Eardley, who seems to say that the external mover for Thomas is the intellect, in "Thomas Aquinas and Giles of Rome on the Will," *Review of Metaphysics* 56 (2003): 836–62, esp. 846–47, and the use of note 31; Calvin G. Normore, "Ockham, Self-Motion and the Will," in *Self-Motion: From Aristotle to Newton*, ed. Mary Louise Gill and James G. Lennox (Princeton, N.J.: Princeton University Press, 1994), 294. For the Aristotelian background to Thomas's view of God's influence on human action, see Flannery, *Acts Amid Precepts*, 136–38.

48. Thomas, *S.T.*, I-II, q. 9, art. 6; Idem, *De Malo*, q. 6, art. 3, resp. et ad 1, 4, 17, 21 (Leonine, 23.149–53); Idem, *De Veritate*, q. 22, art. 8–9 (Leonine, 22.3.630–34).

49. Thomas, *S.T.*, I-II q. 10, art. 4; Idem, *De Malo*, q. 6, art. 3, resp. et ad 3 (Leonine, 23.149–50). For other texts and a discussion, see Thomas M. Osborne Jr., "Premotion and Contemporary Philosophy of Religion," *Nova et Vetera*, English Edition 4 (2006): 607–32; Idem, "Augustine and Aquinas on Foreknowledge through Causes." *Nova et Vetera*, English Edition 6 (2008): 219–32.

50. Thomas, *S.T.*, II-I I, q. 95, art. 5. See also Idem, *S.T.*, I-II, q. 9, art. 5.

the celestial bodies. Thomas thinks that the celestial bodies can influence the passions, but since the passions cannot efficaciously move the will, even the celestial bodies do not intrinsically and efficaciously cause the will's self-motion. Only the first mover, namely God, can do so. God both gives the will its nature by creating it and he is the universal good to which the will is naturally ordered.

Some contemporaries of Thomas, and certainly members of the following generation, are concerned to avoid the position that the known object determines the will's movement efficaciously, which might be thought of as a kind of psychological or intellectual determinism.[51] In his later writings, Thomas may have emphasized the control of the will, and this emphasis may be in response to these concerns. Nevertheless, Thomas himself consistently emphasizes throughout his career that the will is a self-mover in the created order. He does think that the root of freedom is in the intellect, in that the ability to understand the good in general both makes it possible to act freely and explains the indeterminacy of the will with respect to particular goods in this life. But Thomas also emphasizes that the will moves the intellect, and that the known object is not strictly speaking the efficacious cause of the will's motion.

JOHN DUNS SCOTUS

John Duns Scotus's treatment of the causation of a human act occurs in a different context, namely that of Franciscan and other theologians who argue against the position that the act of willing is determined by the object, whether it be the presentation of the object through an image/sensory representation or the external object itself.[52] This position was targeted by the bishop of Paris's condemna-

---

51. Although many scholars discuss a "psychological determinism," it is not clear that any held such determinism. Even such "intellectualists" as Godfrey of Fontaines and Siger of Brabant were not determinists, although their contemporaries may have worried that their views would lead to determinism. See François-Xavier Putallaz, *Insolente liberté: Controverses et condamnations au xiiie siècle* (Fribourg: Éditions Universitaires; Paris: Cerf, 1995), 249–51.

52. For a recent discussion of the vast literature on the subject, see Bonnie Kent,

tion of 1277 and, perhaps more importantly, by those theologians who were behind the condemnation. But later the masters at Paris also agreed to a *propositio magistralis*, which stated that rectitude in the intellect is in some way incompatible with error in the will. Although the historical and philosophical effects of the condemnation and even the *propositio* are debated, there is general agreement that they express a late thirteenth-century concern with some form of determinism, or at least a concern that determinism ultimately results from the view that liberty is formally in the intellect rather than the will.[53] Scotus develops his views at least in part by reacting to the threat of such determinism.

It is also important to note a particularly Franciscan concern with Thomas's emphasis on the role of the intellect in human action.[54] In 1282, the Franciscan Order made William de la Mare's *Correctorium fratris Thomae*, a list and correction of Thomas's supposed errors, required reading for those who wished to study Thomas. Whereas the 1277 and related condemnations were primarily local and probably concerned with the Arts Faculty, the Franciscan adoption of the *Correctorium* was geographically widespread and explicitly directed at what William thought were Thomas's own positions. Many Domini-

"Evil in Later Medieval Philosophy," *Journal of the History of Philosophy* 45 (2007): 177–205; Kent Emery and Andreas Speer, "After the Condemnation of 1277: New Evidence, New Perspectives, and Grounds for New Interpretations," *Nach der Verurteilung von 1277: Philosophie und Theologie an der Universität von Paris im letzten Viertel des 13. Jahrhunderts*, ed. Jan Aertsen, Kent Emery, and Andreas Speer, Miscellanea Mediaevalia 28 (Berlin/New York: de Gruyter, 2001), 3–19. For the view that the condemnation plays a central role, see Stephen D. Dumont, "Time, Contradiction, and the Freedom of the Will in the Late Thirteenth Century," *Documente e studi sulla tradizione filosofica medievale* 3 (1992): 561–97; Edward P. Mahoney, "Reverberations of the Condemnation of 1277 in Later Medieval and Renaissance Philosophy," in *Nach der Verurteilung*, 902–30, esp. 914–15; Peter S. Eardley, "The Problem of Moral Weakness, the *Propositio Magistralis*, and the Condemnation of 1277," *Mediaeval Studies* 68 (2006): 161–203.

53. For the historical roots of this tension in the early thirteenth century and before, see especially Putallaz, *Insolente Liberté*, 1–14; Colleen McCluskey, "The Roots of Ethical Voluntarism," *Vivarium* 39 (2001): 185–208. For the relationship between the 1277 condemnation and Siger of Brabant's view that liberty is formally in the intellect, see Putallaz, *Insolente Liberté*, 15–91.

54. Kent, *Virtues of the Will*, 81–84, 123–39; Putallaz, *Insolente Liberté*, 93–126.

cans argued that the *Correctorium* often misrepresented Thomas's work.[55]

Scotus, like William, does not target Aristotle's moral psychology for criticism. Scotus is concerned with certain more or less Aristotelian views defended by such thinkers as Godfrey of Fontaines and perhaps even Giles of Rome, who were seen by many as giving a deterministic account of the object's influence on the will. Scotus offers an alternative Aristotelian account by using Aristotle's description of rational potency to explain how the will as a power can be open to opposites.

What is the root of human freedom according to Scotus's account? Unlike Thomas, Scotus thinks that it is at least conceptually possible for there to be an intellectual appetite that is not free. How then does Scotus distinguish between the intellect and the will? Previous Franciscan thinkers had defended the position that the soul's powers are identical with the soul itself.[56] In contrast, Scotus applies in this context his wider theory of the formal distinction, which is a distinction between things that are not really distinct, even though there is a real formal basis for this distinction.[57] According to Scotus, this formal distinction allows us to hold that the powers of the soul are

55. See, for example, the many comments in the Dominican John of Paris, *Le Correctorium Corruptorii "Circa,"* art. 51–54 (54–57), ed. Jean-Pierre Muller, Studia Anselmiana 12–13 (Rome: Pontificium Institutum S. Anselmi, 1941), 258–74.

56. For the earlier Franciscan tradition, see Pius Künzle, *Das Verhältnis der Seele zur ihren Potenzen: Problemgeschichtliche Untersuchungen von Augustin bis und mit Thomas von Aquin* (Freiburg: Universitätsverlag Freiburg, 1956), 116–41. For a discussion of Godfrey of Fontaines's position, see John F. Wippel, *The Metaphysical Thought of Godfrey of Fontaines: A Study in Late Thirteenth-Century Philosophy* (Washington, D.C.: The Catholic University of America Press, 1981), 202–7; Peter Eardley, "The Foundations of Freedom in Later Medieval Philosophy: Giles of Rome and His Contemporaries," *Journal of the History of Philosophy* 44 (2006): 364–70. For the general historical background to Scotus's understanding of the will, see Ernst Stadter, *Psychologie und Metaphysick der menschlichen Freiheit: Die ideengeschichtliche zwischen Bonaventura und Duns Scotus* (München: Schoningh, 1971).

57. Maurice J. Grajewski, *The Formal Distinction of Duns Scotus: A Study in Metaphysics* (Washington, D.C.: The Catholic University of America Press, 1944). For the application to the soul's powers, see especially 155–78. This discussion should be treated with caution, as he relies partially on questionable texts.

truly causal powers formally and not really distinct from the soul as such.[58] The will is an active power of a particular kind, namely a rational potency, which was discussed by Aristotle. For Scotus, the will is the only active potency in the fullest sense.[59]

Scotus provides a detailed commentary on Aristotle's description of a rational potency in his *Quaestiones super libros metaphysicorum Aristotelis*, Book IX, q. 15.[60] Aristotle's *Metaphysics* may seem to us

58. Unfortunately, the most explicit statement of this can be found not in the *Ordinatio*, but in what may be William of Alnwick, *Additiones Magnae* II, d. 16, nn. 17–19 (Wadding ed., 6.2.772–73). William's *Additiones* are now thought to be at least a faithful report of Scotus's Parisian lectures. The Scotistic Commission's edition of the *Reportationes* may shed more light on what this work really is. Both Grajewski's discussion and that of Richard Cross depend in large part on what Luke Wadding published as the *Opus Oxoniense*, which is not included in the Vatican edition of the *Ordinatio*, as it seems to be from the *Additiones Magnae* or from a *reportatio* of Scotus's Parisian lectures. See Richard Cross, "Philosophy of Mind," in *The Cambridge Companion to Scotus*, 268–71, 281, n. 30, nn. 35–37, 39. Although this work is not part of the *Ordinatio*, it is a description of Scotus's teaching. For the source of this work, see the Vatican Edition of Scotus, 8.89*–92*. But Scotus did hold the position. Cross points to other edited texts in which Scotus presents a similar position, such as Scotus's *Quaestiones super libros metaphysicorum Aristotelis*, lib. 4, q. 2, n. 143, and lib. 9, q. 5, nn. 12–18 (OPh, 3.355, 4.562–65). The date of this work is uncertain, but it may be very early. The position is also stated in passing in 2 *Ord.*, d. 1, q. 6, n. 321 (Vat., 7.156). For the rejection of the traditional Franciscan distinction between the powers, see also Olivier Boulnois, *Être et représentation: Une généalogie de la métaphysique moderne à l'époque de Duns Scot (XIIIᵉ–XIVᵉ siècle)* (Paris: Presses Universitaires de France, 1999), 199–200.

59. For a discussion of the will as a rational potency, see especially Allan B. Wolter, "Duns Scotus on the Will as Rational Potency," in Wolter, *The Philosophical Theology of John Duns Scotus*, ed. Marilyn McCord Adams (Ithaca, N.Y.: Cornell University Press, 1990), 163–80; Marilyn McCord Adams, "Duns Scotus on the Will as Rational Power," in *Via Scoti: Methodologiae ad mentem Joannis Duns Scoti 1993, Atti del Congresso Scotistico Internazionale Roma 9–11 Marzo 1993*, ed. Leonardo Sileo, Studia scholastico-Scotistica 5 (Rome: Edizioni Antonianum 1995), 839–54; Hannes Möhle, *Ethik als Scientia Practica nach Johannes Duns Scotus: Eine philosophische Grundlegung*, Beiträge zur Geschichte der Philosophie des Mittelalters n.f. 44 (Münster: Aschendorff, 1995), 161–73; Mary Beth Ingham and Mechtild Dreyer, *The Philosophical Vision of John Duns Scotus* (Washington, D.C.: The Catholic University of America Press, 2004), 146–72. In general, see Walter Hoeres, *Der Wille als Reine Vollkommenheit nach Duns Scotus*, Salzburger Studien zur Philosophie 1 (München: Pustet, 1962). Aristotle's discussion of rational potency is in *Metaphysics* 9.2, 5.

60. This text can be found in Scotus, OPh, 4.675–99.

a strange place to look for an account of the will, but Scotus is following an older tradition. For instance, William de la Mare had used Aristotle's account of a rational potency in order to attack Thomas's understanding of the will.[61] Scotus follows Aristotle's division of active potencies between the rational and the nonrational.[62] Nonrational potencies are capable of a kind of self-movement, but they are always moved by another, as are the sense powers and the sense appetites. In contrast, a rational potency is a power for opposite objects. Scotus explains that the intellect cannot be a fully rational potency, because although it can think about opposite objects, it cannot determine itself to opposite objects.[63] The ability to think or not think about something does not imply an ability to move oneself to think or not to think. The rational ability for self-determination belongs solely to the will.

This ability of the will to determine itself to opposites is at the heart of Scotus's understanding of the distinction between nature and the will.[64] Natural powers are always moved by something else. Consequently, although nonrational potencies can be active, they must have a cause. But there is no cause of the will's movement to one good rather than another. If the will did not have this power with respect to opposites, then it would be incapable of contingent and therefore free acts. Scotus emphasizes that the will determines and controls the intellect's indeterminacy.[65]

The will as a nature has an appetite for its own perfection, just as

61. William de la Mare, *Correctorium*, art. 51 (55), 52 (56), in John of Paris, *Correctorium Corruptorii "Circa,"* 263, 267.

62. Aristotle, *Metaphysics* 9.3.1046b2–6.

63. John Duns Scotus, *Super libros metaphysicorum*, lib. 9, q. 15, n. 36 (OPh, 4.684–85).

64. Tobias Hoffmann, "The Distinction between Nature and Will in Duns Scotus," *Archives d'histoire doctrinale et littéraire du moyen âge* 66 (1999): 184–224; Thomas M. Osborne Jr., *Love of Self and Love of God in Thirteenth-Century Ethics* (Notre Dame, Ind.: University of Notre Dame Press, 2005), 174–86. See also Thomas Williams, "How Scotus Separates Morality from Happiness," *American Catholic Philosophical Quarterly* 69 (1995): 426–27; Idem, "The Libertarian Foundations of Scotus's Moral Philosophy," *The Thomist* 62 (1998): 197–200.

65. Scotus, *Super libros metaphysicorum*, lib. 9, q. 15, n. 41 (OPh, 4.686).

other natures do.[66] This inclination is not an elicited act but an ever present inclination *(inclinatio)* for it own perfection, and is a willing *(velle)* only in the broadest sense. This natural inclination is like that of a stone, which wants to move toward the center of the earth, and is merely passive. But since the will is not merely natural but also free, it can have an act of willing *(velle)* in the strictest sense, which is an elicited act. Aside from the use of "natural will" to describe the passive inclination, and a second use to distinguish the natural will from a supernatural power, there is also a third use of "natural will" to describe an elicited act that is in conformity to such an inclination.[67] Such a "natural will" is an elicited act for that which is advantageous *(commodum)* to itself. The will is free to elicit or not elicit this act of willing for the advantageous. Consequently, the will can act against its natural inclination.

This distinction between willing in accordance with natural inclination *(inclinatio)* and not so willing is connected to Scotus's appropriation of Anselm's distinction between the inclination for the advantageous *(affectio commodi)* and the inclination for the just *(affectio iustitiae)*.[68] This distinction between these inclinations *(affectiones)* is based on the distinction between two kinds of goods, namely that which is good for the agent and that which is good in itself. There is scholarly disagreement over how Scotus's account of these inclinations is related to his understanding of the will as a nonrational potency, and whether the existence of these two inclinations is even necessary for the will's freedom.[69] Nevertheless, in at least some texts,

66. Scotus, *Ord.* 3, d. 17, n. 13 (Vat., 9.566–68); Idem, *Lect.* 3, d. 17, q. 1, n. 9 (Vat., 20.424–25); Idem, *Collatio* 16, nn. 1–2 (Wadding ed., 3.381); Idem, *Ord.* 4, d. 49, q. 10, nn. 2–3 (Wadding ed., 10.505–6). See especially Parthenius Minges, *Ioannis Duns Scoti doctrina philosophica et theologica*, 2 vols. (Ad claras aquas: Collegium S. Bonaventurae, 1930), 276–84.

67. Scotus, *Ord.* 3, d. 17, n. 15 (Vat., 9.568); Idem, *Lect.* 3, d. 17, q. 1, n. 11 (Vat., 20.425–26).

68. For Scotus and Anselm, see Douglas Langston, "Did Scotus Embrace Anselm's Notion of Freedom?" *Medieval Philosophy and Theology* 5 (1996): 145–59. For the connection between the two inclinations and the distinction between the will as a nature and the will as free, see Hoffmann, "Nature and Will," 209–12.

69. The position that there is no necessary connection between the two inclinations

Scotus states that if the will were to have merely the inclination to the advantageous, then it would not be free. Scotus uses an example from Anselm to illustrate his point:

> If it were understood—according to that fictive example of Anselm in the *De casu diaboli*—that there would be an angel "having the inclination for the advantageous and not for the just" (that is, having merely an intellectual appetite as such an appetite and not as free), such an angel would be unable not to will the advantageous, nor even not to will such things in the highest way; nor would it be imputed to it as a sin, since that appetite would be related to its cognitive power in the same way that the appetite for the seen thing is related to sight, in necessarily following what is presented by that cognitive power and the inclination [*inclinatio*] to the highest thing shown by such a power, because it does not have anything to control itself ... the "inclination for the just" is the liberty innate to the will, because it itself is the first moderator of such an inclination [*affectio*] [for the advantageous].[70]

The sin of an angel is possible precisely because the angel has not only a natural inclination to the advantageous, but also an inclination to the just by which the natural inclination can be regulated.[71] The

---

and freedom can be found in Adams, "Scotus on the Will and Power," 844–45; Eadem, "Ockham on Will, Nature, and Morality," in *The Cambridge Companion to Ockham*, 253; John Boler, "Transcending the Natural: Duns Scotus on the Two Affections of the Will," *American Catholic Philosophical Quarterly* 67 (1993): 109–26. For various opposed positions, see Michael Barnwell, *The Problem of Negligent Omissions: Medieval Action Theories to the Rescue* (Leiden/Boston: Brill, 2010), 190–201; Hoffmann, "Nature and Will," 209–12; Severin Kitanov, *Beatific Enjoyment in Scholastic Theology and Philosophy, 1240–1335* [diss.], (Helsinki, 2006), 230–49; Langston, "Did Scotus Embrace Anselm's Notion?" 156–58; Sukjae Lee, "Scotus on the Will: The Rational Power and the Dual Affections," *Vivarium* 36 (1998): 40–54; Williams, "Libertarian Foundations," 198–99; Idem, "From Metaethics to Action Theory," in *The Cambridge Companion to Scotus*, 342–49.

70. "Si enim intelligeretur—secundum illam fictionem Anselmi *De casu diaboli*—quod esset angelus 'habens affectionem commodi et non iustitiae' (hoc est, habens appetitum intellectivum mere ut appetitium talem et non ut liberum), talis angelus non posset non velle commoda, nec etiam non summe velle talia; nec imputaretur sibi ad peccatum, quia ille appetitus se haberet ad suam cognitivam sicut modo appetitus visivus ad visum, in necessario consequendo ostensionem illius cognitivae et inclinationem ad optimum ostensum a tali potentia, quia non haberet unde se refrenaret ... 'affectio iustitiae' est libertas innata voluntati, quia ipsa est prima moderatrix affectionis talis"; Scotus, *Ord.* 2, d. 6, q. 2, n. 49 (Vat., 8.48–49).

71. In addition to the above text, see Scotus, *Lectura* 2, d. 6, q. 2, nn. 36–37 (Vat.,

will is a rational potency only in that it has the two inclinations. The thought experiment about the angel with only the inclination for the advantageous shows that if there were an only an inclination for the advantageous, then the will would be determined in the way that animal appetites are. The intellectual appetite in this passage is identified with the inclination for the advantageous, and as such is not free. It is not just the intellectual appetite that is the source of freedom, but the will as a rational potency. The inclination for the just is present only in free creatures. The inclination for the advantageous is common to everything that has a cognitive power, including even animals.[72]

A significant contrast between Scotus and Thomas on this issue is that Scotus thinks that the distinction between the *bonum in se* and the *bonum sibi* requires two distinct inclinations *(affectiones)* of the will. For Thomas, someone can will what is good for its own sake because the object of the will is what is good and not merely what is advantageous.[73] Additionally, Thomas thinks that any nature is directed to God and the common good of the universe more than its own good. Consequently, the difference between Thomas and Scotus is not merely one over the nature of intellectual appetite, but also over whether all of nature is primarily self-directed.[74]

With respect to free choice, an important point is that Scotus seems to think that a determined intellectual appetite is at least conceptually possible. Scotus sharply differs from Thomas, who thinks that every intellectual creature must be free. There is an underlying disagreement over the way in which the intellect grasps the good. Thom-

---

18.381–32); R. P. 3, d. 18, q. 1, n. 23; William of Alnwick, *Additiones Magnae* 2, d. 6, q. 2, nn. 9–11 (Wadding ed., 11.1.289–90).

72. Scotus, R. P. 4, d. 49, q. 4, n. 5 (Watting ed., 11.2.901).

73. Thomas, 2 *Sent.*, d. 3, q. 4, ad 2–3 (Mandonnet ed., 2.645).

74. Osborne, *Love of God and Love of Self*, 94–112, 174–86, 198–200; Rude A. te Velde, "*Natura in se ipsa recurva est*: Duns Scotus and Aquinas on the Relationship between Nature and Will," in *John Duns Scotus: Renewal of Philosophy*, ed. S. P. Bos, Acts of the Third Symposium Organized by the Dutch Society for Medieval Philosophy Medium Aevum, May 23 and 24, 1996, Elementa, Schriften zur Philosophie und ihrer Problemgeschichte 72 (Amsterdam: Rodopi, 1998), 155–69.

as emphasizes the indeterminacy of the good in general, which is the object of the will. The immateriality of the intellect and this universality of will's object help to explain the freedom of choice. For Thomas, the ability to choose between different actions is rooted in the intellect's ability to think about different possible goods. In contrast, the distinction between the good in general and particular goods does not play the pivotal role in Scotus's account. Scotus thinks that the intellect could grasp the good and be determined to it. There are different possibilities precisely because the will can choose between two options, namely the advantageous and the just. The very possibility of an intellectual but not free creature shows that for Scotus freedom is rooted not in the intellect but in the will as a rational potency with two distinct inclinations.

Scotus rejects the view that free agents necessarily will happiness and the good in general and are only free with respect to particular goods.[75] According to Scotus, someone can fail to elicit an act of willing happiness *(non velle)*, although he cannot will against or flee *(nolle)* happiness.[76] He can "not will" happiness in two ways.[77] First, the agent might not think of happiness. Second, the agent might will something that is not ordered and cannot be ordered to happiness, such as fornication. Someone who wills to fornicate is not willing against happiness, since it is impossible to will against happiness or indeed against any good. But, according to Scotus, he is willing something other than happiness.

Scotus's distinction between nature and reason has a significant consequence for his view of the way in which even those who see God in heaven retain their freedom. He criticizes a position, such as we

75. Scotus, *Ord.* 4, d. 49, q. 10, nn. 4–10 (Wadding ed., 10.512–14). The source of Wadding's text is unclear, but it may be a *reportatio*. See the Vatican editors, Vat., 1.27*–28*.

76. It seems to me that a failure to distinguish between *non velle* and *nolle* partially mars the discussion of Scotus and eudaimonism in Irwin, *Development of Ethics*, 1.659–71. For a criticism of the view that Scotus rejects eudaimonism (properly understood), see Osborne, *Love of Self and Love of God*, 174–86, 209–14.

77. Scotus, *Ord.* 4, d. 49, q. 10, n. 15 (Wadding ed., 10.540). See also Idem, *Collatio* 17, n. 8 (Wadding ed., 3.384).

find in Thomas, that the blessed adhere to God through enjoyment *(frui)* because God is the universal good. Scotus objects that the way in which the will moves is incompatible with any such natural necessity.[78] Although the intellect by necessity understands a proportional object that is present to it, the will does not by any necessity enjoy this object. He does allow that there is a certain *secundum quid* necessity in the beatific vision, but this necessity does not violate the will's freedom.[79] How does Scotus explain this kind of necessity? In his late Quodlibet 16, he does not side with any one explanation, but leaves open the possibility that the blessed might will the ultimate end through some sort of supernatural necessity.[80] He is only certain that the divine will necessarily wills its own good. In Book IV of his *Ordinatio*, he states that although the ability to sin remains in the blessed, they are incapable of moving from potency to act because God prevents the exercise of their secondary causal power.[81] The ability to sin remains, but it cannot be exercised given God's refusal to act. Whereas Thomas uses the will's natural inclination to the universal good in order to explain the impeccability of the blessed, Scotus's distinction

78. Scotus, *Ord.* 1, d. 1, p. 2, q. 2, n. 80 (Vat., 2.60).

79. Scotus, *Ord.* 4, d. 49, q. 6, n. 9 (Wadding ed., 10.433). See also n. 22 (Wadding ed., 10.476). For a general discussion, see R. Prentice, "The Degree and Mode of Liberty in the Beatitude of the Blessed," in *Deus et Homo ad mentem I. Duns Scoti. Acta tertii Congressus Scotistici internationalis Vindebonae 28 Sept.–2 Oct. 1970*, Studia scholastico-Scotistica 5 (Rome: Societas internationalis Scotistica, 1972), 327–42; Douglas C. Langston, *God's Willing Knowledge: The Influence of Scotus' Analysis of Omniscience* (University Park: Pennsylvania State University Press, 1986), 39–44; Christian Trottmann, "La vision béatifique dans la seconde école franciscaine: De Mathieu d'Aquasparta à Duns Scot," *Collectanea Franciscana* 64 (1994): 175–78; Richard Cross, *Duns Scotus* (New York/Oxford: Oxford University Press, 1999), 149–51; Gaine, *Free Will in Heaven*, 51–70; Kitanov, *Beatific Enjoyment*, 219–30.

80. Scotus, *Quod* 16, n. 30, ed. Timothy B. Noone and H. Francie Roberts, in "John Duns Scotus' *Quodlibet*: A Brief Study of the Manuscripts and an Edition of Question 16," in *Theological Quodlibeta in the Middle Ages: The Fourteenth Century*, ed. Christopher Schabel, Brill's Companions to the Christian Tradition 7 (Boston/Leiden: Brill, 2007), 131–98, at 174–75. For a discussion of the relevant kinds of necessity, see Calvin G. Normore, "Duns Scotus's Moral Theory," in *The Cambridge Companion to Duns Scotus*, 141–45.

81. Scotus, *Ord.* 4, d. 49, q. 6, n. 11 (Wadding ed., 10.455).

between nature and will makes such an explanation impossible. In general, Scotus seems to think that God is a partial cause of any free act, although God's causality belongs to a higher order.[82]

What is distinctive about Scotus's understanding of contingency in the context of human action? Some scholars have described the difference between Thomas's understanding of freedom and that of Scotus as in part based on a new understanding of contingency and time.[83] According to this view, Thomas and earlier Scholastics hold a "diachronic" notion of contingency, according to which different alternatives are possible at different periods of time. For instance, Socrates is able to sit and not sit because he can do so at different moments of time. But while he sits, the sitting is necessary. According to this view, Scotus and later thirteenth-century thinkers develop a notion of "synchronic contingency," partially in the context of debates over the relationship between the intellect and the will. Synchronic contingency is a possibility for opposites at the same instant of time. Synchronic contingency is used to defend the will's liberty, since on this view someone can retain the possibility of one option even while actually willing another incompatible option. According to those who emphasize these two kinds of contingency, it is important that for Thomas the present is necessary, if only in a weak sense, whereas for Scotus even the present can be contingent.

Whatever the value of this distinction as a description of medieval modal notions, it is true that Scotus distinguishes between a power

82. The texts are at times indecisive. With respect to God's causality in the context of sin, see especially Scotus, *Lectura* 2, dd. 34–37 (Vat., 19.325–70; Idem, *Ord.* 2, dd. 34–37 (Vat., 8.368–447); William of Alnwick, *Additiones Magnae* 2, d. 37 (Wadding ed., 11.1.399–403).

83. Stephen D. Dumont, "The Origin of Scotus's Theory of Synchronic Contingency," *The Modern Schoolman* 72 (1995): 149–67; Idem, "Time, Contradiction, and Freedom," passim; Jakob Schmutz, "Du péché de l'ange à la liberté d'indifférance: Les sources angélogiques de l'anthropologie moderne," *Le Études philosophiques* 2 (2002): 179–86; Antonie Vos, *The Philosophy of John Duns Scotus* (Edinburgh: Edinburgh University Press, 2006), 414–29; Thomas Williams, "Libertarian Foundations." Relevant issues can be found in the illuminating account by Timothy Noone, "Nature, Freedom, and Will: Sources for Philosophical Reflection," *Proceedings of the American Catholic Philosophical Association* 81 (2008): 1–23.

for opposites at successive instants of time and a power for opposites at the same instant of time.[84] He does not think that it is possible at the same time to will for and against the same object, but that someone retains the power of not willing an object at the same time that he wills the object. In order for there to be this power for opposites at the same instant of time, there must a priority of nature at that same instant of time. For instance, if Socrates wills to sit, his will is in first act such that it is capable of willing not to sit. But, at the same time, the will is in second act such that it actually wills to sit. At the same instant of time there is a natural priority of the first act, which is the power of willing, over the second act, which is the actual willing. He is not saying that it is possible that someone can both will to sit and not to sit at the same time, but that someone who wills to sit has a naturally prior power to will not to sit at the same instant of time.

For Scotus, this is an important point, although it does not play so prominent a role in his thought as it plays in some contemporary accounts of Scotus. Nevertheless, there are problems with using the distinction between the kinds of contingency as a key for understanding Scotus's thought on the causation of human action in contrast with that of Thomas and Ockham. First, the two kinds of contingency simply do not map on to Thomas's account of the various kinds of contingency. Thomas did not hold a solely "diachronic" view of contingency.[85] Moreover, the necessity of the present is unimportant for the

---

84. Scotus, *Lect.* 1, d. 39, qq. 1–5, nn. 50–52 (Vat., 17.495–96). It is also instructive to look at a parallel text interpolated in some versions of the *Ordinatio*, which is reprinted in Appendix A of Vat., 6.417–19. In additions to the literature cited in the preceding note, see Langston, *God's Willing Knowldge*, 26–33.

85. See Harm J. M. J. Goris, *Free Creatures of an Eternal God: Thomas Aquinas on God's Infallible Foreknowledge and Irresistible Will*, Publications of the Thomas Instituut te Utrecht, New Series 4 (Nijmegen: Stichting Thomasfonds, 1996), 257–75; Alejando Llano Cifuentes, "Aquinas and the Principle of Plenitude," in *Thomas Aquinas and His Legacy*, Studies in Philosophy and the History of Philosophy 28 (Washington, D.C.: The Catholic University of America Press, 1994), 131–48. Some problems with the denial of any notion of synchronic contingency to Thomas can be found in Tobias Hoffmann, "Aquinas and Intellectual Determinism: The Test Case of Angelic Sin," in *Archiv für der Geschichte der Philosophie* 89 (2007): 122–56; McCluskey, "Intellective Appetite," 453–54. Scott MacDonald criticizes Dumont's position in his "Synchronic

way in which human action is contingent.[86] If Socrates sits, then it is necessary that he sits. But this kind of necessity is irrelevant to deeper concerns over the will's freedom. Both Scotus and Thomas admit that the present has a weak kind of necessity.[87] The important issue is whether there is a causal sequence in which the cause necessitates the effect. The sitting is contingent in the sense that it was not necessitated by its causes. Second, there is no tight conceptual connection between a position on these modal notions and a rejection of intellectual determinism. For instance, Ockham attacks Scotus's view on the natural priority of the will's ability to its act at one instant in time, but Ockham's criticism does not incline Ockham to any sort of intellectual determinism.[88] Scotus's description of this natural priority is an interesting part of Scotus's understanding of contingency and human freedom. But it should not cloud the main issue that separates him from Thomas, which concerns the different ways in which the will and the known object are both causes of human action.

Although Scotus emphasizes that human freedom is rooted in the will as a rational potency, unlike Thomas, he often attributes efficient causality to the known object.[89] At least in his early work, Scotus ar-

Contingency, Instants of Nature, and Libertarian Freedom: Comments on 'The Background to Scotus's Theory of the Will,'" *The Modern Schoolman* 72 (1995): 169–75.

86. Thomas M. Osborne Jr., "Augustine and Aquinas on Foreknowledge through Causes," *Nova et Vetera*, English Edition 4 (2006): 227–31. For Thomas's different modal notions, see J. J. MacIntosh, "Aquinas on Necessity," *American Catholic Philosophical Quarterly* 78 (2004): 371–403.

87. Thomas, *Expositio libri Peryermenias* I, lect. 15 (Leonine, 1*.80–81); Scotus, *Lectura* I, d. 39, qq. 1–5, n. 58 (Vat., 17.499).

88. For the attack on Scotus's understanding of the instants of nature, see Ockham, *Ord.* 1, d. 38, q. un. (OTh, 4.578–83); Schmutz, "Péché de l'ange," 186–87; G. Seel, "Der antike modallogische Determinismus und Ockhams Kritik an Duns Scotus," in *L'homme et son univers au Moyen Âge*, Actes du VIIe Congrès international de philosophie médiévale, 20 août–4 septembre, ed. Charles Wenin (Louvain-la neuve: Editions de l'Institut supérieur de philosophie, 1996), 2.510–20. Nevertheless, the plausibility of distinct instants of nature at the same instant in time does play some role in later debates. See Schmutz, "Péché de l'ange," 183–86.

89. It seems to me that this point is neglected in the insightful comparison by Patrick Lee, "The Relationship between Intellect and Will in Free Choice according to Aquinas and Scotus," *The Thomist* 49 (1985): 322–42.

gues that the intellect and will together concur as one total cause of a free human action, although the will plays a greater role. He discusses the causal relationship between the will and intellect at length in two passages from two different periods of his career. In his early *Lectura* on the Sentences, d. 25, Scotus develops the view that the known object is a partial efficient cause of the act.[90] But in Scotus's later Paris lecture on this very same topic, he states that the will alone is the total cause of the act. The Vatican editors of the *Lectura* argue that the distinction between the two positions is primarily verbal.[91] In contrast, Steven Dumont suggests that Scotus's Parisian lecture was influenced by the climate at Paris, in which Scotus was lecturing under a Franciscan who, as many Franciscans did, defended Henry of Ghent's view that the known object is merely a cause *sine qua non*.[92] Dumont argues that this later discussion contradicts the earlier statements of the *Lectura*. Mary Beth Ingham agrees with Dumont against the Vatican editors that Scotus changes his mind on the causal role of the known object, but she holds that this development occurred because Scotus arrived at a deeper understanding of what it means for the will to be rational.[93] It is not necessary here to adjudicate between the different historical claims, but rather to look at the philosophical points that are made in these two works.

In the *Lectura*, Scotus takes a middle view between two positions. The first position is that the cause of the will's activity is the known object, and the second is that the known object is merely a cause that is *sine qua non*.[94] The first position was held in different ways by Godfrey of Fontaines and others, whereas the second was held by Henry of Ghent and many in the Franciscan tradition.[95] Scotus argues for the

90. Scotus, *Lect.* 2, d. 25 (Vat., 19.229–63).

91. Vat., 19.38*–41*. See also Vos, *John Duns Scotus*, 421–23.

92. Steven Dumont, "Did Duns Scotus Change His Mind on the Will?" in *Nach der Verurteilung von 1277*, 719–94, esp. 773–84.

93. Mary Beth Ingham, "Did Scotus Modify His Position on the Relationship of Intellect and Will?" *Recherches de théologie et philosophie médiévales* 69 (2002): 88–116.

94. Scotus, *Lect.* 2, d. 25, nn. 22–68 (Vat., 19.234–52).

95. For the positions of Godfrey and Henry in their historical context, see Kent, *Virtues of the Will*, 137–43; Putallaz, *Insolente liberté*, 177–252. For Scotus's relation-

position that the known object is an efficient cause, but is not by it-self the total cause of the will's activity.[96] The will is also an efficient cause. Both concur as partial causes in one total cause. He is careful to state that the causal role is not equal. Both have a causality that is perfect in their own order, but the will is the principal cause and the known object is the less principal.

What does it mean for two partial causes to concur in one total cause?[97] Scotus thinks that there are many examples of such concurrence, but the important examples in this context are those in which one partial cause is more important than the other, although they both play significant roles. The two causes are not merely accidentally conjoined, but neither is it the case that one partial cause has its efficacy from the other. Scotus gives examples to illustrate this concurrence. First, according to Scotus's biology, the father plays a more important causal role in the production of a child than the mother does. Nevertheless, the mother causes this production in her own order, even though it is less significant. Another example is that of the way in which a man and a woman rule a household. The principal ruler is the father. But the mother also plays a causal role in a way that the children or servants do not. In this case the father is the more important principle of ruling, whereas the mother is a real but less principal cause. In these cases the will is like the father in reproduction or the man in ruling the household, whereas the known object is like the mother or the wife. These examples may not be so helpful in a contemporary biological and social context, but the point is clear. Both causes are necessary in their own order and together form one total cause of the effect.

The reasons that Scotus gives for this position are connected with his criticisms of the two extreme positions. Against the position that

---

ship to these views, see Kent, *Virtues of the Will*, 143–49. For a detailed account of Godfrey's dispute with Henry, see Lottin, *Psychologie et morale*, 1.304–31. Cf. John F. Wippel, *Metaphysical Thought of Godfrey of Fontaines*, 192–202.

96. Scotus, *Lectura* 2, d. 25, n. 69 (Vat., 19.253). See also Idem, *Collatio* 3, nn. 2–5 (Wadding ed., 3.354–55).

97. Scotus, *Lectura* 2, d. 25, nn. 71–73 (Vat., 19.253–54).

the known object is the efficient cause, Scotus relies on his understanding of the way in which the will is a nonrational potency.[98] A natural cause acts in a uniform way. For instance, a red object causes redness in the sight. Seeing redness is not a result of a free choice by the power of sight. When we freely look at an object, the freedom requires a determining principle on the part of the agent, which can only be the will. The will uses the power of sight to see the red object. The freedom is the ability to look at the object or not.

If the intellect is merely a partial cause of the willing, then why does Scotus refuse to follow Henry's description of the intellect as a *sine qua non* cause? Against Henry, Scotus argues that if the known object or the mind were merely a *sine qua non* cause of willing, then "free choice would be blind (since the one willing, inasmuch as he is freely willing, would be blind)."[99] According to Scotus, Henry's position not only contradicts Augustine's authority, but it is also unreasonable. The object gives the willing its content. If the object known were only a *sine qua non* cause, then there would be no difference between loving a present object and loving an absent object.[100] This position has absurd consequences, one of which is that the blessed in heaven would not love God more than those who now living do. The difference between the two loves is in part based on the different ways in which God is present as an object.

According to Scotus, two of the most significant problems with Henry's view are (1) that it does not account for why the will acts at one time rather than another, and (2) that it does not account for the way in which acts are specified. Scotus claims that if the known object were not a moving cause, then there would be no explanation of why the will cannot act on its own independently from the object.[101] It would be possible for the will to always be in act. Henry might re-

---

98. Scotus, *Lectura* 2, d. 25, n. 74. For the will as a nonrational potency, see n. 80 (Vat., 19.256–57). For the connection with his arguments against Godfrey, see nn. 36–37 (Vat., 19.239–40).

99. "liberum arbitrium esset caecum (quia libere volens, in quantum libere volens est, esset caecus)"; Scotus, *Lect.* 2, d. 25, n. 78 (Vat., 19.78). See n. 68 (Vat., 19.252).

100. Scotus, *Lect.* 2, d. 25, nn. 67, 79 (Vat., 19.252, 256).

101. Scotus, *Lect.* 2, d. 25, n. 55 (Vat., 19.247).

ply that the known object as a *sine qua non* cause is necessary for the will's activity.[102] Scotus states that he does not know what kind of cause it would be, since the *sine qua non* cause would have to be reduced to one of the four causes, or some new genus of causes. The explanation of the known object's role as a *sine qua non* cause merely states that the intellect is in some way necessary for the will's act, but it does not explain the way in which it is necessary. Indeed, the statement that the will's act is impeded by the lack of this cause endangers the very causal priority of the will that the position claims to defend.[103] A superior cause is not impeded by an inferior cause.

Henry's position not only fails to explain how the will is moved from potency to act, but also to explain why one such act differs from another.[104] The distinction between discrete acts of willing comes from the object, and in order to account for such a distinction the objects must be *per se* active causes. Why is the will a *per se* cause? If the object were merely a condition of willing, then the object could not specify the will's acts. Scotus states that if, as in Henry's view, the object played no *per se* causal role in the willing, then similar acts of the will could be elicited concerning different objects. The intensity or perfection of love could be independent from the object loved. According to Scotus, an interesting consequence of Henry's position would be that the love of a mouse could be more intense and perfect than the love of God in the beatific vision. In general, Scotus thinks that Henry's position would make it impossible to distinguish between one act of willing from another. So although Scotus in this text does not give the known object a principal role in the causation of willing, he does think that it is an active partial cause. Scotus thinks that Henry's view ultimately implies that free action does not occur in any way through cognition, which seems obviously false.

Scotus largely relies on his understanding of the will as a rational and therefore self-determining potency in order to attack the view that the will must be merely passive with respect to opposite alterna-

102. Scotus, *Lect.* 2, d. 25, nn. 56, 58 (Vat., 19.248).
103. Scotus, *Lect.* 2, d. 25, n. 59 (Vat., 19.249).
104. Scotus, *Lect.* 2, d. 25, nn. 60–63 (Vat., 19.250).

tives.[105] Much of Scotus's argument is against Godfrey of Fontaines's personal view that sense information or images of the sense appetite move the will, since the mover, namely the sense information or image, must be distinct from the moved, namely the will.[106] Scotus, as many other Scholastics including Thomas, does not want to argue that the will's action is directly caused by a lower potency. For our purposes, Scotus's more interesting arguments are not against Godfrey's view of the causal importance of the sensory information or image, but against the more general view that the known object is the only or at least principal efficient cause of the act. Scotus is concerned to argue against any sort of intellectual determinism.

The controversy over intellectual determinism concerns the way in which the intellect and the will interact. Scotus argues that someone might say that although the will is not free to choose with respect to first principles, it is free with respect to particular conclusions about the good.[107] This position is close to that of Thomas. Scotus's argument against this view is that it gives no explanation of what the ultimate cause of the act is. On the one hand, if understanding is not ultimately caused by the will's activity, then the will is determined by the intellect and not free. On the other hand, if the understanding is ultimately caused by the intellect, then the will and not the intellect is the cause of its own acts.

Until this point, Scotus's argument against intellectual determinism might work against an account that holds that the known object determines the will through efficient causality, but it does not touch Thomas's position that the known object is the final and not the efficient cause of the act.[108] Nevertheless, in criticizing this position

105. Scotus, *Lect.* 2, d. 25, nn. 28–37 (Vat., 19.236–40).
106. Scotus, *Lect.* 2, d. 25, nn. 38–50 (Vat., 19.241–44).
107. Scotus, *Lect.* 2, d. 25, nn. 28–35 (Vat., 19.236–39).
108. For the view that this argument works against Godfrey but not against Thomas, see Capreolus, *Defensiones* 2, d. 25, art. 3, ad secundum argumentum Scoti (4.240). Lottin argues (to me unconvincingly) that Thomas's view when followed to its logical conclusion leads to a view like that of Godfrey, see Lottin, *Psychologie et morale*, 1.331–39, 247–52. Putallaz draws attention to the weaknesses of Lottin's account in his *Insolente liberté*, 184–87, 247–52.

about the efficient causality of the known object, Scotus attacks an assumption that is shared by Thomas, namely that liberty has its source in the intellect's ability to present different alternatives. Scotus uses the example of Anselm's angel to attack this point.[109] Such an angel could reason, yet if it had only the inclination to the advantageous, it would not be free. This argument is the first one that we have examined which concerns Thomas's view of freedom. Its success depends upon whether it is possible for there to be an intellectual appetite that is not free.[110]

Scotus gives another argument that also touches on Thomas's position. This argument is based on the way in which the intellect is capable of presenting opposite objects to the will. Scotus thinks that a demonstrative syllogism is not free with respect to alternatives.[111] Consequently, when the intellect presents opposite objects, the reasoning behind one of them must be defective. He thinks that if the liberty of the will had its root in the intellect's freedom, then this liberty would be based only on defective knowledge. But Scotus rejects the view that freedom depends on a defect.

This important difference between Thomas and Scotus has not been sufficiently recognized. They have contradictory views over whether the indeterminacy of the intellect's presentation of alternative goods results from a mistake. Although Thomas does not think that such a mistake is necessary for freedom between alternatives, he does think that one kind of the will's indeterminacy depends on defective knowledge, namely the freedom to choose between a true and a merely apparent good. But for Thomas this freedom is not as important as the freedom to choose between different means to or instances of happiness, or the freedom to exercise the will's act. The choice between joining one religious order and another is not based on a deduction from principles about happiness, but rather is a choice between different instantiations of happiness. So although

109. Scotus, *Lect.* 2, d. 25, n. 33 (Vat., 19.238–39).

110. Capreolus makes this point in his *Defensiones* 2, d. 25, art. 3, ad quartum argumentum Scoti (4.242).

111. Scotus, *Lect.* 2, d. 25, n. 35 (Vat., 19.239).

Scotus's argument touches on one aspect of Thomas's understanding of freedom, it does not meet his argument in similar terms.[112] As in the case of whether there can be an unfree angel, the difference between Thomas and Scotus depends not so much on the validity of the arguments, but on underlying assumptions. In Scotus's *Lectura*, two important issues between them are not developed, namely whether there can be an intellectual being without freedom, and the way in which freedom is related to the distinction between particular goods and happiness in general.

In a later work Scotus discusses the very same question of the will's causation in a different way. This discussion is found in a parallel section of his Paris lecture on the *Sentences*.[113] The structure of the

112. McCluskey, "Happiness and Freedom in Aquinas," 79–83.

113. We have four or perhaps five disussions of this Paris lecture on Book II, d. 25, which seem now to be either *reportationes* or discussions partially taken from *reportationes*. Three of them are now considered by some to be taken from William of Alnwick's *Additiones Magnae*, which are generally considered to be at least an accurate record of Scotus's thinking and reflective of what has been called R. P. IIA. The three possible editions or partial editions of *Additiones Magnae* 2, d.25 are in Carlo Balic, *Les commentaires de Jean Duns Scot sur les quatres livres de Sentences: Étude Historique et Critique* (Louvain: Bureaux de la Revue, 1927), 264–301; Wadding, *Ord.* 2, d. 25; Wadding, R. P. 2, d. 25. For the relationship between Wadding's *Ordinatio*, the *Additiones Magnae*, and the *Reportationes Parisiensis*, see the editors of the Vat., 8.89*–91*. For the relationship between Wadding's R. P. 2 and the *Additiones Magnae*, see for now Hechich, "Il Problema delle 'Reportationes,'" 77. Scholarly opinion seems to be very fluid and we can expect future changes. Timothy Noone and Tobias Hoffmann have kindly provided me with preliminary transcriptions of the R. P. IIA, d. 25 and Timothy Noone with what has been called R. P. IIB, d. 25. R. P. IIB is less complete and contains a much shorter discussion of some of the arguments also found in R. P. IIA, whereas it is very different from Balic's version of the *Additiones Magnae*, and there are further differences in Wadding's *Ordinatio* 2, d. 25. As far as I can tell, the arguments and comments of what has been called R. P. IIA, d. 25, are in substance and in their order (although not always in grammatical structure or in phraseology) exactly the same as those found in Wadding's edition of R. P. II, which is now regarded as being derived from the *Additiones Magnae*. Not only is Wadding's version close to IIA, but it also seems to differ greatly from the manuscripts which were used in Balic's edition, five of which are now regarded as important manuscripts of the *Additiones Magnae*. For the manuscripts, see Balic, 264, Hechich, 77–78. Since the Wadding edition of R. P. II, d. 25 is so close to that of IIA and different from Balic's edition of the *Additiones Magnae*, and the Wadding edition is now widely available, I will cite from

discussion differs from the earlier one in that it primarily consists in an attack on the view that the known object causes the will's act, and more particularly Godfrey's position that sense information or images *(phantasmata)* play some such role. The tenor of this discussion may result from academic politics at the University of Paris, where Franciscans held or perhaps were expected to hold Henry's view that the known object is a *sine qua non* cause. Whereas Scotus had previously claimed that the known object is a less principal but nevertheless partial efficient cause of the will's act, in this text he argues that "no created thing other than the will is the total cause of the act of willing in the will."[114] In his defense of this alternative position, Scotus uses many of the arguments for his older position, such as the argument that the indeterminacy on the part of the intellect results from unsound arguments.[115] His later use of this point is slightly different in that he does not restate that such indeterminacy would be a poor kind of freedom, but instead states that the contingency would not come from the will itself but rather from a weakness of the intellect. The focus on the importance of the will's ability to move itself is thus made sharper. He also argues not merely for the thesis that the known object is a less principal efficient cause than the will, but for the stronger thesis that only the will is the total efficient cause of the act.

Scotus does not deny that the known object plays a role in the act's production. He states that the intellect and the will concur in the act. But he notes that the intellect's contribution is insufficient for the determination of the act. Again, he refers to the example of Anselm's angel, which would have "an intellectual appetite incapable of determining itself, but desiring according to the mode of nature."[116] He

---

the Wadding edition and refer to this edition as the "Paris lecture" in the text. But it should be kept in mind that at this time the common opinion is that Wadding's edition of the "*Reportatio Parisiensis* II" is the *Additiones Magnae* 2, but this opinion may change soon. I am particularly grateful to Timothy Noone for his generous comments on this issue, and his emphasis that we really do not know what texts Wadding used here, or even whether the manuscipts on which they are ultimately based are extant.

114. "nihil creatum aliud a voluntate est causa totalis actus volendi in voluntate"; Scotus, R. P. II, d. 25, n. 20 (Wadding ed., 11.1.371).

115. Scotus, R. P. II, d. 25, n. 20 (Wadding ed., 11.1.372).

116. Scotus, R. P. II, d. 25, n. 20 (Wadding ed., 11.1.372).

uses the same thought experiment as before, but in order to make a seemingly stronger point. The basic argument is simple and based on his belief that the will is the only power that can determine itself, and he states that this position can be found in Aristotle's understanding of a rational potency.

Most of the later arguments against Godfrey's position resemble those of the earlier discussion. However, since in this text he does not criticize Henry's description of the known object as a mere *sine qua non* cause, he must come up with a new response to Godfrey's argument that if the known object is merely a *sine qua non* cause, then the will is always in act. Scotus cannot use his previous response to Godfrey, namely that the known object is a partial but not total cause, because he now rejects this terminology. Instead, in this later text he points out that there is often a dependence of one effect on another without causal priority.[117] For instance, the intellect often depends on a kind of sense information *(phantasma)* for understanding, and yet the intellect's knowledge is not efficiently caused by this sense information. There is also a certain noncausal priority of the intellect with respect to an instant of nature, since the object must be known before it can be willed. This "before" is not temporal, but it indicates a dependence. This dependence of the will on the known object is not a causal dependence with respect to the action because the will, unlike the senses or even the intellect, is a fully self-determining power. The will is sufficient for moving itself from potency to act.

Scotus in this passage resolves one of his previous objections to Henry's position, which was that the known object is needed as a cause to help explain the will's movement from potency to act. He does not similarly address a second major criticism of Henry's position, which is that the object must be a cause if we are to account for the difference between the will's acts. However, he does discuss the importance of the known object's role in his response to another position, which is that the exterior object in the soul is the cause of the act. Scotus argues that the role of the known object could be understood in two ways.[118] First,

117. Scotus, R. P. II, d. 25, nn. 15–16 (Wadding ed., 11.1.370–71).
118. Scotus, R. P. II, q. 25, n. 19 (Wadding ed., 11.1.371). There is a different account

it could be held that the object in the soul is an efficient cause and that the object itself is a final cause, but that as an efficient cause it is not the total cause. This first possibility resembles his earlier view in the *Lectura*. The second approach is to hold that the object is a cause *sine qua non*, and he argues that in this case it is an efficient cause per accidens.

This hesitancy between considering the known object as a partial cause and as a *sine qua non* cause can be found also in a probably very late section of Scotus's *Ordinatio*.[119] One of the arguments against Henry in the *Lectura* is that if the object were merely a *sine qua non* cause, then the enjoyment of God in this life and in heaven would be the same. In the Paris lecture, Scotus claims that the distinction between the two kinds of enjoyment could be explained either with the object as a partial cause, as in the earlier works, or as a *sine qua non* cause.[120] In Book IV of the *Ordinatio*, which is probably later than the *Reportatio Parisiensis*, Scotus similarly mentions that if one wishes to distinguish between the two kinds of enjoyment as belonging to different species, which probably should be done, then either approach could be used as the basis for such a distinction between species.[121] It seems that Scotus in his later works is more willing to accept the description of the object as a *sine qua non* cause, although he is hesitant and it is not clear that his understanding of such a cause is the same as that of Henry.

What is Scotus's understanding of a *sine qua non* cause? He previously had attacked the view that the known object is such a cause because he thinks that this kind of causality is either reducible to other kinds or to some strange new kind of cause. It has no real explanatory value. In at least some versions of the later lecture, Scotus seems to

---

in IIB, in which Scotus is repored as arguing that the known object might not be a being, in which case it could not exercise causal efficacy.

119. For a consideration of the argument and additional texts, see Dumont, "Did Scotus Change His Mind?" 778–83.

120. R. P. II, d. 25, n. 4 (Wadding ed., 11.1.373). This argument is also not contained in IIB. It is interesting that the primary places in which Scotus mentions two distinct possibilities of understanding the known object's role are missing in IIB.

121. Scotus, *Ord.* 4, d. 49, q. 5, nn. 4–5 (Wadding ed., 10.425–26).

answer his previous query as to the nature of the object's *sine qua non* causality by stating that it is a kind of efficient causality. This position not only resembles to some extent his earlier view that the known object exercises efficient causality, but it glosses Henry's view in such a way as to explain the *sine qua non* causality of the object as efficient causality.

In this later lecture Scotus does not settle on one explanation or another, but it is significant how the first possibility, namely that the object is a partial efficient cause, resembles his earlier view, and that Scotus's description of the second possibility explains Henry's *sine qua non* causality in a way that avoids the objections that he previously raised against Henry. Nevertheless, even though he introduces elements that are similar to his early position, both explanations seem compatible with his statement in this later text that the will is the total cause of its own act.

There is one more section in which Scotus discusses the possibility of efficient causation by the object. In his response to an objection that is based on Aristotle's statement that the appetible object moves the appetite, Scotus also entertains the position that the object is an efficient cause, although he denies that it is the total cause and presumably even a part of the total cause. He states that, interpreted in this way, Aristotle's statement supports his own position that the will and not the object is the total cause.[122] But Scotus does not decisively defend this explanation of the known object's efficient causality. He also considers another interpretation of Aristotle's statement, namely that the appetible object is a final cause that moves the will only metaphorically. This second possible interpretation of Aristotle's statement would contradict not only the words but also the substance of his earlier position in the *Lectura* that the object has not only a final but also an efficient causal role. But Scotus does not clearly endorse this view.

Although Scotus clearly changed his mind over the question of whether the will can be described as the sole total cause of its act, it is

---

122. Scotus, R. P. II, d. 25, n. 21 (Wadding ed., 11.1.372). In the beginning of IIB, he mentions only the possibility that the object moves metaphorically.

difficult to determine how much this change is merely verbal and how much it expresses a real theoretical shift. In general, the tone of the Paris lecture is more cautious and the position is less fully developed. In the *Lectura* both the will and the known object are partial efficient causes of the will's act, although the will is more important and the source of contingency is in the will's ability to determine itself. In the Paris lecture, the will is not simply the principal partial cause, but is itself the total cause of the will's act. The role of the object in the production of the act is to a great extent unexplained. He defends Henry's view that it is a *sine qua non* cause, but it is not clear that he shares Henry's understanding of *sine qua non* causes. His earlier concerns about this kind of causality are not addressed. Moreover, he allows for the possibility that the known object exercises some sort of efficient causality, although he modifies this claim by stating that it cannot be a per se efficient cause and it is not even part of the act's total cause.

It is also difficult to show that the discussion in the Paris lecture is philosophically better or more consistent with his thought, or that it expresses Scotus's own more mature view. The Vatican editors have shown how in another late text, namely his revision of the *Ordinatio*, Scotus still refers to the position that the known object is a partial cause that along with the will forms one total cause.[123] How are these remarks consistent with the Paris lecture? It is at least significant that Scotus describes the known object as a partial efficient cause both in his early and in his late works. Moreover, we will see that Ockham attributes to Scotus only the view that the known object is a partial efficient cause.

Although Scotus did later discuss the known object as a *sine qua non* cause, Scotus's description of this known object as partial efficient cause remains important for two reasons. First, the change may be only verbal. Even if there is a real theoretical shift, it has not yet been shown that this shift present an alternative view that is clearly

123. Scotus, *Ord.* 2, d. 7, n. 44 (Vat., 8.95–96). For other texts, see Vat., 19.40*–41*. But Dumont, "Did Scotus Change His Mind?" 758–66, convincingly argues that these references do not definitively show that Scotus did not change his view.

superior either with respect to Scotus's thought as a whole or with respect to the difficulties that need to be addressed. Second, the position that the known object is a partial efficient cause is often later attributed to Scotus, and may be more influential. We do not need to settle the historical dispute over whether there was any theoretical shift in order to give greater weight to Scotus's view that the known object is a partial efficient cause of an act, even though it is helpful to know that Scotus himself may have seen difficulties with this view.

Even though Scotus's treatment of the causation of the human act is not always consistent, certain themes are constant. First, he thinks that the freedom and the contingency of the human act are entirely rooted in the fact that the will itself is a fully rational potency that can determine itself to opposites. This capability for self-determination does not conceptually follow from the description of the will as an intellectual appetite, since it would not be a logical contradiction for an angel to have an intellectual appetite that is determined merely to its own advantage. Second, Scotus refuses to locate the source of indeterminacy in the will's capacity for opposites because the intellect influences the act as a rational and not logical agent, and the intellect's indeterminacy is found in its ability to construct or follow unsound arguments. Third, he often states or is open to the position that the known object exercises at least some efficient causality in the production of the will's act. More frequently, Scotus holds that the known object acts as a partial efficient cause that is perfect in its own kind but less important than the will, which is the other efficient cause. Although in a later work he seems to retract this view or at least this terminology, he remains open to the suggestion that the known object exercises a *per accidens* efficient causality that is distinct from the will's total causality.

WILLIAM OF OCKHAM

As shall be shown, William of Ockham follows the Franciscan tradition in denying that the will and the intellect are really or even formally distinct powers, or that the powers of the soul are distinct from the soul. His view concerning the real identity of the intellect and the will causes him to reject Scotus's theory that human freedom is rooted in the will as a formally distinct rational potency with two distinct inclinations. But William of Ockham adopts the position that is most frequently expressed by Scotus, which is that the known object and the will concur together as the total cause of the will's act. According to Ockham, freedom is rooted in the ability of the intellectual creature to will for or against any object presented to it by the intellect, including happiness.

Ockham defends the position that the act of the intellect is a partial cause of the act. He differs from Scotus first perhaps in his thesis that the real partial efficient cause is not the object but the act of understanding.[124] This approach might solve the problem of how an object existing outside the agent can efficiently cause something within the agent. More importantly, Ockham rejects Scotus's position that the choice is free because one of the partial causes, namely the will, is free. Ockham writes that "the intellect and the will in no way are distinguished on the part of the thing, but however according to him [Scotus], the intellect necessarily causes understanding, and the will contingently and freely causes volition."[125] Ockham denies that one in the same act can have both a natural and a free cause.[126] Since the object is distinct from the moved will, it cannot be a natural cause of the will's free movement. The cause must be free. He also rejects a view common to Thomas and Scotus, namely that the will has a natural inclination toward its own perfection, and especially Scotus's view that freedom is possible because the intellect has not only the natural inclination, which Anselm describes as the inclination to the advantageous, but also an inclination for the just.[127] Ockham argues that the distinction between the two inclinations is merely a distinc-

124. "actus intelligendi est vere causa efficiens respectu volitionis et non obiectum extra"; Ockham, *Rep.* 3, q. 12 (OTh, 6.396).

125. "intellectus et voluntas nullo modo distinguuntur ex parte rei, et tamen secundum istum intellectus necessario causat intellectionem, et contingenter et libere voluntas causat volitionem"; William of Ockham, *Ord.* 1, d. 1, q. 6 (OTh, 1.491).

126. Ockham, *Ord.* 1, d. 1, q. 6 (OTh, 1.492–93).

127. Ockham, *Ord.* 1, d. 1, q. 6 (OTh, 1.507).

tion between acting in accordance with right reason or against it.[128] It is strange that Ockham does not seem to recognize that for Scotus an act in accordance with the inclination for the advantageous can be also in accordance with right reason and even meritorious.[129] Generally speaking, Ockham rejects the complexities of Scotus's account: the will is not even formally distinct from the intellect, nor does it have two different inclinations.

Although Ockham denies that there is a real distinction between the will and the intellect, he argues that there is a distinction between the sensitive soul and the intellectual soul in human beings.[130] His argument is not a demonstration from propositions that are known through their terms. Nevertheless, he thinks that he can give sufficient reasons for his thesis. The reasons shed light on other issues, such as the distinction between the intellect and sense. Unlike Thomas, he does not use the distinction between particulars and universals to distinguish intellect from sense. Since Ockham thinks that even in this life the intellect also directly knows particulars, this argument cannot work.[131]

His first argument is that the intellectual appetite can restrain the sense appetite.[132] For instance, someone can wish to eat a cake but can choose not to through his intellectual appetite. This conflict between the appetites shows not only a distinction between the appetites themselves, but also a real distinction in the subjects to which they belong. This first argument is important because it shows how Ockham can use a distinction between appetites to argue for a dis-

---

128. Ockham, *Ord.* 1, d. 1, q. 6 (OTh, 1.502). See Armand Maurer, *The Philosophy of William of Ockham in Light of Its Principles*, Studies and Texts 133 (Toronto: Pontifical Institute of Medieval Studies, 1999), 451–60; Holopainen, *Foundations of Ethics*, 3–16; Vesa Hirvonen, *Passions in William Ockham's Philosophical Psychology*, Studies in the History of Philosophy of Mind 2 (Dordrecht: Kluwer, 2004), 35–46.

129. See, for instance, Scotus, *Ord.* 3, d. 31, nn. 22–23 (Vat., 10.124); Ibid., 3, d. 26, q. un., n. 110 (Vat., 10.35–36).

130. Ockham, Quod 2, q. 10 (OTh, 9.156–61).

131. For Ockham's new focus on the primacy of the individual, see Maurer, *Philosophy of William of Ockham*, 490–96.

132. This argument can also be found in his *Rep.* 2, q. 20 (OTh, 5.444).

tinction between the cognitive powers and the forms that the appetites accompany. The second argument is a *reductio*. If the two souls were not distinct, then every act of sensation would be an act of the intellect, which is obviously false. Another absurd consequence would be that God would be able to conserve sensation in souls that are separated from the body through death. Ockham thinks that it is contradictory for these separate souls to sense. The third argument is based on the way in which the sensitive soul is extended. According to Ockham, the sensitive soul is extended and material. Indeed, in another passage he states that the soul's powers are distinguished only to the extent that they belong to different parts of the body. [133] The fact that a blind man can hear shows that the power of sight is distinct from that of hearing. Sight and hearing are distinct in part because their bodily organs are in distinct locations. This understanding of the local distinction between the sense powers underlies the third argument, which is based on the way in which one soul is extended and the other is not. Ockham notes that the intellectual soul does not exist in any one part of the body. Consequently, it must be different from the sensitive soul, which does have parts.

Ockham uses the principle of parsimony to argue against positing unnecessary distinctions between powers, and also unnecessary distinctions between powers and the soul.[134] According to Ockham, although there is some basis for distinguishing in reality between the sense powers, there is no such reason to distinguish in reality between the intellect and will as powers. The description expressing what "intellect" names is the "'substance of a soul capable of understanding.' The description of 'will' is that which is 'the substance of a soul capable of willing.'"[135] Ockham does allow that the distinction is real in the sense that willing is really distinct from understanding. Consequently, the connotation of the word "will" differs from that of

---

133. Ockham, *Rep.* 3, q. 4 (OTh, 6.136–39).

134. Ockham, *Rep.* 2, q. 20 (OTh, 5.436–37).

135. "'intellectus est substantia animae potens intelligere.' Descriptio voluntatis est quod est 'substantia animae potens velle'"; Ockham, *Rep.* 2, q. 20 (OTh, 5.435). See especially Holopainen, *Foundations of Ethics*, 16–20.

the word "intellect" because although they both refer to or denote the same subject, namely the intellective soul, they do connote really distinct acts. The distinction between the two is simply a distinction between the two acts, and only to this extent is the distinction real. Positing separate powers complicates the issue without providing any better explanation of how the acts are caused. It should be noted that Ockham is not denying a distinction between the will and the intellect. He agrees with Aristotle that distinct objects require distinct parts of the soul.[136] But he argues they are called "parts" merely because of the real distinction between the acts themselves, and not on account of any real distinction in the soul.

Since the will and the intellect are not really distinct powers, and the will does not have different inclinations, it seems that Scotus's example of an intellect with merely a natural appetite would be impossible. According to Ockham, the ability to identify an object as good or evil implies an ability to desire it or to have aversion toward it.[137] Although cognitive and appetitive acts are distinct, the objects are the same. For instance, the hamburger that I apprehend as good is the same hamburger that I desire to eat. The distinction between acts does not require a distinction between powers in the soul. Consequently, there are as many appetitive powers as there are cognitive powers, and the appetites are distinguished from each other only to the extent to which the cognitive powers are distinct. For instance, the appetite that follows on sight is different from the one that follows on hearing. We have already seen that these two cognitive powers are distinct because they are connected with distinct bodily organs. Similarly, there is a real distinction between the appetite that follows on intellectual cognition, namely the will, and the sensitive appetites, because of the real distinction between senses and the intellect. But with respect to the intellectual substance, there is no distinction between intellect and will. The ability to know the good entails an ability to make a decision about it. Ockham writes that "no object, neither

136. Ockham, *Rep.* 2, q. 20 (OTh, 5.440–41).
137. Ockham, *Rep.* 2, q. 20 (OTh, 5.447).

good nor bad, can be known by some sensitive or intellectual cognition unless the appetite following such a power can have an act concerning the same object."[138]

What is the root of freedom? Ockham focuses on the ability to produce contingent effects. For Scotus, as for Thomas, free human actions are contingent. But Scotus thinks that the Holy Spirit is freely and necessarily produced.[139] Freedom is compatible with necessity in this case because the causality is not natural. Scotus thinks that freedom is a perfection. Against Scotus, Ockham argues that freedom is not distinct from the ability to cause contingent effects.[140] The word "freedom" denotes either the will itself or "an intellectual nature in connoting that something can be done contingently by it."[141] Ockham again uses the principle of parsimony to argue that freedom is not something that exists apart from the will, which is the same as the intellectual substance. As with previous thinkers, Ockham's discussion of an act's causation focuses on the relationship between the will and the act of knowing. But for Ockham, this relationship is between the acts themselves, and not two distinct faculties. Nevertheless, the discussion of the acts is also a discussion of the relationship between the "intellect" and the "will," if these two terms are correctly understood as denoting the same intellectual substance but as having different connotations that are based on the real distinction between the acts produced.

Although every act of the will requires intellectual cognition, not every intellectual cognition requires willing. Knowledge and will are the immediate efficient causes of willing and willing against.[142] Ock-

---

138. "nullum obiectum, nec bonum nec malum, potest congosci ab aliquo cognitione sensitiva vel intellectiva quin appetitus sequens talem potentiam possit habere actum circa idem obiectum"; Ockham, *Rep.* 2, q. 20 (OTh, 5.447).

139. Scotus, *Ord.* 1, d. 10, nn. 30–32 (Vat., 4.352); Idem, *Quod* 16, art. 2 (Noone and Roberts ed., 176–80). For the compatibility of this necessity with freedom in God, see Gaine, *Free Will in Heaven*, 39–50.

140. Ockham, *Ord.* 1, d. 10, q. 2 (OTh, 3.335–44).

141. "importans ipsam voluntatem vel naturam intellectualem connotando aliquid contingenter posse fieri ab eadem"; Ockham, *Ord.* 1,, d. 10, q. 2 (OTh, 3.344).

142. Ockham, *Rep.* 2, q. 20 (OTh, 5.441–42); *Rep.* 3, q. 12 (OTh, 6.396).

ham writes, "the two drag one and the same ship."[143] The act of under-standing is a partial efficient cause of willing. In this sense, an act of understanding is always prior to an act of willing. However, the intellect itself is a merely passive potency. The contingency of the action comes from the will, which is active. Although the act of understanding is an efficient cause of the act, the act of willing's efficient causality explains the act's contingency. Perhaps Ockham's position here results from his tendency to reduce the role of final causality. In general, Ockham represents a shift from an earlier medieval emphasis on final causes to an emphasis on efficient causes.[144]

A distinctive characteristic of intellectual creatures is the ability to reflect on one's own knowledge. As we have seen, Thomas at times uses the intellect's ability for reflection on itself as an explanation for the way in which freedom is rooted in the intellect.[145] According to Ockham, this distinctive ability for intellectual reflection is based on the will's efficient causality.[146] By the intellect I know something without knowing that I know it. In order for the intellect to know its own act, the will must will that this unreflective act be known by a reflective act of the intellect.

The will can even cause reflection on its own acts without any extra causal input from the intellect, even though an object must be known to be willed.[147] Suppose that someone might love another without perceiving that he loves that other person. He knows the person and loves him, but does not know that he loves him. According to Ockham, the reflection on this loving can be caused by the will alone.

---

143. "duo trahunt unam et eandem navem"; Ockham, *In libros Physicorum Aristotelis*, lib. 2, cap. 5 (OPh, 4.287).

144. Marilyn McCord Adams, "Ockham on Final Causality: Muddying the Waters," *Franciscan Studies* 56 (1998): 1–46; Stephen F. Brown, "Ockham and Final Causality," in *Studies in Medieval Philosophy*, ed. John F. Wippel, Studies in Philosophy and the History of Philosophy 17 (Washington, D.C.: The Catholic University of America Press, 1987), 249–72; Maurer, *Philosophy of William of Ockham*, 412–17.

145. Thomas Aquinas, *De Veritate*, q. 24, art. 2, resp. (Leonine, 22.685). For more texts and an analysis, see Gallagher, "Aquinas on the Will," 569–74.

146. Ockham, Q. V., q. 5 (OTh, 8.177–79); Quod 2, q. 12 (OTh, 9.165–67).

147. Ockham, Q. V., q. 5 (OTh, 8.178–79).

Ockham argues that if the unreflexive act of understanding on its own caused the reflective act, then every act of understanding would also be an act of understanding that one understands, which is false. Some cause other than an additional act of understanding is needed. Ockham states that willing on its own causes the reflective understanding by moving the intellect to think about its own acts. Although the will is required for such reflective acts, the original intellectual act is also necessary. But the reflective act of understanding follows naturally once the will has elicited it. The knowledge through reflection is an effect of the will alone.

In this reflective knowledge, there are different orders of causality. If someone wills to think about his own act, the self-knowledge is caused immediately. What are the causes of this self-knowledge that occurs immediately? The first unreflective act of loving is caused by the cognition of the loved object and the will. The second act of willing to know about one's willing is caused not only by the will, but also by the loving and knowing that constitute the first unreflective act. In these cases the will plays the active role in moving the agent to reflexive understanding, but the first act of cognition retains some causal role.

Ockham grants a greater role to an intellectual act as an efficient cause of a free act than Thomas does. Nevertheless, Ockham grants a greater independence to the will in that he thinks that the will can act against judgments of reason without necessarily forming new judgments. Although previous thinkers had recognized that the will can choose something other than what was previously judged to be good, they seem not to hold that the will can perform different actions given the same intellectual judgment.[148] For Ockham, although the will's act presupposes intellectual activity, it is largely independent from knowing.[149] This independence can be seen especially in his description of the will's freedom: "I call freedom the ability by which I am able indifferently and contingently to posit diverse courses, such that

148. For instance, see Colleen McCluskey's comments on Philip the Chancellor (d. 1236) in Eadem, "Ethical Voluntarism," 197–200.

149. Ockham, *In libros Physicorum*, lib. 2, cap. 8 (OPh, 4.319–21); Idem, *Rep.* 3, q. 11 (OTh, 6.355); Idem, Q. V., q. 4 (OTh, 8.133–34).

I am able to cause and not to cause the same effect, with no difference existing somewhere else outside this power."[150] This notion of freedom has been described by Servais Pinckaers as the "liberty of indifference," since its focus is on the autonomy of the will and its indifference to opposite alternatives.[151] Just as Thomas and Scotus do, Ockham contrasts the will with a natural power in that the will can be a source of its own action. But Ockham's understanding of the will's self-motion separates the will further from the judgment of reason and any natural ordering to the good.

In one text, Ockham suggests that human choice is not limited to the threefold division of the good into the pleasurable, the useful, and the upright *(honestum)*.[152] He states that the will must will the good only in the sense that anything that is willed is good. In another text, Ockham argues that the will is able to at least will against any good, even if the good object has no aspect of badness in it.[153] In yet

150. "voco libertatem potestatem qua possum indifferenter et contingenter diversa ponere, ita quod possum eumdem effectum causare et non causare, nulla diversitate existente alibi extra illam potentiam"; Ockham, Quod 1, q. 16 (OTh, 9.87). This is the "philosophical" notion of freedom. See Ockham, *Ord.* 1, d. 1, q. 6 (OTh, 1.501–2). For a more detailed account, see Osborne, "Ockham on Freedom and Happiness," 435–56.

151. Servais Pinckaers, *The Sources of Christian Ethics*, trans. Mary Thomas Noble (Washington, D.C.: The Catholic University of America Press, 1995), 240–53. For a defense of some of Pinckaers's general claims in the light of contemporary scholarship, see Thomas M. Osborne Jr., "William of Ockham as a Divine Command Theorist," *Religious Studies* 41 (2005): 1–22. For the contrast with Ockham's predecessors, see Maurer, *Philosophy of William of Ockham*, 510–15; Marilyn McCord Adams, "William of Ockham: Voluntarist or Naturalist," in *Studies in Medieval Philosophy*, ed. John F, Wippel, Studies in Philosophy and the History of Philosophy 1 (Washington, D.C.: The Catholic University of America Press, 1987), 228–34; and with caution Normore, "Ockham, Self-Motion, and the Will," 297–99. The textual evidence for Normore's interpration of Thomas is unclear as he focuses in large part on the synchronic/diachronic distinction, and does not adequately distinguish Thomas's position from one similar to or the same as that which we can find in Godfrey.

152. Ockham, Q. V., q. 8 (OTh, 8.442). For a contrast of Ockham with Thomas Aquinas, see Linwood Urban, "William of Ockham's Theological Ethics," *Franciscan Studies* 33 (1973): 336–39.

153. Ockham, Q. V., q. 8 (OTh, 8.445).

another text, he states that the will is free with respect to any end.[154] Whereas Thomas and Scotus explain the will's activity with recourse to the good, in at least some cases Ockham thinks that the good is such merely because it is willed by the agent. In at least these cases, the good is explained with recourse to the will.

Ockham's rejection of this natural ordering to the good can be seen in his defense of the view that someone can will against both happiness in general and happiness in the particular. With respect to happiness in general, Ockham argues that in at least some cases of suicide the agent wills against his own happiness, since the suicide wills against it in willing not to exist.[155] Whereas Scotus had followed a traditional view that the suicide at least wills against his own misery, Ockham separates the suicide's act from any explanation in terms of the agent's happiness. Ockham also argues for his view by pointing out that an agent might think that happiness is impossible and consequently not will it, and a Christian through some mortal sins might simply just will to suffer eternal punishment rather than to be happy. Ockham denies the position, common to both Thomas and Scotus, that happiness cannot be the object of willing against *(nolle)* and unhappiness cannot be the object of willing *(velle)*, just as he seemingly denies their common belief that anything willed is willed under the formality of the good.

Ockham's general arguments for the view that happiness can be willed against or rejected also provide particular instances of his appeal to experience to show that the human will is free. Thomas explains freedom with an appeal to the different ways in which the good can be known, and the need for the will to efficiently cause the act. Scotus appeals to experience, but he also explains freedom in terms of the will's different inclinations and its status as a rational potency. Additionally, Scotus rejects the view that in this life we can know our-

---

154. Ockham, *In libros Physicorum*, lib. 2, cap. 13 (OPh, 4.402–3).

155. Ockham, *Ord.* 1, d. 1, q. 6 (OTh, 1.503–4). The centrality and existence of this difference between Ockham and Scotus is neglected in Irwin, *Development of Ethics*, 1.702–4.

selves directly without using sense experience and sense organs.[156] In contrast, Ockham does not find it necessary to explain how freedom is possible because he thinks that the ability to choose between alternatives is easily known through direct experience. No other explanation or argument is clearer than this primitive experience.[157] The examples of the suicide and the Christian who chooses eternal damnation are for him clear examples of how even happiness can be willed against.

With respect to the enjoyment of God in heaven, Ockham agrees with Scotus against those such as Thomas who argue that there is a natural necessity of the end, since the end completely fulfills the will's desire for the good. But whereas Scotus is indecisive about the explanation of this impeccability and even suggests that there is some sort of *secundum quid* necessity for loving God in these cases, Ockham thinks that his arguments for the position that happiness in general can be willed against also show that someone can simply choose against happiness in the particular.[158] Moreover, he gives additional arguments that shed some light on his understanding of the relationship between the will, happiness, and ethics. For instance, Ockham writes that God might will that someone lack enjoyment in the beatific vision. But since any will can conform to the divine will, it follows that someone can will against his own enjoyment.

How does Ockham explain the impeccability of the blessed in heaven? He argues that God is the pure cause of their happiness. God is the total cause of such happiness in such a way that the will and the intellect do not play that active efficient role that they do in the present life; they are purely passive.[159] Ockham holds this view seem-

156. Boulnois, *Être et représentation*, 175–88.

157. Ockham, Quod 1, q. 16 (OTh, 9.88). For a related argument from reason, see Ockham, *In libros Physicorum*, lib. 2, cap. 8 (OPh, 4.320).

158. Ockham, *Ord.* 1, d. 1, q. 6 (OTh, 1.504–5).

159. Ockham, *Rep.* 2, q. 20 (OTh, 5.443); Idem, *Rep.* 4, q. 15 (OTh, 7.336). For the necessity of the beatific vision, see the two questions wholly devoted to the topic, Idem, *Ord.* 1, d. 1, q. 6 (OTh, 1.486–507), and Idem, *Rep.* 4, q. 16 (OTh, 7.340–61), as well as the discussion of "securitas" in Q. V., q. 6, art. 11, dub. 6 (OTh, 8.312–13). For a summary, see Gaine, *Free Will in Heaven*, 71–85; Kitanov, *Beatific Enjoyment*, 266–85. Ockham's

ingly because he believes both in the eternity of the beatific vision and that the will can choose against any good. If the intellect or will played an active role in the beatific vision, then the agent would be able to reject this vision.

Ockham emphasizes the will not by limiting the efficient causality of the cognitive act in the production of the free action, but by giving the will an active role that is independent from anything outside of it. The two efficient causes of the act are the knowledge and the will, but the will is the source of the act's contingent production. Ockham does not deny that there may be other causes involved. For instance, in many cases an act of the sensitive appetite is an immediate effective partial cause of a free act, but it exercises its causality only through its influence on the will, which is entirely free. It is easier to act with the sense appetite rather than against it, but the sense appetite in no way determines the will.

With respect to God's causal contribution, Ockham thinks that we know through faith that God concurs immediately in every secondary cause.[160] Ockham seems to deny what Thomas holds and Scotus suggests in some passages, namely that God is a universal cause of the human act and yet as such does not violate the act's contingency. For Thomas, the movement of the human will by God is unproblematic, although the will can be moved immediately and efficaciously by no extrinsic created cause. For Ockham, God directs human affairs through providence by adding or withholding his causal contribution to the human action.[161] Just as Scotus had appealed to God's withdrawal of his causal activity as a possible explanation of the impeccability of the blessed in heaven, Ockham uses it to explain why the Virgin Mary did not sin. If she had chosen to sin, then God would

position that the beatific vision is passive may have additional roots in the Franciscan tradition. See Trottmann, "La vision béatifique dans la seconde école franciscaine," 148–52.

160. Ockham, *Rep.* 2, qq. 3–5 (OTh, 5.50–87).

161. Ockham, *Rep.* 3, q. 8 (OTh, 6.206); Idem, *Rep.* 3, q. 5 (OTh, 6.153–56). See Lucan Freppert, *The Basis of Morality according to William of Ockham* (Chicago: Franciscan Herald Press, 1988), 37–38.

have prevented it by not concurring in the production of the action. Ockham thinks that divine concurrence is necessary for an act, but he seems to think that God cannot exercise his providence over free acts except through the exercise of a separate causal contribution. In a sense, Ockham thinks that the human will cannot be totally efficaciously caused by God, even though he thinks that God can choose to concur or not in the act itself.

In summary, Ockham shifts the causal importance in the production of an act to the will, which is not really distinct from the intellectual substance. He does not emphasize the will by reducing the known object to merely a *sine qua non* cause, as did Henry of Ghent and perhaps even the later Scotus. Indeed, Ockham more precisely focuses on the act of the intellect rather than on the object itself. He claims that the act of the intellect, like the will, is an immediate partial efficient cause of the act. Ockham's shift is in the separation of the will's causal exercise from any external determination, whether it be an external good, the known object, or even God. The will is free because it is indifferent with respect to alternatives even when everything outside of the will is the same, including the intellect's judgment. Moreover, not only is the will free with respect to external efficient causality, but it is also free with respect to the end. If presented with any good, the will is capable of choosing or rejecting it, just as the will is free to reject not only happiness in particular but also happiness in general.

TRAJECTORY OF THE POSITIONS

The above summary shows how the three figures differ in their views on (1) the root of freedom, (2) whether the known object is an efficient cause of the act, and (3) the relationship between freedom and the good. First, Scotus is the only figure to think that it is conceptually possible for an intellectual appetite to be unfree. He does not think that there are any such cases, but his use of Anselm's thought experiment, in which an angel could have an appetite only for the advantageous and not for the just, illustrates that for Scotus the will is not merely any intellectual appetite, but rather an intellectual appetite with two different inclinations. For Scotus, created freedom requires a distinction between the inclination for the advantageous and the just. The will is truly a rational potency because it can move itself in accordance with either inclination. In contrast, Thomas and Ockham think that all intellectual creatures must be free. For Thomas, freedom is rooted in the intellect's ability to grasp the good in general, and to choose not only between true and merely apparent goods, but also between different true goods. For Ockham, there is no real distinction between the intellect and the will, but they both connote different ways in which an intellectual substance can act. Moreover, the distinction between sense and intellect is not exactly reflected in the distinction between the particular and the universal. The ability to grasp good or evil through intellectual knowledge entails the ability to direct oneself toward or against the known object. The human ability to act in this way is known directly through experience.

Second, Thomas is the only one of the three to argue that only the will is an efficient cause of its own act. He argues that the known object is not an efficient cause, but rather exerts influence in the order of final causality. In contrast, Scotus (more often than not) and Ockham state that the known object is an efficient cause of a free human act. Generally speaking, Scotus thinks that the known object is a partial efficient cause of the act that is less principal than the will, although the will and the intellect together form one total cause of the act. In one later text, Scotus states that the will itself is the only created total cause of the act, but even in this discussion he considers it possible that the known object is a per accidens efficient cause. Like Scotus, Ockham also thinks that the will and the known object together are immediate partial efficient causes of the act. In general, Ockham limits the role of final causality in merely philosophical explanations. Whereas Thomas thinks that freedom requires that efficient causality be reserved to the will alone, at least in the created order, Scotus and Ockham think that freedom merely requires that the will must be a more principal efficient cause.

Third, Ockham thinks that freedom is primarily a freedom of indifference with respect to different alternatives. Both Thomas and Scotus think that human actions are limited to the goods presented by the intellect, and that different actions require that there be different judgments by the intellect. Although Ockham thinks that the known object is necessary for an action, he also thinks that the will is free for alternatives even when there is no difference outside the will. Consequently, the will can somehow act independently of the intellect's judgments.

The above considerations indicate that there are limitations to explaining the differences between the figures in terms such as "voluntarism" and "intellectualism." In one sense, Thomas could be described as more "voluntarist" than Scotus or Ockham because he thinks that only the will can be the immediate efficacious cause of its own act. Moreover, it is hard to compare Thomas's discussion of free choice with that of the others, because Scotus and Ockham do not share Thomas's distinction between the liberty of specification, which is based on the intellect's ability to present different goods, and the liberty of exercise, which is based on the will's efficient causality. In another way, Thomas could be described as more "intellectualist" than Scotus because Thomas thinks that this freedom is ultimately rooted in the intellect's ability to present not just true and false goods, but even different true goods to the agent. The possibility of specifying different acts results not just from the possibility of intellectual error, but also from a real diversity of goods that could be presented. But again it is difficult to directly compare the two figures. Scotus does not discuss this presentation of different particular but true goods. He merely assumes that the intellect's indeterminacy would result from some sort of defective argument.

In one respect, Scotus could clearly be called more "voluntarist" than Thomas or Ockham because he thinks that the existence of an intellectual appetite as such is not sufficient for freedom. The will is a rational potency not merely because it is an intellectual appetite, but rather because it has two distinct inclinations. God could create an angel with an unfree intellectual appetite. In yet another sense, Ockham could be described as more "voluntarist" than Scotus or

Thomas, in that he emphasizes the independence of the will from any other cause. Although the trajectory from Thomas through Scotus to Ockham could be described as being from intellectualist to more voluntarist positions, this terminology does not do justice to the distinctive features of each thinker's approach.

Despite these reservations, the three themes of the book are illustrated by the positions discussed in this chapter. First, a clear progression can be seen in the separation of willing from natural inclination. Thomas argues that the will has a natural inclination to the good in general, and when happiness in particular is presented to it, the will chooses it by a necessity of the end. In contrast, Scotus explains happiness by arguing that the will has an inclination for the just that is distinct from ordinary natural inclinations, which he thinks are self-directed. Ockham continues the separation of willing from natural inclination and even final causality by arguing that the will is a self-mover when it is really independent and can choose any good that is presented to it. Does Ockham think that evil can be willed? Ockham does think that happiness is willed against in the case of some mortal sins. Moreover, according to one passage, any chosen object might be good merely in the sense that it is willed. Ockham at least moves in the direction of a contemporary notion of freedom that does not understand freedom in terms of a preestablished order of goods, but rather in terms of an ability to choose indifferently between alternatives in spite of natural teleology, reason's dictates, or the object's goodness. There is a trend toward a concern with intellectual determinism.

The perceived problem of intellectual determinism brings up the second theme of this book, which is an increased emphasis on the explanatory role of the will. Scotus and Ockham are concerned with describing the known object's efficient causality in such a way that it does not impede the will's self-motion. This concern may have roots in the 1277 condemnation of intellectual determinism and its backers. In contrast, the issue is less problematic for Thomas because he denies that the known object is an efficacious cause. The third theme, a changing view of mental causation, is illustrated by this same difference over whether the known object or the act of knowing is primarily an efficient cause. For Thomas, the causal contributions of the will and the intellect are interrelated and cannot compete with each other. According to Ockham and Scotus's more frequently expressed position, the intellect and the will are both involved in efficient causality. The point is not, as in Thomas, that there are distinct and cooperating kinds of causality, but that in the line of efficient causality the intellect's role is subordinated to that of the will.

2

PRACTICAL REASON

Different views on the relation of the intellect and will to some extent affect descriptions of the role that practical reasoning plays in the production of an act, which involves disagreement over a host of problematic questions. For instance, what is the relation of a conclusion to an action? Can the conclusion of a practical syllogism be the action itself, or must the agent elicit an entirely separate act of the will for there to be an action? According to the first view, the practical reasoning has a stronger appetitive aspect, whereas in the other it is merely cognitive. A related question is whether the premises of practical reasoning are intrinsically practical, or whether they are made practical by the activity of the agent. There are further problems involving the relationship between moral science and practical reasoning as a whole, as well as prudence in particular. Is moral science practical simply because it is used in practical reasoning? How does it differ from prudence? Are its principles intrinsically distinct from those that belong to speculative reason?

The first key issue is the way in which the conclusion of a practical syllogism is related to an agent's choice. Thomas, Scotus, and Ockham all not only make the Aristotelian distinction between theoretical and practical reason, but they also make his distinction between speculative and practical syllogisms. A *speculative syllogism* reaches a conclusion through necessary premises. For instance, the following is an example of a speculative syllogism: All mammals have lungs (major premise); all humans are mammals (minor premise); therefore, all humans have lungs (conclusion). By contrast, a *practical syllogism* leads to a choice or a judgment about an action that can be chosen. For instance, Thomas states that an intemperate person might employ this syllogism: Every pleasurable thing should be done (major premise); this act of fornication is pleasurable (minor premise); this act of fornication should be done (conclusion).[1] The minor premise of a practical syllogism provides either an instance of or a means to the good that is indicated by the major premise. The practical syllogism at least resembles the speculative in its structure, but differs with respect to its connection with desire and action. In general, medieval thinkers do not explicitly separate psychological activities from logical activities in the way that some later thinkers do.[2] For instance, Thomas and Scotus both connect the different parts of logic to different mental operations.[3] They do not think that logic is a psychological description, but they do closely connect logic with mental acts.

Recent scholars disagree over how to understand Aristotle's account of the practical syllogism.[4] Many of these recent disagreements are similar or identical to disagreements expressed by medieval think-

1. Thomas, *De Malo*, q. 3, art. 9, ad 7 (Leonine, 23.97).

2. See G. E. M. Anscombe, "Practical Inference," in Anscombe, *Human Life, Action and Ethics*, ed. Mary Geach and Luke Gormally, St Andrews Studies in Philosophy and Public Affairs (Exeter, U.K.: Imprint Academic, 2005), 4.109–47; Idem, *Intention*, 2nd ed. (Cambridge, Mass.: Harvard University Press, 2000), nn. 41–43, 78–80.

3. Thomas Aquinas, *Expositio libri Peryemenias*, lib. 1, lect. 1 (Leonine, 1*.1.5); Idem, *Expositio libri Posteriorum*, lib. 1, lect. 1 (Leonine, 1*.2.4–5); John Duns Scotus, *Quaestiones in librum Porphyrii Isagoge*, q. 3 (OPh, 1.11–20); Idem, *Quaestiones in libros Perihermenias Aristotelis*, q. 1, n. 1 (OPh, 2.43–44).

4. For discussions of Aristotle's understanding of the practical syllogism in light of the voluminous contemporary scholarship, see especially the now "classic" discussions by Anthony Kenny, *The Anatomy of the Soul: Historical Essays in the Philosophy of Mind* (Oxford: Blackwell, 1973), 28–50; Martha Nussbaum, *Aristotle's De Motu Animalium* (Princeton, N.J.: Princeton University Press, 1978), 165–220. More recent Aristotelian scholarship is taken into account in discussions of Thomas's appropriation of the practical syllogism. See Daniel Westberg, *Right Practical Reason: Aristotle, Action,*

ers. Whereas some contemporary scholars think that the major premise of a practical syllogism can indicate goods that are possible to attain, others argue that in many cases the major premise is merely a rule that should be applied. Some authors suggest that both instances can be found in Aristotle. A related disagreement is over whether mere deliberation about the way in which a good is to be obtained takes the form of a practical syllogism, or whether practical syllogisms are found only in the kind of reasoning that leads to a particular action. A further dispute is over whether the conclusion of the practical syllogism is the action or choice itself, or whether it is a judgment about an action that can be chosen.

The different views of understanding deliberation and the practical syllogism's conclusion are especially important for thinking about the relationship between the intellect and the will. How is deliberation under the will's control? Does deliberation end in choice itself, or does the intellect merely conclude deliberations with a judgment that the will can accept or reject?[5] Deliberation will be more fully discussed in chapter 3. Nevertheless, these differences should be understood in the context of the more general discussion of how to distinguish between practical and speculative reason. Is practical reasoning intrinsically distinct from theoretical reasoning, or is it distinct merely in that something other than the intellect, namely the will, can decide to act on it?

This contrast between practical and speculative knowledge is also important for the understanding of the role of prudence in an act's production. For Aristotle, *prudential knowledge* is a kind of practical knowledge about the good life as a whole. Another kind of practical knowledge belongs to technical skills, which are directed to particular ends, such as boat building or sculpting. Aristotle distinguishes between the knowledge of a technical skill that one acquires through

---

and Prudence in Aquinas (Oxford: Clarendon Press, 1994), 17–25; Flannery, *Acts Amid Precepts*, 3–24.

5. Nussbaum, *Aristotle's De Motu Animalium*, 186, n. 35, suggests that Walter Burley may have been among the first to interpret Aristotle's *De Motu Animalium* as maintaining that the conclusion of a practical syllogism is a proposition rather than an action.

study and that which one acquires through experience. The knowledge acquired through study is more universal but less useful. What about the difference between the moral knowledge of the prudent person and that of the philosopher? Does the moral virtue of prudence differ from philosophical knowledge about moral matters merely because prudence is less universal, or does this knowledge have a characteristic feature that more strongly connects it to action?

THOMAS AQUINAS

Thomas Aquinas accepts the standard Aristotelian view that practical reason is distinct from speculative reason because of the end to which it is directed. He sometimes refers to this distinction between the two kinds of reason as between the practical and the speculative "intellect."[6] The distinction is the same as the distinction between reason and intellect that was indicated in the previous chapter, according to which "intellect" applies also to God and the angels, whereas reason is specifically human. The distinction between the practical and the speculative intellect is not a real distinction between powers, but between the ways in which one intellect apprehends different kinds of truth. "Reason" or "intellect" indicates not the reasoning process itself but the agent's ability to reason. How are the speculative and practical intellects distinct? Thomas writes:

For the speculative intellect is that which orders what it apprehends not to a deed, but only to the consideration of the truth; and that intellect is called "practical" which orders what it apprehends to a deed. And this is what the Philosopher says in the *De Anima*, III, that "the speculative differs from the practical by the end."[7]

6. Thomas, *S.T.*, II-II, q. 39, art. 5, ad 3; Idem, *Sentencia libri De Anima*, lib. 3, cap. 8 (Leonine, 45.243); Idem, *De virtutibus in communi*, art. 7, resp. (Marietti ed., 2.724). For possible development and many texts, see John Naus, *The Nature of the Practical Intellect* (Rome: Libreria Editrice dell'Universita Gregoriana, 1959), 17–34.

7. "Nam intellectus speculativus est, qui quod apprehendit, non ordinat ad opus, sed ad solam vertitatis considerationem: practicus vero intellectus dicitur, quid hoc quod apprehendit, ordinat ad opus. Et hoc est quod Philosophus dicit in III De Anima, quod 'speculativus differt a practico, fine'" (Thomas, *S.T.*, I, q. 79, art. 11, resp.).

Practical reason not only apprehends the truth but it causes or can cause action, which involves an end.[8] Consequently, practical truth requires a connection with the rational appetite. As we have seen in the previous chapter, the exercise of an act depends on the will's activity and not just on knowledge. This connection with the appetite means that the correctness of practical reason is more complicated than that of speculative reason.[9] Speculative reason errs when someone makes a judgment about the way the world is. Its rectitude consists in the intellect's conformity to the world. In contrast, practical reason's rectitude depends not only on the truth of judgments but also on the appetite's rectitude and consequently the possible rectitude of a chosen action. Speculative error in itself is purely cognitive. Someone could make a merely speculative error about whether cyanide is poisonous or not. Error in practical reasoning can involve a disorder in the agent's appetite. The judgment that an innocent person should be poisoned may be false in many ways, but one defect might only consist in that agent's willingness to kill an innocent person and his consequent judgment that, at least in this particular case, murder is a good.

The distinction between practical and speculative knowledge is also connected to the distinction between (1) the necessary and the universal and (2) the contingent and the particular.[10] The knowledge that cyanide can be poisonous is based on the kind of thing that cyanide is, and is not about any particular bottle of cyanide. In contrast, someone who uses cyanide to murder must make a judgment about *this* use of *this* particular cyanide. Although this distinction is important for Thomas, it should not be concluded that science does not involve particulars, or that the practical reason only makes judgments about particulars. The difference is in the way in which the particular

8. Thomas, *S.T.*, II-II, q. 83, art. 1, resp.; Idem, *In De anima*, lib. 3, cap. 8 (Leonine, 45.243).

9. Thomas, 3 *Sent.*, d. 33, q. 1, art. 1, sol. 2 (Mandonnet ed., 3.1020); Idem, *S.T.*, I-II, q. 64, art. 3, resp.; Idem, *Sententia libri Ethicorum*, lib. 6, lect. 2 (Leonine, 47.w2.336–37).

10. Thomas, *S.T.*, I-II, q. 57, ad 3; Idem, *Sententia libri Ethicorum*, lib. 6, lect. 3 (Leonine, 47.2.340–42).

is considered.[11] Speculative reason considers particulars such as this particular bottle of cyanide insofar as it instantiates universal and unchanging properties. Practical reason considers universal and necessary truths about cyanide, but only insofar as they are relevant to a particular act, such as poisoning one's colleague.

The distinction between known objects does not determine whether knowledge is completely practical, but it does demarcate speculative from practical reason. If the known object is not subject to action by the knower, then it is not fully practical.[12] Fully *(simpliciter)* speculative knowledge is about things that cannot be changed, and knowing the truth is its end or goal. In contrast, knowledge is fully *(simpliciter)* practical when it is ordered to an end. But not all knowledge neatly falls into one of these categories. For instance, Thomas states that astronomers use their knowledge about the heavenly bodies to arrive at a conclusion about what to do in the case of an eclipse. Furthermore, we might study human actions in moral philosophy without having an end immediately in mind. Thomas accounts for these instances in part by distinguishing between the different ways in which knowledge can be speculative and practical.

Thomas distinguishes between degrees of speculative and practical knowledge by distinguishing between the knowledge's object, mode, and end.[13] If the object is not subject to action, the knowledge of it can still be practical if it is considered as influencing human action (mode) or if it is used for a practical end. In such a case, the knowledge is practical to the extent that it is directed to action, but speculative to the extent that the object is not subject to choice. Consequently, such knowledge is in one respect *(secundum quid)* prac-

11. Thomas, *De Veritate*, q. 14, art. 12, ad 1 (Leonine, 22.2.473); Idem, *S.T.*, I, q. 86, art. 3; Idem, *Expositio Libri Posteriorum* I.16 (Leonine, 1*.2.61–62); Idem, *Sententia libri Ethicorum*, lib. 6, lect. 3 (Leonine, 47.2.334).

12. In addition to the texts cited below, see Thomas, *Super Boetium de Trinitate*, q. 5, art. 1, ad 4 (Leonine, 50.140). For a collection of texts and a comparison, see Naus, *Practical Intellect*, 151–69; William Wallace, *The Role of Demonstration in Moral Theology: A Study of Methodology in St. Thomas Aquinas* (Washington, D.C.: Thomist Press, 1962), 71–94.

13. Thomas, *S.T.*, I, q. 14, art. 16.

tical and in another respect *(secundum quid)* speculative. Similarly, some objects that are themselves subject to human action might be known in a way that is not directed to action. For instance, someone might study the structure of a house (object) without considering how to build it (mode), or he might even study how to build a house but yet have no intention of building one (end). In these cases, the knowledge has an object that is subject to human action, but either the mode or the end is not practical. This knowledge is also in one respect speculative and in another respect practical. Knowledge is fully speculative if and only if the object is not subject to human action and the end is truth. Knowledge is fully practical if and only if it is ordered to a deed. Other kinds of knowledge share characteristics of both.

An important consequence of these distinctions is that for Thomas knowledge can to some extent be practical even if the knowledge is never used by any agent to produce an action. This characteristic of being able to be used in action is intrinsic to the knowledge and not a result of the use to which the knowledge is put. This point is clearly brought out in Thomas's discussion of how God knows those things that he could make but does not make.[14] God does know these possibles, and this knowledge is not merely speculative. But it cannot be fully practical since he never uses this knowledge to make them. Thomas argues that God has virtually practical *(in virtute)* knowledge of these possibles, just as humans can have knowledge that is virtually practical in that it is not actually directed to an end. Although knowledge must be directed to an end by the agent for that knowledge to be fully practical, knowledge can be virtually or even habitually practical apart from such actual ordering.

When looking at Thomas's description of the practical syllogism, it is important to remember that there are degrees of practical knowledge. Sometimes Thomas discusses the practical syllogism in the context of any deliberation, whereas in other passages he describes it as concluding or completing part of an action.[15] In these cases, the

14. Thomas, *De Veritate*, q. 2, art. 8 (Leonine, 22.1.69–70); Ibid., *De Veritate*, q. 3, art. 3 (Leonine, 22.1.106–9).

15. Westberg, *Right Practical Reason*, 155–60.

practical syllogism could be described as an "operative syllogism." The difference between these accounts does not necessarily imply that he is inconsistent or has changed his mind, since some contexts involve knowledge that is practical in only one respect, whereas in other contexts he is concerned with fully practical knowledge. Another important point for Thomas is that the practical syllogism is only quasi-syllogistic.[16] He presumably makes this point to indicate that the practical syllogism does not share all of those characteristics that are possessed by the syllogisms used in a necessary and fully deductive science.

Thomas writes that the practical syllogism's conclusion is a "judgment or [seu] choice, or [vel] operation."[17] How can the conclusion of a syllogism be a choice, which is an act of the will? Thomas's texts can be unclear. In one text he is clear that choice is like (quasi) the conclusion of a practical syllogism.[18] In another text he states that the judgment that is the conclusion of a practical syllogism falls under choice, which follows it.[19] The relationship between choice and deliberation will be discussed in the next chapter. But it is clear that for Thomas some practical syllogisms end in the action itself, whether we indicate that it is the judgment that choice follows, the choice itself, or the operation that is chosen. In the first chapter we saw how for Thomas the known object plays a specifying role, whereas the will moves to action. In the case where the practical syllogism's conclusion is a choice or operation, the conclusion is intellectual in that it gives content to what is chosen, but the will's exercise is also part of the conclusion. How would Thomas address the contemporary question of whether the conclusion of a practical syllogism is a proposition or an action? In some partially practical syllogisms, the conclusion will be about an action but not itself an action, as in some kinds of deliberation and practical reasoning that is not fully practical. But in fully practical syllogisms, the conclusion is an action in the sense

---

16. Thomas, *De Malo*, q. 3, art. 9, ad 7 (Leonine, vol. 97).

17. "iudicium seu electio vel operatio"; *S.T.*, I-II, q. 76, art. 1, resp. See Westberg, *Right Practical Reason*, 158–60.

18. Thomas, *S.T.*, I, q. 86, art. 2, ad 2.   19. Thomas, *S.T.*, I-II, q. 13, art. 3.

that the judgment specifies the choice, although the specifying aspect of the action is expressed propositionally. Thomas does not seem to think that all practical syllogisms fall under the same category in this respect.

The distinctive characteristic of any practical syllogism is the connection to action. Since actions are singular, practical syllogisms are distinctive in their relation to judgments about particular and contingent events. A practical syllogism that has a choice or operation as its conclusion consequently has a conclusion that is particular and not universal. The universal premise is a general statement about what should or should not be done. The minor premise makes possible the application of the universal premise to a particular operation. Consider the following practical syllogism: one's father should not be killed; this man is my father; this man should not be killed.[20] Here the major premise is a universal premise that indicates a good that should be sought or an evil that should be avoided.

Is the universal premise a rule or a good? In the context of a discussion concerning how law belongs to reason, Thomas explains that universal premises of a practical syllogism are laws.[21] Those premises that are known by human reason and based on human nature are described as "the natural law."[22] Consequently, the premises and principles of practical reason are also "precepts" that indicate what should be done. The agent then applies these precepts or universal premises to his situation in order to arrive at a conclusion. When the deliberation leads to choice, the conclusion is the choice itself or the action.

The universal precepts of the natural law follow on the basic goods of human nature, which are the objects of natural inclination.[23] The natural law's primary precepts follow from these inclinations. Deliberation is not about the ends that are given by nature, but about the means to these ends. Other secondary precepts follow from the primary precepts either deductively or through some sort of further determination by practical reason.[24] For instance, the commands of the

20. Thomas, *S.T.*, I-II, q. 76, art. 1.
22. Thomas, *S.T.*, I-II, q. 94, art. 1.
24. Thomas, *S.T.*, I-II, q. 94, art. 3–4.

21. Thomas, *S.T.*, I-II, q. 90, art. 1, ad 2.
23. Thomas, *S.T.*, I-II, q. 94, art. 2.

Decalogue belong to the natural law in a primary way. Although primary, they also have more common principles in the precepts to love God above all things and one's neighbor as oneself. Thomas writes that "these two precepts are the first and common precepts of the law of nature, which are known through their terms to human reason, whether through nature or through faith."[25] Other moral precepts, such as those also not only known by reason but also revealed by the Mosaic law, are accessible to reason but harder to know and more remote from the principles.[26]

Thomas states that these precepts or principles of practical reason are intrinsically distinct from speculative principles. This distinction is made clear in his comparison of the first principles of speculative and practical reason. The first principle of speculative reason is the principle of noncontradiction. This principle is presupposed in every instance of speculative reasoning. The first principle of practical reason is "Do good and avoid evil." Just as speculative statements depend in some way on the principle of noncontradiction even when the knower has not even explicitly formulated the principle of noncontradiction, so do practical statements depend on this primary principle. For instance, the principle "Borrowed items should be returned" presupposes that the good should be sought even though it more narrowly indicates a kind of good, which is the just act of returning borrowed items. The first principle is presupposed in some way, but it is not generally used as a distinct premise. Thomas discusses this first practical principle in the context of natural law, but it is used in all practical reasoning, including that which belongs to technical skill. Nevertheless, since other kinds of practical reasoning are subordinate to practical reasoning about the good life of the whole, it seems appropriate to describe the first practical principle as "moral."[27]

25. "illa duo praecepta sunt prima et communi praecepta legis naturae, quae sunt per se nota rationi humanae, vel per naturam vel per fidem"; Thomas, *S.T.*, I-II, q. 100, art. 3, ad 1.

26. Thomas, *S.T.*, I-II, q. 100, art. 1, 3.

27. Ralph McInerny, "The Principles of Natural Law," *American Journal of Jurisprudence* 25 (1980): 1–15; Russell Hittinger, *A Critique of the New Natural Law Theory* (Notre Dame, Ind.: University of Notre Dame Press, 1987), 10–92; Flannery, *Acts Amid*

The distinction between practical and speculative principles can be seen in Thomas's use of the term "*synderesis*" to describe a distinct ability to grasp the various first practical principles, which are the primary precepts of the natural law and directive of all human operations.[28] These principles are the ends of the various moral virtues.[29] Prudence is the virtue by which these principles are applied to concrete situations. The prudent agent uses a practical syllogism in which the major premise indicates a truly good end to be attained and the minor premise indicates the concrete way in which it can be obtained.[30] The relationship between *synderesis* and prudence is like that between the understanding of speculative principles and speculative knowledge.[31]

For Thomas Aquinas, the practical judgment of prudence should not be mistaken for conscience, which in this context is a judgment about the worth of a particular act.[32] In such a case, correct judgment

---

Precepts, 25–49; Guiseppe Butera, "The Moral Status of the First Principle of Practical Reason in Thomas's Natural Law Theory," *The Thomist* 71 (2007): 609–31. For an alternative interpretation, see John Finnis and Germain Grisez, "The Basic Principles of Natural Law: A Reply to Ralph McInerny," *American Journal of Jurisprudence* 26 (1981): 21–31; Germain Grisez, "The Structures of Practical Reason: Some Comments and Clarifications," *The Thomist* 52 (1988): 269–91; John Finnis, *Aquinas: Moral, Political and Legal Theory* (Oxford: Oxford University Press, 1998), 123–29.

28. Thomas, *S.T.*, I-II, q. 94, art. 2, ad 2; Idem, *S.T.*, I, q. 79, art. 12; Idem, *De Veritate*, q. 16, art. 1 (Leonine, 22.2.501–7). Paul Morrisset, "Le syllogisme prudentiel," *Laval théologique et philosophique* 19 (1963): 65–71. For historical sources and different interpretations of the term "synderesis," see Lottin, *Psychologie et morale*, 2.103–349; Timothy C. Potts, "Conscience," in *The Cambridge History of Later Medieval Philosophy: From the Rediscovery of Aristotle to the Disintegration of Scholasticism: 1100–1600*, ed. Norman Kretzmann, Anthony Kenny, and Jan Pinborg (Cambridge: Cambridge University Press), 687–704.

29. Thomas, *S.T.*, I-II, q. 13, art. 3; Idem, *S.T.*, II-II, q. 47, art. 6, resp. Paul Morrisset, "Prudence et fin selon saint Thomas," *Sciences écclesiastiques* 15 (1963): 450–58.

30. Morriset, "Le syllogisme prudentiel," 74–76.

31. Thomas, *S.T.*, II-II, q. 47, art. 7, ad 3. It seems to me that this contrast between *synderesis* and prudence, as well as their distinction from conscience, is neglected in Robert Pasnau, *Thomas Aquinas on Human Nature*, 244–49.

32. For the term *conscientia* and its background, see Douglas Langston, *Conscience and Other Virtues: From Bonaventure to MacIntyre* (University Park: Pennsylvania State University Press, 2001), 7–69.

does not necessarily require moral virtue in the agent. In contrast, although prudence is an intellectual virtue, it depends on a correct order to the human being's ultimate end.[33] This correct ordering has its root in the moral virtues, which perfect the appetitive parts. The proper act of prudence is not just a judgment about whether an act should be done, but the command or choice to do it. The act of prudence is distinguished from conscience because the judgment of conscience is merely cognitive, and conscience often errs. Conscience is the purely cognitive conclusion of a practical syllogism.[34] But prudence presupposes rectitude and it leads to action. Its principal act is to command action, but it works alongside other virtues that have different cognitive acts. These other virtues are (1) *eubelia*, which concerns deliberation; (2) *synesis*, which is about judgments involving normal events; and (3) *gnome*, which involves judgments about unusual situations.[35] There is much scholarly debate over whether the proper act of prudence, which can be translated as "command" *(praeceptum)*, is properly that command *(imperium)* by which the intellect orders the execution of an act, or whether it is the intellectual component of the act of choice *(iudicium electionis)*.[36] According to either interpretation, the prudent agent judges correctly in choice and commands right action.

Thomas's position on the exact extent to which practical reasoning shares the deductive characteristics of the speculative syllogism is unclear. We will see that he thinks that some agents, namely the incontinent and the continent, use practical syllogisms with four propositions. One other important difference concerns the validity of some practical syllogisms. His distinction between primary and secondary

33. Thomas, *S.T.*, II-II, q. 47, art. 13. For texts and a discussion, see Thomas M. Osborne Jr., "Perfect and Imperfect Virtues in Aquinas," *The Thomist* 71 (2007): 39–64.

34. Thomas, *De Veritate*, q. 17, art. 2, resp. (Leonine, 22.2.520). Ralph McInerny, *Aquinas on Human Action: A Theory of Practice* (Washington, D.C.: The Catholic University of America Press, 1992), 220–39; Leo Elders, "La doctrine de la conscience de saint Thomas d'Aquin," *Revue Thomiste* 83 (1983): 553–57; Morriset, "Le syllogisme prudential," 82–86.

35. Thomas, *S.T.*, II-II, q. 48, art. 1, resp. For a discussion, see Westberg, *Right Practical Reason*, 191–97.

36. Westberg, *Right Practical Reason*, 176.

premises affects the validity of practical syllogisms.[37] In deductive speculative reasoning, the conclusions always rightly follow from the premises. It makes no difference whether the premises are more or less universal. Practical reasoning from the more common principles also has this rectitude according to which a correct conclusion always follows from the premises. Consider the following practical syllogism: Adultery is to be avoided; this act is adultery; this act is to be avoided. The conclusion will never be false if the second premise is true. Thomas argues that with respect to the most universal principles, those premises that lead to the judgment of conscience entail the conclusion as clearly as the principles of speculative reason entail a speculative conclusion.[38]

Thomas in different texts gives different or at least apparently different accounts of which acts should be judged to be evil on account of such practical premises, and whether God can dispense from the precepts. The problem often occurs in the context of problematic divine commands, such as the commands for Abraham to kill Isaac, which would normally be murder; for the Israelites to take goods from the Egyptians, which would normally be theft; and for Hosea to have relations that would otherwise be fornication. In two texts Thomas appeals to Bernard of Clairvaux's position that God can dispense with commandments that belong to the second tablet of the Decalogue, namely, those which concern one's neighbor.[39] But in other passages Thomas states that not even God can dispense from such precepts of the natural law.[40] In these latter texts, which belong to the same period as the former, he states that the character of the act changes when God gives the command. For instance, when God orders Abraham to kill Isaac, Abraham can licitly do so because he is an agent of God,

37. Thomas, *S.T.*, I-II, q. 94, art. 4. For a discussion of this aspect of practical reasoning, see Flannery, *Acts Amid Precepts*, 195–210; Westberg, *Right Practical Reason*, 172–74.

38. Thomas, *De Veritate*, q. 17, art. 2, resp. (Leonine, 22.2.520).

39. Thomas, 1 *Sent.*, d. 47, q. 1, art. 4 (Mandonnet ed., 1.1071–74); Idem, *De Malo*, q. 3, art. 1, ad 17 (Leonine, 23.68–69).

40. Thomas, 3 *Sent.*, d. 37, art. 4, ad 3 (Moos ed., 3.1248); Idem, *De Malo*, q. 15, art. 1, ad 8 (Leonine, 23.272); Idem, *S.T.*, I-II, q. 94, art. 5, ad 2; Idem, *S.T.*, I-II, q. 100, art. 8.

who can justly kill anyone on account of original sin. Similarly, since God is the supreme authority on marriage laws, he can make what would otherwise be fornication a just act. It is likely that the two texts in which Thomas discusses dispensations of the second tablet are ultimately invoking the fact that such acts that would ordinarily be murder or fornication are no longer such if they have been commanded by God, since the character of murder or fornication no longer belongs to them. It is not that murder would be good, but that killing Isaac would not be murder. As Steven Jensen notes, the material descriptions of the act are the same, but the formal descriptions differ.[41] For example, without the divine command, the killing of Isaac is the killing of an innocent person by someone who has no authority. With the divine command, the killing of Isaac would be that of a deputy who is inflicting a just penalty. The difference between the formal descriptions rests not only on God's will, but also on the fact that God has the right to kill Isaac. Whatever the interpretation, Thomas clearly holds that there are exceptionless premises that the agent can use in practical reasoning.

Universal premises can be found in both practical and speculative syllogisms. The problem for practical reasoning is that its primary principles are universal and do not immediately yield conclusions about many particular acts. This problem is especially acute with respect to affirmative precepts. Primary negative precepts apply at all times and in all situations. Once the badness of the act is known, many particular acts can be excluded from any deliberation. In contrast, positive precepts, such as the precept to love God, do not directly indicate what should be done in many particular situations. Secondary precepts are needed, but secondary precepts introduce the possibility of error because they cannot cover all the contingent features of a situation.[42] Consider this practical syllogism: Borrowed items should be returned; this gun is a borrowed item; this gun should be returned. Normally the conclusion is correct. However, if an enemy

---

41. Steven J. Jensen, *Good and Evil Actions: A Journey through Saint Thomas Aquinas* (Washington, D.C.: The Catholic University of America Press, 2010), 180–95.

42. Steven J. Jensen, "When Evil Actions Become Good," *Nova et Vetera*, English Edition, 5 (2007): 747–64.

of the political community asks for the gun back, the conclusion is false. Speculative syllogistic reasoning from more particular but true principles never leads to a false conclusion, but practical syllogistic reasoning from secondary precepts can yield an incorrect conclusion.

Prudence and practical technical skill *(ars)* differ from each other because prudence is concerned with the reasoning that leads to a virtuous act that perfects the agent, whereas technical skill is concerned with making a product. Following contemporary usage, Thomas uses the word *ars,* which was used to translate Aristotle's word for technical skill, *techne,* to refer not merely to productive skills but also to branches of the medieval educational curriculum, such as logic. In this wider sense, not all technical skill is practical. For example, logic is a technical skill that has the knowledge of truth as its end rather than action.[43] Logic follows determinate paths, and its truths are not contingent. Although productive skills do have contingent objects, they resemble speculative skills such as logic in that they are concerned with more determined means to an end.[44] For instance, the writer does not need to deliberate about forming letters, and the cithara player does not deliberate when he performs. The perfect exercise of a technical skill makes many kinds of deliberation unnecessary and even counterproductive.

Practical technical skill is judged by the goodness of what is produced, whether it be a bed, or a sculpture, or a piece of music, whereas imprudence is bad for the agent.[45] The person with practical skill needs prudence if he wishes to use his technical skill well.[46] It is never correct to act imprudently, but it can sometimes be correct to err in one's technical production. For instance, the prudent woodworker might make a mistake in woodworking in order to teach a student how such mistakes are made and avoided. The mistake is not a result of his poor skill but rather voluntary. Both prudence and art are

43. Thomas, *S.T.,* q. 47, art. 2, ad 3.

44. Thomas, *In octo libros Physicorum Aristotelis,* lib. 2, cap. 8, lect. 14, n. 8 (Leonine, 2.96). Aristotle, *Physics* 2.8. See also Thomas, *Sententia super libros Ethicorum,* lib. 3, lect. 7 (Leonine, 48.1.140).

45. Thomas, *Sententia super libros Ethicorum,* lib. 2, lect. 4 (Leonine, 48.1.87–88).

46. Thomas, *Sententia super libros Ethicorum,* lib. 6, lect. 4 (Leonine, 48.2.345–47).

concerned with goods. But prudence is concerned with the nature of the good even formally considered, namely insofar as it is a good that should be chosen by the particular agent.[47]

This concern of prudence with the good life as a whole points to another difference between prudence and technical skill, namely that there are many species of technical skill and yet there is only one species of prudence.[48] Technical skills are separable. For instance, a good shoemaker might be unable to build boats. But someone who has fully developed prudence with respect to one of the major common virtues has prudence with respect to them all. For example, someone who has fully developed prudence with respect to courage is also prudent with respect to temperance. The reason is that even though different virtues are about different matters, these matters are interrelated. Someone might be lead to an intemperate act through fear, or to an unjust act through temperance. If he is tempted through fear to sin against chastity, he will be able to judge that he should resist the temptation. Like technical skills but unlike prudence, the speculative sciences are also separable.[49] For instance, someone might know geometry but not physics. It is possible that someone might lack prudence in some area, but such a defect is also a defect for prudence in every area. Such prudence is underdeveloped or "imperfect."[50] Prudence with respect to one of the common virtues cannot be isolated from prudence with respect to the other virtues, and indeed the good life as a whole.

The virtuous prudent person and the vicious imprudent person each employ practical syllogisms with two premises and a conclusion. For instance, the temperate person might reason: "No fornication should be committed; this act is fornication; this act should not be done." The intemperate person might reason: "Every pleasurable thing should be

47. Thomas, *S.T.*, II-II, q. 47, art. 4, resp.

48. Thomas, *S.T.*, I-II, q. 65, art. 1, ad 4; Idem, *De virtutibus cardinalibus*, art. 2, ad 4 (Marietti ed., 2.819–20). See Thomas M. Osborne Jr., "Thomas and Scotus on Prudence without All the Major Virtues: Imperfect or Merely Partial?" *The Thomist* 74 (2010): 166–70.

49. Thomas, *S.T.*, I-II, q. 65, art. 1, ad 3; Idem, *De virtutibus cardinalibus*, art. 2, ad 8 (Marietti ed., 2.820).

50. Thomas, *S.T.*, II-II, q. 47, art. 13. Osborne, "Perfect and Imperfect Virtues," 57–62.

enjoyed; this act is pleasurable; this act should be enjoyed." But some practical syllogisms have three premises and a conclusion. Following Aristotle, Thomas thinks although some agents are virtuous and others are vicious, there are many agents who are neither.[51] Continent agents act well, but they think about what they should not do because their desires are disordered. Incontinent agents act poorly, but they are generally aware of what they should do. But the continent and the incontinent think about both universal premises. Consequently, their practical syllogisms have four propositions, namely, universal premises, the minor premise, and the conclusion.[52]

How is it possible for a syllogism, or at least something like a syllogism, to have three premises and a conclusion? Thomas considers both the continent and the incontinent to have practical syllogisms with the same two universal premises. The difference comes from the use of the major premises. The continent is aware of that universal premise that is used by the vicious, but he does not use it to draw a conclusion. Presumably he reasons: "Every pleasurable thing should be enjoyed; no fornication should be committed; this act is fornication; this act should not be done." The incontinent is aware of that universal premise which is used by the temperate, but he does not use it. The incontinent is led by his passion to consider fornication as pleasurable rather than as a sin. Presumably the incontinent reasons: "Every pleasurable thing should be enjoyed; no fornication should be committed; this act is pleasurable; this act should be enjoyed." Thomas considers both the continent and the incontinent to have practical syllogisms with the same two universal premises. The difference between the practical syllogisms is in the major premise actually used, the minor premise, and

51. This passage follows the discussion in Thomas, *De Malo*, q. 3, art. 9, ad 7. But see also Idem, *S.T.*, I-II, q. 77, art. 2; Idem, *Sententia super libros Ethicorum*, lib. 7, lect. 3 (Leonine, 48.2.390–93). For discussions, see especially Westberg, *Right Practical Reason*, 204–13; Tobias Hoffmann, "Aquinas on the Moral Problem of the Weak-Willed," in *The Problem of Weakness of Will in Moral Philosophy*, ed. Tobias Hoffmann, Jörn Müller, and Matthias Perkams (Leuven: Peeters, 2006), 230–36; Steven J. Jensen, "The Error of the Passions," *The Thomist* 73 (2009): 349–79; Bonnie Kent, "Aquinas and Weakness of Will," *Philosophy and Phenomenological Research* 75 (2007): 70–91.

52. Wallace, *Role of Demonstration*, 113–19.

the conclusion. In fact, in these cases the agents use only two of the three premises. The unused universal premise seems to be in a way only potentially fitting in the practical syllogism.

Thomas's discussion of incontinence is important for practical reasoning because it clearly shows how persons with different moral habits reason differently. Moreover, it illustrates how Thomas closely connects the cognitive and the appetitive aspects of moral action. For instance, although Scotus also distinguishes between the different kinds of character, he does not explicitly explain this difference in terms of the practical syllogisms that are used.[53] As we shall see, Scotus is more concerned with the relationship between the will's act and the conclusion of a practical syllogism.

Although Thomas's explanation of the incontinent agent is significant, it is not central to his understanding of free action. Virtuous and vicious agents also choose freely although they deliberate less because their patterns of acting follow more fixed paths. Indeed, the virtue of prudence is particularly important for Thomas's understanding of practical reasoning. Its connection to command or choice sheds greater light on the practical syllogism and is a better illustration of how the knowledge of the end and means lead to choice. The prudent person acts once he sees an appropriate means to the true good.[54] This habitual reasoning does not mean that the prudent person does not need the practical syllogism, or that he never deliberates. But in many cases the prudent person's deliberation will be short or even unnecessary, and there is no intermediate step between the deliberation and the choice. Similarly, the vicious person also uses the practical syllogism without much or any deliberation. For instance, an intemperate person chooses fornication once he sees that it is possible. In general, both good and bad habits simplify but do not take away the process of practical reasoning. The end of the agent is determined

53. Timothy Noone, "Duns Scotus on *Incontinentia*," in *The Problem of Weakness of Will*, 285–305; Tobias Hoffmann, "L'akrasia' selon Duns Scot," in *Duns Scot à Paris: Actes du colloque de Paris, 2–4 septembre 1992*, ed. Olivier Boulnois et al. (Turnhout: Brepols, 2004), 487–516.

54. Thomas, *De Veritate*, q. 24, art. 12, resp. (Leonine, 22.3.716).

in such a way that when the end is seen, the means or instances are chosen unless some further deliberation intervenes.

What is the relationship between prudence and moral science? Thomas insists that moral science is directed to action and that it considers human action insofar as it is ordered to an end.[55] Nevertheless, moral science is not fully practical. Someone might possess moral science without prudence and the inclination to right action.[56] Moral science is acquired through study, whereas prudence is mostly acquired through action. The difference is the extent to which the knowledge is practical, and the contrast between them reflects Thomas's distinction between the degrees of practical knowledge.[57] Since moral science does not always lead to action, it is not fully practical. Its practical syllogisms will lead to conclusions that are purely cognitive. But moral science is to some degree practical because its ultimate goal is right action.

Daniel Westberg has interpreted the difference between the incompletely practical syllogisms of moral science and the fully practical syllogisms of an acting agent as a distinction between the deductions of moral science and the psychological process of an agent.[58] This point is important for practical reasoning in general because the difference between at least one kind of practical reasoning and speculative reasoning would be not so much a difference between kinds of reasoning as between logical relations and a psychological process.

It seems to me that although the fully practical syllogism does move the agent, the syllogism itself is not about psychological states

---

55. Thomas, *Sententia super libros Ethicorum*, lib. 1, lect. 1(Leonine, 48.1.3–6); Ibid., lib. 2, lect. 2 (Leonine, 47.1.80–81); Idem, 3 *Sent.*, d. 35, q. 1, art. 3, sol. 2 (Mandonnet ed., 3.1184). See M.-Michel Labourdette, "Connaissance practique et savoir moral," *Revue Thomiste* 48 (1948): 142–79. For the general historical context, see Georg Wieland, *Ethica—Scientia Practica: Die Anfänge der philosophischen Ethik im 13. Jahrhundert*, Beiträge zur Geschichte der Philosophie und Theologie des Mittelalters, n. f. 21 (Münster: Ashendorff, 1981).

56. Thomas, *S.T.*, I, q. 6, art. 3, ad 3. For the limits of such acquisition, see Wallace, *Role of Demonstration*, 119–28.

57. Morriset, "Le syllogisme prudentiel," 82–89.

58. Westberg, *Right Practical Reason*, 153–55.

or mechanisms. Even though the agent must actually will in order for the syllogism to be fully practical, the premises are not about the agent's own willing, unless this willing belongs to another act. We should keep in mind two points that Elizabeth Anscombe made about the practical syllogism.[59] First, the relationship between the principles and the conclusions is logical rather than psychological. Statements about whether a cloak warms or an item is borrowed are not made true by the agent's psychological states. The fact that practical reasoning is not often fully deductive results from the connection between practical reasoning and contingent actions. Practical reasoning is often nondeductive, but this nondeductive character does not make it into a psychological process. Moreover, it seems to me that this nondeductive character applies not only to fully practical syllogisms but also to many practical syllogisms used by moral science. Second, although the major premise indicates a desired good, the major premise is not about the desire for the good. The practical syllogisms' terms do not include the psychological states as terms. So although the production and use of the syllogism depend partly on whether the agent is or is not disordered, the conclusion is not a merely psychological effect of the premises. Consequently, although the difference between *secundum quid* practical syllogisms and fully practical syllogisms depends on whether the end is actually pursued by the agent, the relationship between the conclusion and the premises is not primarily psychological.

JOHN DUNS SCOTUS

Scotus to some extent separates the cognitive element of practical reasoning from the will's activity. In general, he thinks that knowledge is practical not intrinsically but because of some further relation of the knowledge to action. Nevertheless, he thinks that the object of practical knowledge is distinct on account of the object known rather than on account of an agent's own use of this knowledge for an end. In general, practical syllogisms are necessary for a free human act.

59. Supra, note 2.

But Scotus does not think that every practical syllogism ends in the act. The will is free to accept or reject the known that is presented to it by practical reason.

Scotus follows Aristotle carefully in his concern to base all science, including practical science concerning contingent beings, on necessary truths.[60] Since the agent's end is accidental to the act known, the end as an end cannot be the subject of practical science.[61] He uses the Greek word *praxis* in order to describe the way in which human action can be the object of a practical science. He states that "praxis to which practical knowledge [*cognition*] is extended is an act of another potency than the intellect, naturally posterior to the intellection, naturally suited [*natus*] to be chosen in conformity to right reason, for this, that the act be right."[62] This description mentions three conditions that shed light on the relationship of praxis to reason.[63] First, the act of another potency must be involved if the intellect is to extend beyond itself. Second, this other potency must be the will, since the other powers of the soul are not ordered to the intellect and they naturally exist prior to the intellect. Moreover, unlike the intellect and the will, other human powers are common to humans and nonrational animals. In contrast, as we have seen in the previous chapter, the will's operation depends on the intellect in such a way that only intellectual beings have wills. The third condition limits praxis to those acts that have been chosen correctly. A science such as ethics is concerned with correct choice and its relation to correct knowledge. One important point about this definition of praxis is that it isolates the will's activity from that of the other powers. Scotus does argue that

60. Scotus, *Ord.*, prol. pars 5, qq. 1–2, nn. 332–44, 350 (Vat., 1.217–25, 226–27); Idem, *Lect.*, prol., pars 4, qq. 1–2, nn. 171–73 (Vat., 16.56–58).

61. Soctus, *Ord.*, prol., pars 5, qq. 1–2, n. 247 (Vat., 1.167–68).

62. "praxis ad quam cognitio practica extenditur est actus alterius potentiae quam intellectus, naturaliter posterior intellectione, natus elici conformiter intellectioni rectae ad hoc ut sit rectus"; Scotus, *Ord.*, prol. pars 5, qq. 1–2, n. 228 (Vat. 1, 155). See also Idem, *Lect.*, prol., pars 4, qq. 1–2, n. 133 (Vat., 16.47). For Scotus's understanding of praxis, see Dreyer and Ingham, *Philosophical Vision*, 127–32; Möhle, *Ethik als scientia practica*.

63. Scotus, *Ord.*, prol., pars 5, qq. 1–2, nn. 228–35 (Vat., 1.155–60); Idem, *Lect.*, prol., pars 4, qq. 1–2, nn. 134–39 (Vat., 16.47–48).

acts of powers can be called praxes in a qualified sense, but only insofar as they proceed from the will. For example, strictly speaking praxis is merely the choice to walk. But praxis in a wider sense extends to the walking itself, because the walking is commanded by the will.

This definition of praxis implies a twofold relation to practical knowledge, namely of priority and conformity.[64] Practical knowledge is prior to praxis because in order to qualify as praxis, the choice must be made in accordance with the knowledge. The relationship of conformity is on account of the way in which practical truth depends on right appetite. These relations are aptitudinal rather than real. Aptitudinally related items are capable of being actually related in a certain way. Whether knowledge actually directs or not is merely a contingent matter that does not affect the kind of knowledge. Nevertheless, practical knowledge is that kind of knowledge that is capable of or "apt for" directing right action.

Scotus rejects the position of those who think that knowledge is practical on account of its order to an end.[65] This ordering would be accidental to the knowledge and could not constitute a formal difference between practical and speculative knowledge. The aptitudinal relation of praxis to the knowledge is made possible by the object of the knowledge. The object must be contingent and subject to human action.[66] The intellect and the object suffice for the knowledge to be practical; the knower's actual ends are irrelevant. The aptitudinal relations to praxis remain whether the knowing agent loves the end or not. Since the aptitudinal relation is not essential to the kind of knowledge, it does not as something belonging to an absolute essence divide knowledge into two species. But in much the same way as a proper passion of a species divides a genus, this aptitudinal relation divides knowledge. This division is similar to how lines are divided into straight lines and curved, and numbers are divided

64. Scotus, *Ord.*, prol., pars 5, qq. 1–2, nn. 236–37 (Vat., 1.161–62).

65. Scotus, *Ord.*, prol., pars 5, qq. 1–2, nn. 241–47 (Vat., 1.165–68); Idem, *Lect.*, prol., pars 4, qq. 1–2, nn. 147–49 (Vat., 16.50).

66. Scotus, *Ord.*, prol., pars. 5, n. 252 (Vat., 1.169–70); Idem, *Lect.*, prol., pars 4, qq. 1–2 (Vat., 16.169–70).

into odd numbers and even.[67] What is the role of the end in Scotus's description of practical science? Practical science often extends to the end of the praxis, but not "insofar as it is an end but insofar as it is an object."[68]

Whereas Thomas thinks that prudence is distinct from moral science on account of its direct connection to the virtuous act, Scotus thinks that the proper act of prudence itself does not entail willing.[69] Prudence is more directive of action than moral science is, but the proximity to direction comes only from the way in which prudence is a less universal kind of knowledge. In some works, Scotus distinguishes between moral science, knowledge from experience, and particular dictates.[70] Basic moral principles are known through their terms, such as "God is to be loved above all things." Moral science includes general principles that by themselves are insufficient for determining what particular act should be done. Consequently, moral science might be described as in a way speculative. Moreover, moral science is universal and actions are particular. Consequently, moral science is not concerned with this or that action. Experience is more valuable than science in directing behavior. In contrast, prudence makes judgments about particular actions. For Scotus, the directive aspect of prudence consists in its proximity to the particular act.

Scotus also differs from Thomas by stating that prudence is like technical skill insofar as it has distinct and separable species.[71] According to Scotus, prudence is one as a genus, but the absence of

67. Scotus, *Ord.*, prol., pars 5, qq. 1–2, n. 238 (Vat., 1.163).

68. "non tamen in quantum est finis sed in quantum est obiectum"; Scotus, *Ord.*, prol. p. 1, pars 5, qq. 1–2, n. 13 (Vat., 1.176).

69. Stephen D. Dumont, "The Necessary Connection of Moral Virtue to Prudence according to John Duns Scotus—Revisited," *Recherches de théologie ancienne et médiévale* 55 (1988): 184–206.

70. John Duns Scotus, *In Metaphysicorum*, lib. 6, q. 1, nn. 67–68 (OPh, 4.26–27); Idem, *Lect.*, prol., pars 4, qq. 1–2, n. 174 (Vat., 16.58); Idem, *Ord.*, prol., pars 5, qq. 1–2, n. 351 (Vat., 1.27–28). Dreyer and Ingham, *Philosophical Vision*, 186–91; Dreyer and Ingham, 188, state that in his later writings Scotus "identifies prudence with practical reason."

71. Scotus, *Collatio* 1, nn. 3–4, 19 (Wadding ed., 3.345–46, 349); Idem, *Lect.* 3, d. 36, q. un., nn. 91–108 (Vat., 21.336–40); Idem, *Ord.* 3, d. 36, q. un., nn. 96–100 (Vat., 10.259–61). See Osborne, "Imperfect or Partial Prudence?" 167, 171–73.

one of its species does not affect the other species. Scotus notes that someone might simply lack the opportunity to acquire prudence in one area. For instance, someone might have the opportunity to develop prudence concerning temperance but never have the opportunity to learn that part of prudence that concerns courage in battle. This prudence would not on its own be imperfect, although it is only part of that wider genus that includes the different prudences. The imperfection of the generic whole consists only in the fact that it does not possess all the parts, and not necessarily in the deficiency of any of the parts that it possesses.

Unlike Thomas, Scotus does not explicitly tie the basic moral principles to natural inclination.[72] He does think that synderesis is an unerring habit of practical reason by which the first principles of practical reasoning are known, but he does not discuss in detail the contrast between the principles of practical and speculative reason.[73] He divides moral principles into two kinds.[74] The first are known simply through their terms. For instance, "God is to be loved above all things" is known by anyone who grasps that God is the highest good. The knowledge of these precepts is prior to any act of the will, including even God's will. Strictly speaking, the natural law consists only of these principles and those principles that can be deduced from them, such as the principle that "Nothing other than God should be worshipped as God." Other precepts do not belong to the natural law strictly speaking, although they are in harmony with it. All of the precepts regarding one's neighbor, including the precepts against adultery and murder, fall under this category. God could make exceptions,

---

72. Scotus, *Ord.* 3, d. 37, nn. 8–15 (Vat., 10.274–79); Idem, *Lect.* 3, d. 27, nn. 6–14 (Vat., 21.350–53). For a contrast between Scotus and Thomas on these principles, see Ludger Honnefelder, "Ansätze zu einer Theorie der praktischen Wahrheit bei Thomas von Aquin und Johannes Duns Scotus," in *Was ist für den Menschen Gute? Menschliche Natur und Güterlehre*, ed. Jan Szaif and Matthias Lutz-Bachmann (Berlin: de Gruyter, 2004), 247–62.

73. Scotus, *Lect.* 2, d. 39, qq. 1–2, n. 24 (Vat., 19.384); Idem, *Ord.* 2., d. 39, qq. 1–2, n. 19 (Vat., 8.462).

74. Scotus, *Ord.* 3, d. 37, nn. 16–29 (Vat., 10.274–84); Idem, *Lect.* 3, d. 37, n. 15 (Vat., 21.353). For Scotus's theory of natural law, see especially Hannes Möhle, "Scotus's Theory of Natural Law," in *The Cambridge Companion to Scotus*, 312–31.

but they almost always hold. Unlike Thomas, Scotus thinks that the commandments of the second tablet of the Decalogue belong to the natural law in only a looser way. Scotus argues that if these commands are known to be true through their terms, then even God knows them apart from his willing and is bound by them. But God has no practical knowledge of creatures, so he cannot be bound by any truths about creatures. The contrast with Thomas is instructive.[75] Thomas at least in some texts argues that the command to kill Isaac is connected with the order of justice. Death is God's just penalty for original sin, and Abraham would be God's instrument for carrying out the penalty. In contrast, Scotus merely states that God can make murder good, since God himself is not bound by anything outside of him.

The relationship between the self-evident moral principles and those principles in harmony with them is unclear. Some scholars think that Scotus attributes the goodness of the precepts and corresponding actions entirely to God's will, whereas others think that prior considerations of justice are involved.[76] Moreover, Scotus is unclear about how the precepts of the second table are known. With respect to Scotus's understanding of practical reasoning, the important point is that these other precepts have their force insofar as they are in harmony with precepts that are known through their terms. Scotus does not entirely separate the first set of precepts from human nature. He emphasizes that humans can love God above all because the good is the primary adequate object of the will and God is the highest instance of the good.[77] The justification of the other precepts consists

75. Klaus Hedwig, "Das Isaak-Opfer: Über den Status des Naturgesetzes bei Thomas von Aquin, Duns Scotus, and Ockham," in *Mensch und Natur im Mittelalter*, ed. Andreas Speer and Albert Zimmerman, Miscellanea Mediaevalia 21.2 (Berlin: de Gruyter, 1992), 2.645–61.

76. Thomas Williams, "A Most Methodical Lover? On Scotus's Arbitrary Creator," *Journal of the History of Philosophy* 38 (2000): 169–202; Idem, "The Unmitigated Scotus," *Archiv für Geschichte der Philosophie* 80 (1998): 162–81; Idem, "From Metaethics to Action Theory," 332–35; Mary Beth Ingham, "Duns Scotus, Morality, and Happiness: A Reply to Thomas Williams," *American Catholic Philosophical Quarterly* 74 (2000): 173–95; Allan B. Wolter, "The Unshredded Scotus: A Response to Thomas Williams," *American Catholic Philosophical Quarterly* 77 (2003): 315–56.

77. Osborne, *Love of Self and Love of God*, 186–206.

in their harmony with those precepts that are known through their terms. Scotus rejects the position that these precepts are based on goods that are indicated by those natural inclinations that are shared with nonrational creatures.

Given what has been said, there might be a division in Scotus between (1) universal principles that are easily known; (2) moral science, which is learned from teaching and reasoning; and (3) prudence, which is learned from experience. Prudence alone would be about particular judgments. What is the relationship between these kinds of knowledge? Not everyone with prudence would have moral science, unless moral science is extended to include knowledge that is possessed by those who have never studied moral science. Furthermore, unless prudence is extended to include even the knowledge that is obtained through study, not everyone with moral science would be prudent. More importantly, much practical reasoning is erroneous. The reasoning of these erring agents is similar to that of the good agents, but their act is not guided by practical knowledge.

An important exception to this threefold distinction arises from the fact that some practical knowledge belongs not to prudence but to a technical skill. The distinction between technical skill and experience is like that between moral science and prudence:

Just as technical skill concerning production [*factibilia*] is related to the habit of the experienced person, so, concerning action [*agibilia*], moral science is related to the habit of prudence, since the habits of a technical skill and moral science are as remote to directing because they are universal; but the habits of prudence and of the [technically] experienced person, since they are generated from acts, are particular and close to directing.[78]

The further directive characteristic of skill and prudence consists in their particularity, which is connected to the way in which they are acquired through particular acts. But someone can have prudence

---

78. "sicut ars se habet circa factibilia ad habitum experti, ita circa agibilia se habit scientia moralis ad habitum prudentiae, quia habitus artis et scientiae moralis sunt quasi remoti ad dirigendum, quia universales; sed habitus prudentiae et experti, quia generati sunt ex actibus, sunt particulares, et propinqui ad dirigendum"; Scotus, *Ord.*, prol., pars 5, qq. 1–2 (Vat., 1.228).

and yet act against it. On Scotus's view, prudence gives a dictate in accordance with right reason, but the agent is still free to accept or reject this dictate.[79] Scotus does not seem to distinguish between the kinds or degrees of practicality in judgments of conscience and judgments of prudence or choice.

For Scotus, the intellect functions well even if the agent chooses poorly. How is it possible for someone to act against prudence's dictates? For Scotus, there are two ways in which the will can blind the intellect.[80] First, the will can distract the intellect's good judgment by thinking about something else. Second, the will can command the intellect to think about how to obtain a bad end. In both cases the will turns the intellect away from what it judges or could judge to be correct, but the ability to judge correctly is not taken away. With respect to its independence from correct willing, prudence resembles moral science.

Some scholars have argued that in a later text, namely *Ord.* 3, d. 36, Scotus "offers an explanation of the relationship of knowledge to choice that dispenses entirely with the distinction between moral science and prudence."[81] Although there may be some truth to this view, it seems to me that in this passage Scotus merely states that the name of "prudence" can be extended even to the knowledge of the first moral principles, since the principles virtually include everything that is relevant to the end.[82] He does here state that prudence is concerned with all the stages of practical reasoning, even if it is not active in every agent's practical reasoning. Moreover, Scotus argues that prudence involves not only particular means but also ends. But the point here seems simply to be that there is a relation between the particular dictates and universal prudence. He still thinks that prudence is

79. Scotus, *Ord.* 3, d. 36, n. 72 (Vat., 10.249).

80. Scotus, *Ord.* 3, d. 36, nn. 74–75 (Vat., 10.249–51). Marilyn McCord Adams, "Scotus and Ockham on the Connection of the Virtues," in *John Duns Scotus: Metaphysics and Ethics*, ed. Ludger Honnefelder, Rega Wood, and Mechthild Dreyer (Leiden: Brill, 1996), 506–7.

81. Dryer and Ingham, *Philosophical Vision*, 188.

82. Scotus, *Ord.* 3, d. 26, nn. 96–97 (Vat., 10.259–60).

practical because it includes particular judgments that are the kind of judgments that can direct right action even if the prudential agent does not choose to act rightly. Moreover, in this later text he states that it is probable that prudence leads to right action because, like technical experience, it is closer to action.[83] He does not claim that prudence and moral science are the same.

Scotus's separation of practical reasoning from the agent's own ends and choice is reflected in his understanding of the practical syllogism and its relation to choice. Only some choices require practical reasoning, although all ordinary human moral choices do. God's choice is not directed by fully practical knowledge.[84] We have seen that for Scotus practical knowledge is directive of practical willing. Praxis is right insofar as it conforms to practical knowledge. But the rectitude of God's willing does not depend on his knowledge. Consequently, God's knowledge cannot be practical in the way that creatures' knowledge can be. Moreover, some created intellects can reason practically but not syllogistically. For instance, Christ's intellect has perfect abstractive knowledge of everything, so syllogistic reasoning is unnecessary for him.[85] Nevertheless, Christ made meritorious choices.

Similarly, Scotus thinks that the angels who sinned lacked deliberation because they willed the impossible, namely to be equal to God. The impossible cannot be chosen by that kind of choice that occurs after deliberation, but only by something that is choice in only a broader sense and is not efficacious.[86] Unlike Thomas, Scotus thinks that angels reason discursively from principles to conclusions. However, he thinks that in this particular case they lacked deliberation because of the kind of choice that it was.

What is the difference between discursive reasoning and deliberation? According to Scotus, Christ's intellect is the only created intellect that does not reason discursively, although the angels' discursive reasoning is distinctive because it moves from potential to actual

83. Scotus, *Ord.* 3, d. 26, nn. 85–86 (Vat., 10.255–56).
84. Scotus, *Ord.*, prol., pars 5, qq. 1–2, nn. 324–31 (Vat., 1.211–17).
85. Scotus, *Lect.* 3, d. 18, n. 41 (Vat., 21.12).
86. Scotus, *Ord.* 2, d. 6, q. 1, n. 15 (Vat., 8.30).

knowledge rather than from ignorance to knowledge.[87] Christ and the angels are similar in that they chose and even choose in accordance with correct practical knowledge that is not syllogistic. Whereas Thomas had used the example of the cithara player to show how deliberation is sometimes unnecessary for the exercise of technical skill, Scotus uses Aristotle's example of a cithara player to illustrate how Christ can choose even though he does not need to deliberate. Someone who has a fully developed ability to play the cithara does not need to deliberate about how he plays. Similarly, Christ's more perfect knowledge made deliberation unnecessary for his acts of choice.

Since Scotus uses an example taken from a technical skill, namely cithara playing, to show how a perfect level of knowledge makes the practical syllogism unnecessary, it would seem to follow that the prudent person also does not need to reason syllogistically when acting. Nevertheless, Scotus explicitly argues that the practical syllogism is necessary for meritorious and demeritorious human actions.[88] In other contexts, Scotus considers the position that a prudent person acts well and yet does not seem to employ the practical syllogism.[89] Scotus rejects this view by stating:

For just as someone does not act humanly unless he acts with understanding, so—concerning that which is for the sake of the end—he does not act well humanly unless by understanding that for the sake of which he acts; this "to understand" is "to deliberate." Therefore the virtuous agent does not act in this way suddenly and without deliberation in the way that nature acts, as described in Book II of the *Physics*.[90]

In this text Scotus indicates the same passage in which Aristotle compares the action of the cithara player to that of a natural ability. Ac-

---

87. Scotus, *Ord.* 2, d. 1, q. 6, nn. 312–14 (Vat., 7.153–54). Cf. Idem, *Ord.*, prol., p. 4, qq. 1–2, n. 209 (Vat., 1.142–43); Idem, *Ord.* 2, d. 7, n. 22 (OTh, 8.84–85).

88. Scotus, *Lect.* 2, d. 41, n. 10 (Vat., 19.396).

89. Scotus, *Ord.* 3, d. 33, nn. 76–77 (Vat., 10.175); Idem, *Ord.* 3, d. 39, n. 20 (Vat., 10.327–28).

90. "Sicut enim non humane agit nisi intelligendo agit, ita—circa illud quod est ad finem—non humane bene agit nisi intelligendo illud propter quod agit; et istud 'intelligere' est 'deliberare.' Unde non sic agit virtuosus repentine et sine deliberatione sicut natura agit, ex II *Physicorum*"; Scotus, *Ord.* 3, d. 33, n. 76 (Vat., 10.175).

cording to Scotus, at least in the context of prudence, the cognitive habit does not eliminate the need for reasoning with practical syllogisms. For those with prudence, and even for those who are habitually imprudent in some respect, the practical syllogism is so quick that it is nearly imperceptible. In these texts that emphasize the necessity of practical syllogisms even for the prudent person, deliberation only seems to be absent because of the shortness of time required for deliberation. But deliberation is required for ordinary free human choice, including that of the prudent person.

Scotus's discussions of the practical syllogism of the prudent agent are brief but they shed light on his understanding of the role of the practical syllogism in practical reasoning. First, deliberation is required for ordinary human choice. Second, this deliberation leads to or takes the form of a practical syllogism. Third, this syllogistic reasoning takes place over a period of time, even if this time is short and difficult to recognize. This third point may indicate that for Scotus the practical syllogism has not only logical but also psychological characteristics.

We have already seen how Scotus thinks that reasoning is practical on account of its subject's aptitude for action, and not because it actually is used by the agent in order to act. Similarly, prudence presents the agent with a conclusion that he can freely accept or reject. These aspects of Scotus's theory show that for Scotus the conclusion of a practical syllogism cannot be a choice or an action, but must be a statement. Moreover, the distinction between moral science and prudence consists merely in the particularity of the reasoning and its proximity to action. Unlike Thomas, Scotus does not seem to think that some kinds of practical reasoning are more practical precisely because of their connection with the will. God does not strictly speaking have practical knowledge either of what he creates or of what he could create because his will is not regulated by the knowledge. God's knowledge is speculative. For Scotus, human action occurs when the agent assents to a conclusion that is capable of directing action, and this ability to regulate action results from the conclusion's particularity. Scotus's account of practical reasoning separates more the cognitive and appetitive aspects of human action.

WILLIAM OF OCKHAM

In some respects, Ockham, like Scotus, separates the cognitive and appetitive aspects of practical reasoning. However, Ockham rejects Scotus's account of praxis as the object of practical reasoning and also previous attempts to distinguish between the sciences on account of the way in which objects are considered. For Ockham, *science,* including moral science, is simply an ordered collection of mental habits and propositions.[91] A science's object is the known proposition, and its subject is only the subject of such a proposition. He represents a shift from thinking about science as a unified habit to thinking about it as primarily a collection of habits and secondarily as those propositions that are habitually known. The difference between practical and speculative science consists primarily in the relationship between their conclusions and human action.

Like Thomas and many other medieval thinkers, Ockham accepts at face value Aristotle's statement that practical knowledge differs from speculative knowledge on account of the end. But Ockham is particularly concerned to reject Henry of Ghent's view that practical knowledge is distinct on account of that end which the science itself has, which is or can be distinct from the knower's own end.[92] According to Ockham, a practical science is the type of science that has conclusions that direct or should direct human action, and practical science shares many of the same propositions that belong to speculative sciences. An end is a final cause, and a science has no end unless it is

---

91. Armand Maurer, "Ockham's Conception of the Unity of a Science," *Mediaeval Studies* 20 (1958): 98–112; Idem, "The Unity of a Science: St. Thomas and the Nominalists," in *St. Thomas Aquinas, 1274–1294: Commemorative Studies,* ed. Armand Maurer (Toronto: Pontifical Institute of Mediaeval Studies, 1974), 2.269–91. For the application to practical and theoretical science, see especially Idem, *Philosophy of William of Ockham,* 142–48.

92. Ockham. *Ord.* 1, prol., q. 11 (OTh, 1.303–6). For Ockham's understanding of practical and speculative knowledge, see Sigrid Müller, *Handeln in einer kontingenten Welt: Zu Begriff und Bedeutung der rechten Vernunft (recta ratio) bei Wilhelm von Ockham,* Tübinger Studien zur Theologie und Philosophie 18 (Tübingen: Francke, 2000), 147–82; Holopainen, *Foundations of Ethics,* 38–61; Freppert, *Basis of Morality,* 15–31.

the end of the knowing agent.[93] Nevertheless, some sciences are such that an agent will have certain ends if he acts in accordance with right reason. For instance, someone might study natural sciences or metaphysics not for the contemplation of the truth but for instrumental purposes, such as obtaining money.[94] Nevertheless, if the agent acts well, he regards the contemplation of truth as the end of his acquisition and exercise of speculative knowledge. Practical and speculative sciences are distinguished by the end that should be pursued in accordance with right reason, and this distinction is not a distinction between the subjects of the science but a distinction between objects, since its propositions are about things that should be done.[95]

Ockham emphasizes that even speculative activity can be considered an action since it is commanded by the will.[96] The difference is that the speculative activity is not about human actions, but rather about those things that are not subject to human action. The object of practical reason is not praxis in the sense understood by Scotus, namely only an act of the will in accordance with right reason.[97] Ockham expands the category of praxis in at least three ways. First, he argues that praxis includes not only choice but also the object of choice. Walking and thinking speculatively are praxes insofar as they proceed from the will. Second, he states that Scotus's arguments are insufficient to prove that praxis should be reserved to action in accordance with right reason. Consequently, Ockham does not focus on the way in which the knowledge is capable of directing praxis according to right reason and right action. Since even speculative reasoning can be commanded by the will, it follows that even speculative activity is praxis. Ockham shifts from Scotus's focus on the object to a different focus on the end that the knower should have. Nevertheless, the connection to an actual end is severed. Third, Ockham extends "praxis" to include every act that can be commanded by the will. The differ-

93. Ockham, *Ord.* 1, prol., q. 11 (OTh, 1.306–10).
94. Ockham, *Ord.* 1, prol., q. 11 (OTh, 1.305).
95. Ockham, *Ord.* 1, prol., q. 11 (OTh, 1.313–14, 321).
96. Ockham, *Ord.* 1, prol., q. 10 (OTh, 1.281–85).
97. For Ockham's understanding of praxis, see Holopainen, *Foundations of Ethics*, 61–72.

ence may be that Scotus was concerned to define praxis in such a way that this praxis could be the basis of real practical knowledge. Acts that are not in accordance with right reason or acts merely commanded by the will do not have this relation to knowledge. For Ockham, the objects of practical reasoning are conclusions about what the agent can do even though not all praxis is correct. Practical knowledge is distinct because of the end to which it could be put by an agent who acts in accordance with right reason.

Ockham does not sharply separate many practical and speculative premises. He denies that the speculative and practical sciences are distinct according to their subjects. For instance, we can have both practical and speculative knowledge of the subject "earth."[98] The statement "earth is hard" can belong to speculative knowledge about how things are, but it can also be used in directing human actions such as farming. The difference is in whether the knowledge directs action, and whether the whole proposition leads to or includes such directive statements. Ordinarily speculative statements can be made practical through their use. If "earth is hard" belongs to reasoning about what cannot be changed by human action, then this statement belongs to speculative knowledge. If the statement "earth is hard" is used by the farmer to guide planting or irrigation, then the statement belongs to practical knowledge. Ockham argues that such premises themselves can be described as virtually (*virtualiter*) practical but simply speaking (*simpliciter*) speculative according to common usage. The word *virtualiter* brings to mind Thomas's discussion of virtually practical knowledge.

Unlike Thomas, Ockham does not think that the consideration of the particular as particular is a characteristic feature of practical knowledge. Ockham states that premises can be speculative even if they are about particulars. Practical reasoning employs not only speculative universal premises, but also speculative particular premises.[99]

98. Ockham, *Ord.* 1, prol., q. 11 (OTh, 1.314–15); Idem, *Summa philosophiae naturalis,* preambula (OPh, 6.151–52).

99. Idem, *Summula philosophiae naturalis,* preambula (OPh, 6.150–51).

Practical knowledge ends in a particular conclusion, but practical knowledge is not distinct merely because it is particular. Consider the following syllogism: Parents are to be honored (major premise); these are parents (minor premise); these should be honored (conclusion). The conclusion directs human action and is particular. The major premise directs human action and is universal. The minor premise is speculative but particular. It does not say anything about what to do about the parents, but merely identifies two individuals as parents. Nevertheless, this speculative minor premise connects the universal premise about how to act with the conclusion about a concrete action. In this respect the knowledge is both speculative and practical. Ockham's distinction between practical and speculative knowledge does not correspond to the distinction between the particular and the universal.

Ockham differs not only from Thomas Aquinas but also from Duns Scotus in that he does not, at least in his academic writings, use the term "natural law" to describe these moral principles. He does discuss natural law or natural right in his later political writings. Scholars disagree over how to understand his later natural law teaching, and how or whether this later natural law teaching is compatible with his earlier academic writings. But our focus is on his academic writings, in which there are no or few explicit discussions of natural law.[100]

What is the difference between the moral principles of prudence and those of moral science? Like Scotus, Ockham rejects the view held by Thomas that prudence is distinct because there is only one species of prudence. He agrees with Scotus that there are as many species of prudence as there are species of habits and acts, and that these species are separable.[101] But Ockham rejects Scotus's position that moral science and art differ from prudence and experience with

100. Kevin McDonnell, "Does Ockham Have a Theory of Natural Law?" *Franciscan Studies* 34 (1974): 383–92; A. S. McGrade, "Natural Law and Omnipotence," in *The Cambridge Companion to Ockham*, 273–301; Müller, *Handeln in einer kontingenten Welt*, 211–16.

101. Ockham, *Rep.* 3, q. 12 (OTh, 6.419); Idem, Q. V., q. 8, art. 2 (OTh, 8.331–33). Note that the latter text concerns the fourth kind of prudence.

respect to the proximity to an action.[102] Ockham agrees that moral science involves universal premises, but he states that its universal premises can come from human experience and lead to action. Both the major premises of prudence and those of moral science need minor premises in order to mediate between the major premise and the conclusion. Although the premises may differ as less and more universal, they both can be used in a syllogism that immediately concerns action. For example, if someone knows a principle of moral science, such that "parents should be loved," and all the requisite circumstances are present and known to be present, then he can immediately draw the conclusion. There is no need for prudence. So although Ockham agrees with Scotus that moral science is more universal than prudence, he does not draw Scotus's conclusion that moral science needs some intermediate habit such as prudence in order to direct action. Although all prudence is practical knowledge, not all practical knowledge is prudence.

Ockham's understanding of prudence is complex. In one text he distinguishes between four different senses of "prudence."[103] If prudence is understood in the first way, it includes any knowledge that mediately or immediately directs action. In this first sense, prudence includes moral science. In the second sense, prudence is evident knowledge concerning a particular action, and this knowledge evidently comes from a universal proposition.[104] He gives the example of the conclusion "Good should be done to such persons," which can follow from the universal premise "Good should be done to those who do good." But moral science also involves this kind of reasoning. In the third sense, prudence is that knowledge which immediately directs action and is known only through experience of such an action. This kind of prudence includes propositions such as "This angry person should be soothed through soft words." This third sense is what

102. Ockham, *Ord.* 1, prol., q. 11 (OTh, 1.318); Idem, *Rep.* 3, q. 12 (OTh, 6.419–20); Idem, Q. V., q. 6, art. 10 (OTh, 8.283–84).

103. Ockham, Q. V., q. 7, art. 2 (OTh, 8.330–31).

104. For Ockham's complicated account of evident assent, see especially Elizabeth Karger, "Ockham's Misunderstood Theory of Intuitive and Abstractive Cognition," in *The Cambridge Companion to Ockham*, 208–9.

Aristotle properly calls prudence when he distinguishes prudence from moral science. According to the fourth sense, prudence is an aggregate of all the directive knowledge necessary for living well. Ockham argues that in this way prudence is simply a collection of the different kinds of knowledge necessary for the exercise of the different moral virtues.

Although moral science and prudence are distinct, there are many ways in which they overlap. In the first two senses of the term "prudence," there is no criteria to distinguish it from moral science. The fourth sense of the term would also seem to overlap with knowledge concerning the particular virtues that could be learned through moral science. The contrast between moral science and prudence is starkest if prudence is taken in its third sense, in which prudence comes from particular experience and is directed to particular actions. This kind of prudence lacks universal or speculative premises, but instead includes only propositions that dictate a particular action. Such prudence is practical knowledge properly speaking. If prudence is limited to such conclusions, then it is clearly distinct from the universal propositions of moral science. But it is also excludes the principles that the prudent person uses to arrive at conclusions.

How do prudence in the looser senses and moral science arrive at the basic moral principles? In one text he distinguishes between two kinds of moral science: one that can be evidently obtained through teaching, the other that can only be obtained through experience.[105] Syllogisms such as the following belong to moral science in the first sense: "To every benefactor, good should be done; everyone who frees someone from death is a benefactor; to everyone who frees someone from death, good should be done."[106] Ockham states that the major premise is known through its terms, although he does not explain why it is so. Someone can be taught to reason to the conclusion even if he lacks the relevant experience. But only through experience can

---

105. Ockham, Q. V., q. 6, art. 10 (OTh, 8.281–83).

106. "Omne benefactori est benefaciendum; sed qualibet liberans aliquem a morte est benefactor; igitur omni tali est benefaciendum;" Ockham, Q. V., q. 6, art. 10 (OTh, 8.181).

someone acquire evident knowledge that an angry person in a particular case needs to be soothed through pleasing words.

With respect to that moral science gained through experience, a certain kind of prudence can overlap. Ockham distinguishes between particular prudence, which excludes moral science, and universal prudence. Properly speaking, prudence is particular:

[Prudence is taken] in one way properly speaking for the evident knowledge of some singular proposition which is held only by means of experience. For example, this evident knowledge [is prudence], "he should be soothed through soft words," which is evident by virtue of this contingent [proposition], "that person is to be soothed by such means," and this [proposition] is known through experience.[107]

Moral science does not include such particular statements. In contrast, universal prudence can also be understood to be the evident knowledge of a universal practical proposition that is known through experience. This universal prudence is the same as that moral science that is learned through experience. Can moral science be obtained through experience even if the agent lacks prudence? Ockham claims that it is at least theoretically possible for moral science to be acquired without prudence, although there is a de facto dependence.[108]

Unfortunately, Ockham gives no detailed account of how the knowledge of principles is acquired. Consequently, it is unclear why some basic moral principles are known through their terms, and how others are learned through experience. In one passage, Ockham gives the following examples of principles that are known through their terms: "Everything upright [honestum] should be done, and everything wrong should be avoided," "the will must conform itself to right reason."[109] Ockham never suggests that such principles could be changed even

107. "Uno modo proprie pro notitia evidenti alicuius propositionis singualris quae solum habetur mediante experientia. Verba gratia, notitia haec evidens 'iste est mitigandus per pulcra verba' quae est evidens virute huius contingentis 'ille mitigatur per talem viam' et hoc cognoscitur per experentiam"; Ockham, Q. V., q. 6, art. 10 (OTh, 8.282).

108. Ockham, Ord. 1, prol., q. 11 (OTh, 1.318).

109. "omne honestum est faciendum, et omne inhonestum est fugiendum"; "voluntas debet se conformater rectae rationi"; Ockham, Quod. 4, q. 14 (OTh, 9.177, 178).

by God. With respect to the divine command, Ockham also states that the principle that one should never lead another to act against God's will also seems to be known through its terms. He does not definitively assert that it is so known, and he does not bring up the question of whether God could change the principle.

Ockham thinks that God can change many principles that can be known through reason, such as the precepts to love God, avoid adultery, and avoid theft.[110] Hating God, committing adultery, and stealing could have been good if God had willed to make these acts good. In one text he qualifies his position by stating that the names would change because the names themselves connote that act's badness by connoting the act's bad circumstances. Perhaps he is taking into account Aristotle's statement that theft and adultery are always bad and that the names themselves indicate the badness.[111] Ockham explicitly claims that his position on the connotation of such terms rightly interprets the "saints and philosophers." We have seen that Ockham states that the moral science not known through experience is that taught by the saints and philosophers. Consequently, one part of moral science, namely that acquired through teaching, contains unchangeable truths, such that the terms "adultery" and "theft" connote wrong actions, and changeable truths, such as that the acts of adultery and theft are intrinsically wrong. But these truths are known by many without the aid of revelation. For Ockham, God could have made a world in which the same acts that are now evil would be good and even meritorious.

Can God change any moral principles that are known through their terms? Although it would seem not, some of the principles that are self-known do not seem obviously different from principles concerning acts that God could change. If God could have made the world

---

110. Ockham, *Ord.* 1, d. 47 (OTh, 4.685); Idem, *Rep.* 2, q. 15 (OTh, 5.352–53); Idem, *Rep.* 4, q. 16 (OTh, 7.352). For the discussion of the divine precept, see also Idem, Q. V. 7, art. 1 (OTh, 8.328); Idem, Quod 3, q. 14 (OTh, 9.255). For problems with Ockham's understanding of the command to love God, see especially Osborne, "Ockham as a Divine-Command Theorist," 12–16.

111. Ockham, *Rep.* 2, q. 15 (OTh, 5.352–53). See Aristotle, *Nicomachean Ethics* 2.7.1107a7–a14.

such that adultery and theft are good, then perhaps he could have made a world in which it is good to harm benefactors and to allow the needy to die. We have already seen one text in which he considers the precept concerning doing good to a benefactor as known through its terms. In another text, he states that the following principle is also known through its terms: "Good should be done to everyone in extreme need lest he should perish."[112] It is unclear why these principles are self-evident, or whether they could ever be false. The distinction between the connotation of the terms and the acts themselves does not seem to help in these examples. But Ockham's position is undeveloped.

Ockham does not give clear criteria concerning the self-evidence of a moral truth, so it is difficult to tell whether a given principle is self-evident or known through experience. It is safe only to say that on his account at least some truths learned in moral science could have been false if God had given different commands. In general, scholars disagree over Ockham's understanding of the ultimate connection between moral principles and the divine commands.[113] Ockham accepts the then commonplace distinction between positive and nonpositive moral science, according to which nonpositive moral science, such as that found in Aristotle, concerns what is known to be good or bad apart from the knowledge of a superior's commands.[114] This distinc-

112. "Omni indigenti extrema necessitate sit benefeciendum ne pereat"; Ockham, Q. V., q. 8, art. 2 (OTh, 8.423).

113. Marilyn McCord Adams, "The Structure of Ockham's Moral Theory," *Franciscan Studies* 46 (1986): 1–35; Eadem, "William of Ockham: Voluntarist or Naturalist?" in *Studies in Medieval Philosophy*, ed. John F. Wippel, Studies in Philosophy and the History of Philosophy 1 (Washington, D.C.: The Catholic University of America Press, 1987), 219–47; Eadem, "Ockham on Will, Nature, Morality," in *The Cambridge Companion to Ockham*, 245–72; Peter King, "Ockham's Ethical Theory," in *The Cambridge Companion to Ockham*, 227–44; Maurer, *The Philosophy of William of Ockham*, 516–39; Osborne, "Ockham as a Divine-Command Theorist," 1–22; Müller, *Handeln in einer kontingenten Welt*, 20–41; Rega Wood, "Göttliches Gebot und Gutheit Gottes nach Wilhelm von Ockham," *Philosophisches Jahrbuch* 101 (1994): 38–54.

114. Ockham, Quod. 4, q. 14 (OTh, 9.177). See especially Osborne, "Ockham as a Divine-Command Theorist," 5–7; Müller, *Handeln in einer kontingenten Welt*, 182–93.

tion is used to delineate the study of law from moral philosophy and theology, and does not explain how nonpositive moral science is acquired. The basic point is that it is not learned through studying laws. Consequently, it is available apart from revelation. For present purposes, two issues are important. First, certain principles are intrinsically practical, and these are either known through their terms or through experience. Second, Ockham qualifies many such ordinarily exceptionless principles with phrases such as "with the divine precept remaining." If he thinks that even some self-evident principles also depend in some way on God's will, he cannot think that they are self-evidently true in the way that Scotus does, such that if one grasps the terms they can never be thought to be false.

Although Ockham denies that moral science and prudence differ with respect to proximity to action, he does make a similar point when discussing the way in which moral science can be about objects that are not in the agent's power.[115] He makes another distinction between two different senses of the term "moral science." According to the first, moral science is concerned only about what is within the agent's power. This moral science is simply practical. According to the second, moral science includes the teaching of Aristotle, the philosophers, and the saints. In this second sense, moral science has both practical and speculative parts. Although such moral science includes speculative truths, these speculative truths can lead to practical conclusions. The important point is that proximity to action is not used to distinguish between moral science and prudence, but rather between different parts of moral science.

Ockham uses something like the proximity of a conclusion to action in order to distinguish between kinds of practical knowledge, but the distinction is between prudence and technical skill.[116] All practical knowledge is directive. This directive knowledge is either ostensive or dictative. Ostensive knowledge is concerned not with whether a work should be done here and now, but rather with how the work

---

115. Ockham, *Ord.* 1, prol., q. 12 (OTh, 1.359–60).
116. Ockham, *Ord.* 1, prol., q. 11 (OTh, 1.316–17); Idem, *Rep.* 3, q. 12 (OTh, 6.420).

should be done. The knowledge of a technical skill is merely ostensive. Ockham gives an example:

The technical skill of building a house shows that the house should be made of wood and stones and from such a foundation and with such walls and such a roof, and so with other things, and it dictates neither that the house should be built nor when it should be built, but to prudence it belongs to dictate that it should be made at such a time, or that it should be done in this way or that.[117]

The distinction between ostensive and dictative knowledge shows that practical knowledge can differ in its relation to praxis. Whereas prudence has praxis itself as an object, technical knowledge is often concerned with the object of praxis itself. For instance, the technical skill of building a house and the praxis of building a house have the very same object. In contrast, prudence is concerned with that human praxis which is building a house. The technical knowledge has answers to the question of how the house can be made. Prudence is concerned with whether the building should be built.

Since logic shows how to reason correctly, Ockham argues that even logic is a directive and ostensive science.[118] Unlike Thomas, he does not think that there are speculative arts. This difference is not so much in their understanding of logic as in their criterion for what counts as speculative knowledge.[119] Ockham does not think that the

---

117. "Sicut ars aedificatoria ostendit quod domus componitur ex lignis et lapidibus et ex fundamento tali et talibus parietibus et tali tecto, et sic de aliis, et non dictat quod domus est facienda nec quando est faciendo, sed ad prudentiam pertinet dictare quod tali tempore est facienda, vel sic est agendum vel sic"; Ockham, *Ord.* 1, prol., q. 11 (OTh, 1.316).

118. Ockham, *Ord.* 1, prol., q. 11 (OTh, 1.317); Idem, *Summula philosophiae naturalis*, preambula (OTh, 6.149–50). See Holopainen, *Foundations of Ethics*, 50–56.

119. For its importance for the Thomistic school and later developments, see Maarten J. F. M. Hoenen, "Late Medieval Schools of Thought in the Mirror of University Textbooks: The *Promptuarium Argumentorum* (Cologne 1492)," in *Philosophy and Learning: Universities in the Middle Ages*, ed. Martin J. F. M. Hoenen, J. H. Josef Schneider, and Georg Wieland, Education and Society in the Middle Ages and Renaissance 6 (Leiden: Brill, 1995), 349–55; Sten Ebbesen, "Is Logic Theoretical or Practical Knowledge?" in *Itinéraires d'Alberte de Saxe: Paris: Vienne au xiv*e* siècle, Actes du Colloque organisé le 18–22 juin 1990 dans le cadre des activités de l'URA 1085 du CRNSà*

speculative nature of reasoning comes from the object or the end of contemplating truth. For Ockham, knowledge is practical merely because it tells someone how or whether to act. Human acts include reasoning, since reasoning itself is subject to human choice.

The distinction between technical experience and learned skill in ostensive knowledge is like that distinction between prudence and moral science in dictative knowledge.[120] On Ockham's account, the experienced person acts with greater certainty not on account of the kind of knowledge that he has, but on account of the bodily organs that he uses in the application of the knowledge. The cithara player makes better use of his knowledge than someone who has merely learned how to play the cithara. He is able to use his knowledge better because his bodily organs are more habituated to playing. Unlike Scotus, Ockham does not use this example to make a wider point about choice or deliberation.

Neither dictative nor ostensive conclusions are described as choices or actions. Ockham agrees with Scotus that prudence ends not in a choice or appetitive command but in a purely cognitive judgment. Prudence is simply right reason concerning what should be done.[121] The will is free to accept or reject the command presented by prudence.[122] On his account, even the prudential agent's practical reasoning ends in the intellect's judgment in commanding that an act should be done. But conformity to this command lies entirely in the will's power. Prudence can exist without the morally virtuous choice. Ockham's understanding of the relationship between the command and choice closely corresponds to his understanding of the known object as a partial cause of the action. Prudence is only a partial cause of a morally virtuous act.[123] Its command is necessary for the action, but ultimately the will makes the decision on its own.

---

l'occasion du 600ᵉ anniversaire de la mort d'Albert de Saxe, ed. Joël Biard, Études de Philosophie Médiévale 69 (Paris: Vrin, 1991), 267–76.

120. Ockham, Ord. 1, prol., q. 11 (OTh, 1.319).

121. Ockham, Rep. 3, q. 12 (OTh, 6.422); Idem, Q. V., q. 8, art. 1 (OTh, 8.413).

122. Ockham, Rep. 3, q. 12 (OTh, 6.421); Idem, Q. V., q. 7, art. 3 (OTh, 8.367–68).

123. Ockham, Q. V., q. 8 (OTh, 6.415).

PRACTICAL KNOWLEDGE, PRUDENCE, AND THE PRACTICAL SYLLOGISM

Thomas, Scotus, and Ockham give three contrasting accounts of practical reason. The differences are most clearly seen in three areas, namely (1) the distinctive feature of practical knowledge, (2) the relationship between moral science and prudence, and (3) the practical syllogism.

The different positions concerning the character of practical knowledge are connected to if not based on different views on the relationship between the object and end of practical knowledge. Thomas's focus on the connection to the end in fully practical reasoning causes him to distinguish between degrees of practical reasoning. The object of all practical reasoning, including that which is fully practical, must be either something subject to the knower's action or somehow used in the action. But fully practical reason requires not only such an object or even a practical way of thinking about it, but the willing of an end. Thomas's distinction between object, mode, and end allows him to hold both that (1) only knowledge used in action is fully practical, and (2) there are other kinds of knowledge that share characteristics of practical reasoning even if they are not fully practical. Although less complete kinds of practical reasoning do not conclude in an action or a judgment of choice, they share the basic indeterminacy of practical reasoning, which is based on the generality of that known good which is desired by the will. In this life, every particular good can be thought of as bad or as incomplete. Consequently, when involved in choice, the intellect is not forced to think of the good as consisting in any one action. The intellect specifies what can be done, and the will causes the act's execution.

In contrast, Scotus thinks that the intellect's activity is indeterminate only insofar as it is controlled by the will. The intellect by itself is not a source of indeterminacy. Freedom consists in the ability to will or not will for a known good. Consequently, it is difficult to see how reasoning can be practical by virtue of some distinctive feature of the knowledge or object. Scotus thinks that the agent's own end is extrinsic to the object of practical reason, and that the end is an object of practical knowledge only insofar as it is included in the object. He does not think that the actual end is an intrinsic characteristic of practical reason. Therefore, he cannot hold that there is an intrinsic difference between that practical knowledge that leads to action and the practical knowledge that does not.

Ockham to some extent gives a more complete account of how both practical and speculative reasoning can be about the same things. He argues that speculative and practical knowledge can have the same subject, and that practical reasoning often depends on speculative premises. Although the agent's actual end is not a distinguishing feature of the knower's practical knowledge, practical science does have an end in the sense that the rightly ordered knower has an end for this science. Although Ockham focuses on the actual end of the knower in practical reasoning, he also separates cognition and willing in such a way that practical reasoning does not have such a distinct object except insofar as its conclusions are capable of directing action. As with Scotus, the connection to action is to some extent broken.

These different views on practical knowledge affect the different explanations of how moral science differs from prudence. All three figures agree that moral science is somehow more universal than prudence, and that it can be learned through study, whereas prudence is learned through experience. But Thomas's distinction between the degrees of practical knowledge makes it possible for him to identify prudence as a fully practical habit. Prudence's command is entirely connected with action. The judgments of conscience and moral science are partly speculative.

Both Thomas and Scotus think that the reasoning involved in technical skill is roughly similar to prudence, although they think that ultimately prudence is concerned with what is generally good, whereas technical skill is concerned with the good of a product. They agree that the house builder can have a technical knowledge of building a house even if he does not actually use this knowledge. Thomas states that although this unused technical knowledge has characteristics of practical reasoning, it is not fully practical since it is not actually ordered to the end. Some technical knowledge may be fully practical on account of the person who has the knowledge. The difference is that prudence is always practical, and good practice presupposes and requires prudence. Technical skill need not be fully practical, and need not always lead to the production of a good product.

Although Scotus, like Thomas, thinks that prudence is closer to an action, he states that this proximity to action results from the necessity of having a habit that mediates between general principles and particular conclusions. Scotus suggests that technical knowledge is practical even though it cannot immediately direct action. In house building as well as other technical skills, experience is needed to mediate between the universal principles and the particular conclusions, just as prudence is needed to mediate between the basic principles of moral science and particular conclusions. But this technical knowledge is practical whether or not the house is built. The agent's actual end does not affect the kind of knowledge. Similarly, Scotus thinks that the judgments of prudence are the same whether or not the agent acts on them. Prudence, like moral science and technical skill, can be possessed apart from action. Therefore, Scotus does not distinguish between technical skill and prudence entirely in the way that Thomas does.

Ockham makes an additional distinction that allows him to distinguish between prudence and technical skill without having to hold that there is a necessary connection between prudence and action. This distinction between ostensive and dictative knowledge is based on the way in which an action is commanded. Whereas moral science and prudence dictate conclusions about what should be done, technical skill and experience give only ostensive knowledge of how something should be done. Moral science and prudence are closer to the action itself because they are dictative. Although Ockham resembles Scotus in his belief that there is no intrinsic difference between the agent's judgments concerning those dictates of prudence that are followed and those that are rejected by an agent, he denies Scotus's thesis that prudence is distinct in its proximity to action. Ockham's account of prudence makes it easier to distinguish prudence from technical skill, but even more difficult to distinguish prudence from moral science. He is similar to his predecessors primarily in their Aristotelian belief that prudence, at least in the strict sense, is learned through experience rather than through teaching.

The different views of practical reasoning lead to different descriptions of the practical syllogism's premises, validity, and conclusions. With respect to the major premises of the syllogism, all figures agree that certain practical principles are immediately evident and known through their terms. Thomas connects these principles with the natural inclination to certain goods. Secondary principles are deduced from or determine these more general practical principles. Practical syllogisms differ from speculative syllogisms because normally valid practical syllogisms can be incorrect in exceptional instances. There are no exceptions to the most general principles, but these principles are insufficient for specifying an act. The agent must know how to identify and apply the relevant principles and circumstances, and the resulting reasoning is not entirely deductive. The good in general can be instantiated in different ways, and often the agent chooses a merely apparent good. Thomas's focus on the contingent object of practical reasoning leads him to think that much practical reasoning is not fully demonstrative in the way that speculative reasoning is. Thomas's distinction between the degrees of practical reasoning makes it necessary to distinguish between different kinds of practical syllogisms. In at least some instances, the conclusion of a practical syllogism seems to be a choice or an action. For instance, the prudent agent chooses the act once he sees an obligatory good of virtue.

Although Scotus and Ockham agree on the demonstrative character of the practical syllogism and its separation from action, they give different accounts of how its principles are known. Scotus does not completely sever the connection between moral principles and human nature, but he stresses that these first principles are logical truths. He gives straightforward examples, such as the command to love God. If God is understood to be the highest good, we immediately know that he should be loved above everything. Secondary principles are in harmony with these first principles. God can make exceptions, but secondary principles almost always hold. Ockham is less clear about how the principles are known, although he is confident that such knowledge can be obtained through instruction and experience. Ockham similarly does not make any reference to natural inclination in his explanation of how some truths are known through their terms. But he gives examples of self-evident truths that are not obviously self-evident, and consequently he allows for the existence of more self-evident practical truths than Scotus does.

Despite this difference over the practical syllogism's principles, both Scotus and Ockham seem to think of practical reasoning and the practical syllogism as a deduction from evident principles that are known through their terms or through experience. They do not distinguish between the rectitude of practical syllogisms and that of speculative syllogisms. In addition, they do not see an intrinsic difference between the conclusion of the agent who acts in accordance with prudence and the conclusion of the agent who rejects this dictate. The conclusion of the practical syllogism is simply a statement about how to do something, or what should be done. There must always be an additional act of the will.

It is easy to see how Ockham and Scotus give accounts of practical reasoning that fit with the first two themes of this book, namely the separation of nature from willing, and the increasing emphasis on the will's activity. For these figures, the intellect is like a nature in that it cannot be the source of freedom. Its acts are determined. In contrast, freedom is about the ability to choose between alternatives, which is based on the will. When discussing what makes knowledge practical, they focus less on what the agent is thinking about and more on the agent's own willing. Ockham's focus on the agent is especially marked. But Thomas does not so clearly root freedom in the will. The will's act is specified by the known object. Since he thinks that practical reasoning is indeterminate, the will's act also has a kind of indeterminacy.

Scotus and Ockham also have a view of practical reasoning that reflects the third theme, which involves disagreement over how to understand mental causation. In the next chapter we look more at the role of the will in deliberations that lead to conclusions, but we have seen in this chapter how on their view the will is involved in the acceptance or rejection of a practical syllogism's conclusion. Thomas's account of the practical syllogism's connection to action is not seen as a conjunction of two distinct efficient causes, namely the intellect's act and an additional and separate act of the will. First, he states that fully practical syllogisms always have conclusions that end in choice. This necessary connection to choice characterizes the practical knowledge itself. Second, Thomas distinguishes the liberty of exercise from the liberty of specification. The intellect specifies the act in the judgment concerning what should be chosen, but the intellect is merely a final and not an efficient cause of the act.

3

THE STAGES OF THE ACT

Thomas, Scotus, and Ockham's views of the relationship between practical reason and the will in the production of an act are partially expressed in their descriptions of an act's stages. They each follow a basically Aristotelian structure according to which human acts have three major components: willing the end, deliberating concerning the means, and choosing Nevertheless, they find these three components to be insufficient for fully elaborating an act's structure. In particular, Thomas adds several stages to Aristotle's account, in part by drawing on the language of his contemporaries, translations of Greek Fathers, and Augustine. In contrast, Scotus accepts the Aristotelian paradigm for only certain instances. He distinguishes between two meanings of the word *choice*; only one clearly corresponds to Aristotle's description. Nevertheless, even though he elaborates a further kind of choice, he does not introduce many new acts to his description of those choices that fall under the basic Aristotelian account. Ockham's description of the act in large part resembles Scotus's account of cases that follow the Aristotelian paradigm, although he more carefully distinguishes between deliberation and that intellectual act that accompanies choice.

THE ARISTOTELIAN BACKGROUND

The key text for Aristotle's discussion of human action consists of the first four chapters of Book III of the *Nicomachean Ethics*. His focus is on choice *(prohairesis)*, which is the act that belongs to virtuous or vicious habits. He divides the whole human act into three component acts, namely (1) will or wish *(boulesis)*, (2) deliberation *(bouleusis)*, and (3) choice *(prohairesis)*. For Aristotle, will or wish *(boulesis)* in this context names an act that is distinct from choice and does not indicate a faculty. Medieval translators used the Latin word *voluntas* to translate Aristotle's *boulesis*.[1] One problem with this translation is that the word *voluntas* carried with it many theoretical associations.

Medieval thinkers thought that will or wish *(boulesis/voluntas)* and choice *(prohairesis/electio)* are acts that belong to one faculty, namely the will *(voluntas)*, for which there was no Greek word in Aristotle's time. It is unclear whether Aristotle himself thinks or needs to think that there is a distinct rational appetite, but medievals believe that he did.[2] Medieval philosophers distinguish between the use of "will" to translate Aristotle's "*boulesis*" and its use as naming a potency. For instance, Thomas writes that "the Philosopher speaks of the will [*voluntas*] insofar as it properly names the simple act of the will: but not insofar as it names a power."[3] Sometimes medieval philosophers use the term "simple willing" *(simplex velle)* to indicate this act.

The historical background and context greatly influenced this interpretation of Aristotle's action theory. For instance, Augustine's discussions of the will and free choice were well known. According

---

1. For the Latin text, see Aristotle, *Ethica Nicomachea, Textus Recognitus*, trans. Robert Grosseteste, ed. René Antonin Gauthier, *Aristoteles Latinus*, 26.1–3, fasc. 4 (Leiden: Brill; Bruxelles: De Brouwer, 1973), 410–18.

2. See T. H. Irwin, "Who Discovered the Will," *Ethics, Philosophical Perspectives* 6 (1992): 453–73; Idem, *Development of Ethics*, 1.173–75, 441–42. For an account that stresses the difference between Aristotle and Thomas, see Kahn, "Discovering the Will," 239–45.

3. "Philosophus loquitur de voluntate, secundum quod proprie nominat simplicem actum voluntatis: non autem secundum quod nominat potentiam"; Thomas, *S.T.*, I-II, q. 8, art. 2, ad 2. Cf. Idem, *S.T.*, I, q. 83, art. 4.

to Sarah Byers, Augustine most often used *"voluntas"* to indicate the Stoic impulse for motion *(horme)*, and especially the impulse of rational beings.[4] She states that Augustine's *"arbitrium"* is used for the Stoics' assent. This Stoic assent resembles Aristotelian choice insofar as it is the source of moral responsibility and present in only rational acts, but it does not require deliberation. Byers remarks that Augustine also uses the word *"voluntas"* for the psychological faculty to which this assent belongs.[5] This use of *"voluntas"* for designating at least some sort of psychological faculty became widespread. Although her description of the Stoic influence may not describe exhaustively the source of Augustine's understanding of *"voluntas,"* it seems clear that Augustine's moral psychology does not have direct roots in Aristotle.[6] By the time of Thomas Aquinas's writing, the same Latin word *voluntas* is used both to indicate the power of the soul that is a rational appetite and a preliminary stage of the human act. According to Thomas, the ability to choose freely *(liberum arbitrium)* involves both the intellect and the will, but is itself the same as the will insofar as it is the will's ability to choose *(vis electiva)*.[7]

What is the relationship between these appetitive acts and cognition? Aristotle merely distinguishes between two appetitive acts, namely will or wish and choice. Before choosing, the agent wills or wishes for an apprehended good. Although this good may be merely apparent, it can only be willed insofar as it is thought of as good.[8] Aristotle states that we can will even those goods that are impossible to attain.[9] For instance, someone might will to be immortal. This appeti-

4. Sarah Byers, "The Meaning of *Voluntas* in Augustine," *Augustinian Studies* 37 (2006): 171–89. For an alternative stress on Augustine's originality, see Dihle, *Will in Classical Antiquity*; Kahn, "Discovering the Will."

5. Byers, "*Voluntas* in Augustine,"187–88.

6. John M. Rist argues for a connection with Platonic love in his *Augustine: Ancient Thought Baptized* (Cambridge: Cambridge University Press, 1994), 148–88.

7. Thomas, *S.T.*, I, q. 83, art. 4; Idem, *De Veritate*, q. 24, art. 6, resp. (Leonine, 22.3.695). For a discussion of Thomas in the context of his contemporaries, see Westberg, *Right Practical Reason*, 81–115.

8. Aristotle, *Nicomachean Ethics* 3.4.1113a15–31.

9. Aristotle, *Nicomachean Ethics* 3.2.1111b20–31.

tive act is will or wish *(boulesis)* and precedes any deliberation about how to obtain the end or any choice concerning the means to this end.

Will or wish by itself does not produce action. The central appetitive act in human action is *"prohairesis,"* which is the act that a virtuous or even a vicious habit produces. *Prohairesis* was translated into Latin as *electio*, which I have translated as "choice." Agents cannot choose an impossible action, such as attaining immortality, or any act that does not fall under the agent's power.[10] Choice has both cognitive and appetitive aspects.[11] The cognitive aspect comes from deliberation *(bouleusis)*. *Bouleusis* was generally translated into Latin as *consilium* rather than as *deliberatio*, and the difference between the two Latin words is not always clear.[12] In this context, I will reserve the English word *deliberation* for translating *consilium*. Choice differs from willing because it follows deliberation about the way in which a willed end can be obtained. Aristotle defines *choice* as "deliberative desire of what comes under our ability."[13] In some passages Aristotle seems to suggest that an agent who acts out of passion or desire, or even just spontaneously, does not truly choose.[14]

Deliberation is an intellectual rather than an appetitive act. It excludes objects that are outside of the agent's power, such as necessarily occurring events, chance events, and even human actions that do not come within the scope of the agent's operation.[15] For instance, the Spartans cannot deliberate about Scythian politics. Deliberation be-

10. Aristotle, *Nicomachean Ethics* 3.2.1111b20–31.

11. Aristotle, *Nicomachean Ethics* 3.2.1112a16–18.

12. See Kevin White, "Aquinas on Purpose," *Proceedings of the American Catholic Philosophical Association* 81 (2008): 136–38.

13. "consiliabile desiderium eorum que in nobis"; Aristotle, *Nicomachean Ethics* 3.4.1113a11–13, trans. Grosseteste, 417. Cf. Ibid., 6.2.1139a23.

14. Aristotle, *Nicomachean Ethics* 3.2.1111b10–11; 7.8.1150b30; 7.9.1151a29–35. For discussions, see G. E. M. Anscombe, "Thought and Action in Aristotle," in R. Bambrough, ed., *New Essays on Plato and Aristotle* (London: Routledge & Kegan Paul, 1965), 143–58; Sarah Broadie, "Introduction" to Aristotle, *Nicomachean Ethics*, trans. Christopher Rowe (Oxford: Oxford University Press, 2002), 42–46.

15. Aristotle, *Nicomachean Ethics* 3.3.

gins with an end, such as health, and then concludes with a means to the end, such as a particular medicine. The agent can will or choose the means that are shown to him by deliberation. Children and other animals are capable of voluntary action, since they desire and know about the ends for which they act.[16] Among the animals, only reasoning humans are capable of virtuous or vicious action, which consists in choice. Distinctively human action is found in choice, which in turn is made possible by deliberation.

Aristotle's threefold distinction between will, deliberation, and choice forms the basis for the late medieval understanding of action. Nevertheless, his account leaves problems that call for further explanation and additions. Three problems are particularly significant. First, Aristotle is unclear about the relationship between these three acts and their underlying psychological faculties, such as the will. Although Aristotle may need something like the will to account for the different kinds of appetitive acts, he does not clearly have such a concept. Second, the relationship between choice and deliberation is unclear. Aristotle seems to think both that choice is the central moral act and that it is the appetitive aspect of deliberation. Nevertheless, there is a need to account for moral acts that do not require deliberation.[17] Third, Aristotle's account ends with choice and does not consider the act's execution.

THOMAS AQUINAS

Although it is clear that Thomas divides the complete human act into a variety of acts or stages, different scholars number the stages differently. The general structure of the division is plain enough in the context of the will's acts. Thomas states that there are three acts of the

16. The Stoics gave somewhat different reasons for this same view that children and animals alike are incapable of action that is subject to moral evaluation. See Brad Inwood, *Ethics and Human Action in Early Stoicism* (Oxford: Clarendon Press, 1985), 72–74.

17. For the contrast between Stoics and Aristotelians over whether rational action requires deliberation, see Inwood, *Ethics and Human Action*, 83–84, 89–91.

will with respect to the end, namely (1) willing, (2) enjoyment, and (3) intention, and three further acts with reference to the means to or instances of the end, namely (4) consent, (5) choice, and (6) use. There is scholarly disagreement over the distinction between these acts and their connection with intellectual acts. One classic account states that for Thomas there are twelve stages. According to this view, six additional intellectual steps belong to these six steps that belong to the will.[18] In contrast, one recent writer thinks that Thomas describes only four stages, although each has two components.[19] On this reading, the first two acts listed above are not distinct stages, and the remaining acts of the will have corresponding intellectual components that are not distinct acts. I will more or less enumerate the stages as the acts of the will listed above with the addition of intellectual acts that Thomas brings up during the discussion. I am not claiming that these acts are always really distinct from each other, but rather that they always have distinct descriptions.

If Thomas had not written the *Prima Secundae,* there would be fewer and simpler scholarly discussions of his account of an act's stages. In his commentary on Aristotle's *Nicomachean Ethics,* Thomas more or less stays faithful to Aristotle's account of the distinction between will, deliberation, and choice. This faithfulness is unsurprising since the work is a commentary. In his earlier works Thomas discusses enjoyment, use, intention, and command, which come from a variety of sources.[20] But only in the *Prima Secundae* does Thomas integrate all of these different steps into one coherent account of the act's stages.

Aside from Aristotle, the three most important influences on Thom-

---

18. See Vernon J. Bourke, *Ethics: A Textbook in Moral Philosophy* (New York: Macmillan, 1951), 57–66. For the historical roots, see Servais Pinckaers, "La structure de l'acte humain suivant saint Thomas," *Revue Thomiste* 55 (1955): 393–412.

19. Westberg, *Right Practical Reason,* 119–35. For a modification of Westberg's schema, see Sherwin, *By Knowledge and by Love,* 85–94. Uncontroversial introductory accounts of the will's acts can be found in McInerny, *Aquinas on Human Action,* 51–74; David Gallagher, "The Will and Its Acts (IaIIae, qq. 18–21)," in *The Ethics of Aquinas,* ed. Stephen Pope (Washington, D.C.: The Catholic University of America Press, 2002), 78–83.

20. Lottin, *Psychologie et morale,* 1.415–20.

as's theory are Nemesius, John Damascene, and Augustine. Scholars have traced in detail how Thomas's understanding of various stages has its roots in these figures, whether directly or through their influence on earlier thirteenth-century accounts of human action.[21] Nemesius (whom Thomas mistakenly took to be Gregory of Nyssa) and Damascene were both Syrian writers who wrote in Greek. These two Syrian writers and Augustine were influenced by Stoicism, and they also absorbed elements from Aristotelian commentators. Damascene seems to have been particularly influenced by Maximus the Confessor. Consequently, the *Prima Secundae* presents a picture of human action with elements taken from disparate and even conflicting sources.

Nemesius and Damascene adopted in large part the Aristotelian description of action, but they modified it with Stoic elements. The influence of Nemesius and Damascene can be seen in Thomas's addition of "consent" *(consensus)* and "command" *(imperium)* to the Aristotelian schema. *Consensus* not only has Greek roots in translations of Nemesius and Damascene, but also in the Latin writings of Augustine.[22] Due to a series of historical accidents, Thomas's interpretation of consent seems to be influenced by the *"gnome"* of Maximus and John Damascene, which they used to indicate the role of character on human choice. This *"gnome/consensus"* precedes choice. Augustine seems to use *"consensus"* as a synonym for "choice" *(electio)*. Following Augustine, Thomas uses "consent" for an appetitive act, but he identifies it with the Latin translation of *"gnome"* as *"sententia,"* which is prior to choice.

21. René-Antonin Gauthier, "Saint Maxime le Confesseur et la psychologie de l'acte humain," *Recherches de Théologie Ancienne et Médiévale* 21 (1954): 51–100; Lottin, *Psychologie et morale,* 1.393–424; Emil Dobler, *Zwei Syrische Quellen der Theologischen Summa des Thomas von Aquin: Nemesios von Emesa und Johannes von Damaskus. Ihr Einfluss auf die anthropologischen Grundlagend der Moraltheologie,* Freiburger Zeitschrift für Philosophie und Theologie 25 (Freiburg: Universitätsverlag Freiburg, 2000). For brief accounts in English, see Vernon J. Bourke, *St. Thomas and the Greek Moralists* (Milwaukee, Wis.: Marquette University Press, 1947), 15–21; Westberg, *Right Practical Reason,* 126–29.

22. Gauthier, "Saint Maxime et l'acte humaine," 89–93.

Two other acts, namely command and use, indicate the act's execution. Thomas's understanding of "command" is close to that of his teacher Albert the Great, identifying it with an act of reason that follows choice.[23] Thomas's understanding of "use" has clear roots in Augustine's doctrine that created goods should be used rather than enjoyed, and perhaps has Stoic sources.[24] It also may have roots in the Greek Fathers. But by "use" Thomas indicates the will's employment of other human faculties in the production of the act. Augustine's "use" has as its counterpart "*frui*," which for Augustine is the enjoyment that properly speaking one should only find in God. Thomas uses "*frui*" in a wider sense to name the will's enjoyment of a good in which it rests. In general, although Thomas borrows names from earlier sources in order to describe an act's structure, he does not clearly retain the original meaning of the names.

Some scholars think that the diverse historical sources of the additional acts might suggest that Thomas does not use them to respond to any philosophical deficiency in the Aristotelian analysis of an action. On this view, the acts seem to be a hodgepodge collection of historical authorities rather than parts of a philosophically coherent and systematic account of human action. For example, R.-A. Gauthier argues that the important stage is choice and that the other elements are philosophically insignificant historical accidents.[25] Similarly, Alan Donagan thinks that Thomas should have left out "use."[26] Whether their criticisms are accurate or not, they are correct to see that not all stages are equal. The two most important acts of the will are simple willing and choice.

23. Gauthier, "Saint Maxime et l'acte humaine," 82–88; Dobler, *Syrichen Quellen*, 247–73.

24. Gauthier, "Saint Maxime et l'acte humaine," 93–98. For the Augustinian background, see especially Rist, *Augustine*, 159–68; Osborne, *Love of Self and Love of God*, 17–21.

25. Gauthier, "Saint Maxime et l'acte humaine," 98–100.

26. Alan Donagan, "Thomas Aquinas on Human Action," in *The Cambridge History of Later Medieval Philosophy: From the Rediscovery of Aristotle to the Disintegration of Scholasticism: 1100–1600*, ed. Norman Kretzmann, Anthony Kenny, and Jan Pinborg (Cambridge: Cambridge University Press), 642–54.

In more general discussions of the will's acts, Thomas often mentions only simple willing and choice. For instance, in his discussion of free choice *(liberum arbitrium)*, Thomas states that just as understanding and reasoning both belong to one power, namely the intellect, so do simple willing and choice belong to one power, namely the will. Free choice and the will name one power with two basic acts.[27] Similarly, in his discussion of Christ's will, Thomas distinguishes only between simple willing *(simplex velle)* and choice.[28] If the will is considered as a nature, then it is ordered to the good simply for its own sake. This simple willing is not free. In contrast, if the will is considered as rational, it can choose the good as ordered to an end. This act is choice. The primary contrast between Aristotle's first and third stages, namely simple willing and choice, is reflected throughout Thomas's works. Why are more acts needed?

Thomas delineates and explains the importance of the will's different acts in the *Prima Secundae*, qq. 8–16. In qq. 8–12 he considers the will's acts with respect to the end, and in qq. 13–16 he considers acts of the will and intellect with respect to that which is for the sake of the end. There is some disagreement over whether qq. 8–11, which are about willing and enjoyment, are descriptions of an act's stages. Servais Pinckaers argues that qq. 8–10 are more about willing in general than about distinct an act of the will.[29] Similarly, David Westberg argues that intention, which is not discussed until q. 12, is the first stage of a human act.[30] It seems to me that Pinckaers is correct to note that for Thomas willing is a wide term that in some way includes the other terms, and that consequently qq. 8–11 are important not only for thinking about a distinct act of the will, but also about all of the will's acts. Moreover, Westberg is correct to the extent that intention is a key first step to an act. Nevertheless, it seems that Thomas himself wishes to distinguish between three different acts with respect to the

---

27. Thomas, *S.T.*, I, q. 83, art. 4. Cf. Idem, *De Veritate*, q. 24, art. 6 (Leonine, 22.3.694–96).

28. Thomas, *S.T.*, III, q. 18, art. 4–5.

29. Pinckaers, "L'acte humaine," 396–403.

30. Westberg, *Right Practical Reason*, 132–33.

end. First, in the introduction to q. 8, Thomas clearly states that he is considering three different acts by which the will is moved to the end. Second, the discussion of simple willing in these first few questions exactly corresponds to Aristotle's *boulesis,* which is not a general act of the will but rather an act that is distinct from choice. Third, Thomas carefully distinguishes intention as an act not only from the act of simple willing but also from enjoyment. Intention is significant because it indicates a willing to arrive at the end through some means. Thomas writes:

> The will regards the end in three ways. In one way, absolutely: and thus it is called "will" [*voluntas*], just as we will absolutely health or something of this sort. In another way the end is considered to the extent that something rests in it: and in this way "enjoyment" regards the end. In a third way the end is considered insofar as it is the term of something that is ordered to it: and in this way "intention" regards the end. For not only do we intend health from this, that we will it, but because we will to come to it through something else.[31]

The difference between willing, intention, and enjoyment is between the different ways in which the end is willed. Simple willing considers the end apart from a means of attaining it or a final enjoyment of it. This willing seems to correspond to what Thomas calls the "*simplex voluntas*" that belongs to the will as a nature. This interpretation is supported by Thomas's claim throughout qq. 8–10 that the will is naturally directed to certain goods. For instance, in q. 10, art. 1, Thomas states that the will naturally desires the good in common, happiness in general, and the good that is fitting to human nature. The fitting good includes being, living, and understanding. The agent does not decide whether to will these goods or not; such willing precedes choice.

---

31. "voluntas respicit finem tripliciter. Uno modo, absolute: et sic dicitur 'voluntas,' prout absolute volumus vel sanitatem vel si quid aliud est huiusmodi. Alio modo consideratur finis secundum quod in eo quiescitur: et hoc modo 'fruitio' respicit finem. Tertio modo consideratur finis secundum quod est terminus alicuius quod in ipsum ordinatur: et sic 'intentio' respicit finem. Non enim solum ex hoc intendere dicimur sanitatem, quia volumus eam; sed quia volumus ad eam per aliquid aliud pervenire"; Thomas, *S.T.,* I-II, q. 12, art. 1, ad 4.

This simple willing can be efficacious, but it need not be. Just as the intellect can move to conclusions from its knowledge of first principles, so the will can move itself to the willing of other objects insofar as it already wills the end to which they are directed.[32] This simple willing can have impossible objects and seems to be the same as Aristotle's *boulesis*. Thomas states that the Latin word *velleitas* can be used for such willing when it is inefficacious or indeed generally any such conditional willing.[33]

There are also many instances in which an agent chooses an object that is incompatible with the goods that he simply wills. For instance, life and health are objects of simple willing. Nevertheless, the agent can choose something else that is ordered to a more important but incompatible good. For example, Christ willed to live in accordance with his will considered as a nature.[34] Nevertheless, he chose to die. He willed his death as a means for the salvation of the human race.

Unlike simple willing, enjoyment is made possible by the possession of the willed good. The very notion of enjoyment implies resting in an end that is in some sense ultimate.[35] Thomas distinguishes between two ways in which an end can be ultimate. First, God is the ultimate end of humans simply speaking. Consequently, the enjoyment of God is also an ultimate end, since it is a way in which humans acquire God as an end. However, any pleasant or morally worthy good can be said to be ultimate in a secondary way. The only good that cannot be an object of enjoyment is a merely useful good. Whereas simple willing is naturally if not temporally first in the sequence of the will's acts, the full enjoyment of the end is last. Nevertheless, some enjoyment can be taken in an end that is present only through the agent's intention.[36]

Intention differs from simple willing because it regards the end in-

32. Thomas, *S.T.*, I-II, q. 8, art. 2, resp.
33. Thomas, *S.T.*, I-II, q. 13, art. 5, ad 1; Idem, *S.T.*, III, q. 21, art. 4, resp.
34. Thomas, *S.T.*, III, q. 18, art. 5.
35. Thomas, *S.T.*, I-II, q. 11, art. 3.
36. Thomas, *S.T.*, I-II, q. 11, art. 4, resp.

sofar as it can be attained through some means.[37] Intention falls between Aristotle's will *(boulesis)* and choice. In his earlier *De Veritate*, q. 22, art. 13, Thomas states that intention differs from simply willing *(simpliciter velle)* inasmuch as willing the end differs from willing something in order to an end.[38] In art. 14, he contrasts different ways in which an end such as health can be the object of simple willing or intention. For instance, I will health both apart from willing any means and when I will to become healthy through taking medicine.[39] The distinction between simple willing and intention in the early *De Veritate* seems to be the same as the distinction between will and intention made in the *Prima Secundae*, qq. 8–10. When I take medicine, the willing of health is intention. Apart from taking medicine, the willing of health is an act of simple willing. Someone can simply will health even if in fact he does not intend to be healthy but rather to die for some greater good.

If intention differs from willing because it is about a means to the end, then how does intention differ from choice? There are two acts concerning the means because there is a difference between willing the end through some means, which is intention, and willing the means, which is choice. The two acts are really distinct when an agent intends an end even if he does not determinately will an instance of or means to this end.[40] Nevertheless, the two acts are not always really distinct, since a movement toward the end can also be a movement toward the means.[41] If intention and choice are the same movement, there is still a distinction of reason between the two. Intention fills a gap between simple willing, which can be for impossible ends or ends that are passed over by choice, and choice, which is entirely of the means to an end. "Intention" was a commonly used word that

37. Thomas, *S.T.*, I-II, q. 12, art. 1. See Westberg, *Right Practical Reason*, 136–46; Jensen, *Good and Evil Actions*, 44–72.

38. Thomas, *De Veritate*, q. 22, art. 12, resp. (Leonine, 22.3.645).

39. Thomas, *De Veritate*, q. 22, art. 14, resp. (Leonine, 22.3.648).

40. Thomas, *S.T.*, I-II, q. 12, art. 4, ad 3.

41. Thomas, *S.T.*, I-II, q. 8, art. 3; q. 12, art. 4. Note that Thomas discusses a similar issue in the context of intention and simple willing in the *De Veritate*, q. 22, art. 14 (Leonine, 22.3.647–48).

could plausibly apply to different acts concerning the willing of an end either by itself or through some means.[42] Thomas uses intention to fill what can plausibly be seen as a lacuna in Aristotle's account of human action.

Each of these three acts of the will has a corresponding intellectual act. Although Thomas does not devote questions or even articles to them, he mentions these intellectual acts in passing. For instance, an act of simple willing implies some sort of knowledge of the good that is willed.[43] Similarly, enjoyment requires a judgment concerning the suitability of that which the agent enjoys.[44] The clearest discussion of the intellectual act that accompanies intention is in the *De Veritate*, in which Thomas states that intention requires a judgment that the good might be obtained through some means.[45] In general, the statement that the will is an efficient cause whereas the known object is a formal and final cause holds not only for complete human acts but also in some way for each act of the will.

In qq. 12, 14, and 15, Thomas discusses the will's three acts in relation to the means or instances of the end, namely choice, consent, and use. The order is not one of natural or temporal priority. Thomas begins with choice because it is the most important act concerning the means. Although consent is treated later, it can precede choice naturally and temporally. Two questions contain explicit discussions of intellectual acts. Q. 13 is entirely about deliberation, which is a bridge between intention and choice. In q. 16, he discusses the intellect's act of command in the context of a more general account of commanded acts.

How are these questions related to the acts that Aristotle discusses? Qq. 12 and 13 reflect Thomas's interpretation of Aristotle's explicit description of choice and deliberation. In q. 14 Thomas introduces

---

42. Bonaventure, 2 *Sent.*, d. 40, art. 1, q. 1, resp., in *Opera Omnia*, 10 vols. (Quaracchi: Collegium S. Bonaventurae, 1882–1902), 2.921.

43. Thomas, *S.T.*, I-II, q. 13, art. 5, ad 1. For the texts cited in this paragraph, see especially Bourke, *Ethics*, 58–64.

44. Thomas, *S.T.*, I-II, q. 11, art. 1, ad 3.

45. Thomas, *De Veritate*, q. 22, art. 13, resp. (Leonine, 22.3.645).

consent to account for a needed volitional act that precedes choice but follows intention. Qq. 15–16, which are devoted to use and command, reflect a post-Aristotelian concern not only with the agent's choice of an act but also its execution.

Even though Thomas alters or clarifies Aristotle's account of the relationship between deliberation and choice, his own account is at times unclear. In some texts Thomas seems to accept Aristotle's definition of choice as "deliberative [*consiliabile*] desire of what is within our power," although in q. 13 he leaves out "deliberative" when he quotes this passage.[46] Thomas in this text uses the authority of Aristotle and Nemesius to argue that choice is an act of the will, and he postpones the discussion of deliberation until the next question.[47] Nevertheless, Thomas also cites Aristotle's statement that choice is "an appetitive understanding, or an understanding appetite."[48] He retains that cognitive aspect by stating that every choice involves both desire and judgment. Thomas does not discuss in detail here the relationship between the judgment of choice and deliberation. He seems to accept Nemesius's view that they are distinct intellectual acts.[49] He suggests that this judgment of choice is the conclusion of an "operative syllogism," which is that kind of practical syllogism that ends in a choice.[50] Moreover, he states that the ordering of what is chosen to an end is accomplished through reason. Consequently, the act of choice is even formally an act of reason. Nevertheless, choice is materially or substantially the act of the will that is a movement of the soul toward the chosen good.

In the *De Veritate*, Thomas makes several remarks about this judgment of choice. The judgment of choice is contrasted with the judgment of synderesis insofar as synderesis is about universals and

---

46. Thomas, *S.T.*, I-II, q. 13, art. 1, sc. He also does not mention "consiliabile" in *S.T.*, I, q. 83, art. 3, sc, but he does so in the article's body.

47. Thomas, *S.T.*, I-II, q. 13, art. 1; Dobil, *Syrische Quellen*, 204–22.

48. "appetitus intellectus vel appetitus intellectivus"; Aristotle, *Nicomachean Ethics* 3.2.1139b4, cited in Thomas, *S.T.*, I-II, q. 13, art. 1, resp.

49. Dobil, *Zwei Syrische Quellen*, 208–9.

50. See also Westberg, *Right Practical Reason*, 147–64.

choice is about particulars.[51] It differs from particular conclusions of speculative science because the judgment of choice is practical.[52] Unlike the judgment of conscience, the judgment of choice is fully practical; it is necessarily connected with the will's act of choice [*electio*], and consequently also called the judgment of free will [*iudicium liberi arbitrii*].[53] Although a universal judgment can be opposed to the will, the judgment of choice cannot. Thomas writes, "But the judgment about this particular thing at the present time that can be done can never be contrary to the appetite. For the one who wishes to fornicate, although he knows in the universal that fornication is bad, yet he judges this act of fornication as good for him, and chooses it under the formality of the good."[54] In *S.T.* I-II, q. 13, Thomas states that this judgment is like the conclusion of the fully practical syllogism, and followed by choice.[55]

Choice is distinct from intention because it is about instances of or instruments toward an end rather than the end itself. Thomas's adoption of Aristotle's position that choice and deliberation are about the means rather than the end has been a source of scholarly and philosophical confusion.[56] Since agents do make choices about how to or-

51. Thomas, *De Veritate*, q. 24, art. 1, ad 17 (Leonine, 22.3.683).

52. Thomas, *De Veritate*, q. 16, art. 1, ad 15 (Leonine, 22.2.507).

53. Thomas, *De Veritate*, q. 17, art. 1, ad 4. (Leonine, 22.2.517–18). McInerny, *Aquinas on Human Action*, 220–39; Leo Elders, "La doctrine de la conscience," 553–57.

54. "iudicium de hoc particulari operabili ut nunc, numquam potest esse appetitui contrarium. Qui enim vult fornicari, quamvis sciat in universali fornicationem malum esse, tamen iudicat sibi ut tunc bonum esse hunc fornicationis actum et sub specie boni ipsum eligit"; Thomas, *De Veritate*, q. 24, art. 2, resp. (Leonine, 22.3.685).

55. "electio consequitur sententiam vel iudicium, quod est sicut conclusio syllogismi operativi"; Thomas, *S.T.*, I-II. q. 13, art. 3, resp. See also Thomas, *S.T.*, I-II, q. 13, art. 1, ad 2.

56. This confusion can be found in Terence Irwin, "The Scope of Deliberation: A Conflict in Aquinas," *Review of Metaphysics* 44 (1990): 21–42, and to some extent perhaps in Ludger Honnenfelder, "Ansätze zu einer Theorie der praktischen Wahrheit bei Thomas von Aquin und Johannes Duns Scotus," in *Was ist für den Menschen Gute?: Menschliche Natur und Güterlehre*, ed. Jan Szaif and Matthias Lutz-Bachmann (Berlin: de Gruyter, 2004), 252–57. A corrective can be found in Westberg, *Practical Reason*, 165–67, and Paul Morrisset, "Prudence et fin selon saint Thomas," *Sciences écclesiastiques* 15 (1963): 73–98.

der their lives, it seems as if they do in fact make choices about their ends and even their ultimate end.[57] Thomas's point here is uncomplicated and should be uncontroversial. He simply notes that what is regarded as a means can also be regarded as a principle, but when it is chosen it is chosen as a means. For instance, someone who practices medicine has health as an end. He chooses not health but the means to health. However, someone who is concerned primarily with the care of souls considers health merely as a means to this end. Consequently, when caring for souls health is no longer a principle of practical reasoning but rather a means to an end. Considered merely as an end, health cannot be chosen. Considered as a means, health can be chosen. The only human good that cannot be chosen because it is never ordered to an end is the ultimate end considered abstractly, namely happiness. But means to and instantiations of this end can be chosen or rejected, and they can often be viewed in other contexts as ends that are assumed in deliberation and choice.

The relationship between the end and the means or instances sheds light on the role that the practical syllogism plays in choice and deliberation. The end is indicated in the practical syllogism's major premise, such as the end of warmth, and the means is indicated in the minor premise, such as the means of a particular cloak. The judgment of choice is the conclusion, which indicates a means that is chosen. Thomas seems to think that the judgment of choice must be the conclusion of a practical syllogism. Any means to or instance of a good is only chosen insofar as it in some way shares in the desirability of this good, which is indicated by the major premise. Nevertheless, the apparent necessity of the practical syllogism does not mean that deliberation over time is required. Deliberation occurs when the agent must inquire into the possible means for an end.[58] Its goal seems to be the correct minor premise of a fully practical syllogism, which when joined with the major premise entails the judgment of choice.

As we have seen in chapter 1, Thomas thinks that choice is indeter-

57. Thomas, S.T., I-II, q. 13, art. 3; Idem, Sententia Ethicorum, lib. 3, lect. 5 (Leonine, 48.1.134).

58. Thomas, S.T., I-II, q. 14, art. 6. Cf. Westberg, Right Practical Reason, 170–72.

minate for the same reason that the will is indeterminate in this life, namely that no particular chosen goods exhaust what it means to be good.[59] Consequently, although no one can choose to be miserable, in this life humans can choose against those particular goods in which their happiness consists, and they can also choose apparent goods that make them miserable. What is the connection between such indeterminacy, deliberation, and choice?

Often the indeterminacy of choice results from the indeterminacy of means to or instances of the end. The judgment that gives specification to choice often results from deliberation, which is a rational inquiry concerning what should be done. Deliberation, like choice, presupposes the intention of an end. Moreover, just as in choice, what is the end of one act of deliberation may itself be not an end but ordered to the end of another act.[60] Deliberation also resembles choice in that it has both cognitive and appetitive components.[61] There are two appetitive aspects to deliberation. First, deliberation is about an act of the appetite. Its goal is to indicate which act of the will should be done. Second, deliberation is moved by desire for the end. For instance, someone who deliberates concerning medicine is moved to such deliberation through willing health. Nevertheless, deliberation is primarily an act of reason, since it is an inquiry concerning the best means to or instances of the desired end. The judgment of choice is not itself deliberation, but the goal of deliberation is to arrive at a judgment of choice.

Thomas gives seemingly conflicting accounts of whether deliberation is required for a choice between alternatives.[62] One reason might be that Aristotle's definition of choice includes deliberation. Another

59. Thomas, *S.T.*, I-II, q. 13, art. 2, 6.

60. Thomas, *S.T.*, I-II, q. 14, art. 2; Idem, *Sententia Ethicorum*, lib. 3, lect. 8 (Leonine, 48.1.143).

61. Thomas, *S.T.*, I-II, q. 13, art. 1, ad 1.

62. I am not discussing those acts that are somehow above deliberation since they are performed under the influence of a divine instinct of the supernatural or perhaps even natural order. See Thomas, *S.T.*, I-II, q. 68, art. 1, resp. For a complete discussion, see Reginald Garrigou-Lagrange, *Christian Perfection and Contemplation: According to St. Thomas Aquinas and St. John of the Cross*, trans. Sister M. Timothea Doyle (St. Louis, Mo./London: Herder, 1946), 285–99.

problem is the relationship between *consilium,* which is the Latin word that was used for Aristotle's *bouleusis,* and the Latin *deliberatio,* which can be used more loosely. Both the Latin *"consilium"* and the Greek *"bouleusis"* are often translated by the English "deliberation." Consequently, I will not use the English "deliberation" for *"deliberatio,"* but instead "thinking over." In general, Thomas holds that choice requires such "thinking over" even though it might not require deliberation. However, in the commentary on the *Nicomachean Ethics,* Thomas repeats Aristotle's statement that choice presupposes deliberation and thinking over, and Thomas in this context seems to think that the words are synonymous.[63] It is not surprising to find him following Aristotle in such a commentary, but he also does so in his early *De Veritate* and in his late *Contra doctrina retrahentium.*[64] In the latter work Thomas writes, "For everything which is done from choice, is done from thinking over or deliberation [*ex deliberatione sive consilio*], since choice is deliberated desire [*appetitus praeconsiliati*], as is said in the third book of the *Ethics.*"[65] Consequently, there are at least three texts from different stages of his career in which Thomas includes deliberation in the definition of choice and regards *deliberatio* and *consilium* as synonymous.

In other texts Thomas states that *deliberatio* has different meanings, and he reserves *consilium* as a technical term for Aristotle's *bouleusis.* In these texts, choice requires only a broad thinking over *(deliberatio)* and not deliberation *(consilium).* For example, in another passage of the *De Veritate,* Thomas discusses the kind of thinking in which Christ engaged when carrying out meritorious acts. He distinguishes between two kinds of thinking over *(deliberatio):*

63. "Praeeligentes quidem sive ex electione operamur illa quaecumque ex praecedenti consilio vel deliberatione facimus; sed illa sunt ineligibilia, id est absque electione facta, quaecumque fiunt impraeconsiliata, id est absque praecedenti deliberatione"; Thomas, *Sententia Ethicorum,* lin. 5, lect. 13 (Leonine, 47.2.310).

64. Thomas, *De Veritate,* q. 24, art. 12 (Leonine, 22.3.716); Idem, *Contra doctrinam retrahentium,* cap. 10 (Leonine, 41.C58).

65. "Omne autem quod ex electione agitur, ex deliberatione sive consilio agitur, quia electio est appetitus praeconsiliati, ut dicitur in III Ethicorum"; Thomas, *Contra doctrinam retrahentium,* cap. 10 (Leonine, 41.C58).

Thinking over [*deliberatio*] has two meanings, namely the perception of reason with the certitude of judgment concerning that about which the thinking over [*deliberatio*] is being made, and so it can be instantaneous in a matter wherein there is no doubt concerning what ought to be done; and thus [thinking over] was in Christ. However it can also be said to be a discussion or inquiry, and this includes a certain discursiveness, whence it cannot be instantaneous; and Christ did not need such thinking over [*deliberatio*], because he was not in doubt concerning what should be done.[66]

What is the relationship between this *deliberatio* and *consilium*? In a later reply of the same question and article, Thomas states that although Christ chose actions he never had deliberation *(consilium)* because he never lacked certitude.[67] In this case *consilium* seems to be similar to or perhaps even the same as the second kind of thinking over *(deliberatio)*, which involves inquiry. This second kind of deliberation seems to be what Aristotle calls *bouleusis*.

In the *Tertia Pars* of the *Summa Theologiae*, Thomas makes a similar point about Christ's choice but does not use the term "*deliberatio*" in a wider sense.[68] The exact words are "*deliberatio consilii*," which might be translated as the "thinking over that belongs to deliberation."[69] He states that Christ does not need to deliberate because he knows what he should do. In another question from the *Tertia Pars*, he not only makes a similar point about Christ's knowledge, but he first mentions "*consilium vel deliberatio*" and then he mentions "*deliberatio consilii*."[70] In the *De Malo*, Thomas not only gives a similar argument for the position that the angels do not need to deliberate in

---

66. "deliberatio duo importat, scilicet perceptionem rationis cum certitudine iudicii de eo de quo fit deliberatio, et sic potest esse in instanti in eo in quo non est dubitatio de agendis; et sic fuit in Christo. Potest enim dicere discussionem sive inquisitionem, et sic imporat discursum quendam, unde non potest esse in instanti; et tali deliberatione Christus non indigebat, qui non erat dubius de agendis"; Thomas, *De Veritate*, q. 29, art. 8, ad 1 (Leonine, 22.3.870–71).

67. Thomas, *De Veritate*, q. 29, art. 9, ad 9 (Leonine, 22.3.871).

68. Thomas, *S.T.*, III, q. 24, art. 3, ad 2.

69. For this and other terminological issues, see White, "Aquinas on Purpose," 143, note 11.

70. Thomas, *S.T.*, III, q. 34, art. 2, ad 2.

order to choose, but he also mentions the absence of deliberation in human arts such as writing.[71] These texts might explain why Thomas, in the *Prima Secundae*, q. 13, art.1, leaves deliberation out of the definition of choice. However, in the *Prima Secundae* and in the *De virtutibus*, he suggests in other contexts that for an act to be a complete human act, such as a mortal sin, there has to be thinking out over time.[72] The thinking out or deliberation *(deliberatio)* necessary for a choice to be mortally sinful seems to require something like *consilium*. This second position fits with Aristotle's inclusion of deliberation in his definition of choice and Thomas's passing references to it.

If we had only the above passages about the relationship between deliberation and choice, it would be unclear whether Thomas thinks that there can be choice without deliberation. Nevertheless, in the *Prima Secundae*, q. 14, art. 4, Thomas explicitly argues that deliberation is only sometimes required for choice. He explains that although rational inquiry is generally necessary for human action, there are two reasons why there can be certitude without such inquiry. First, the means to the ends might follow determined ways. He uses the example that he also uses in the discussion of an angel's choice, which is that of a writer who does not need to deliberate over how to form letters. Second, Thomas notes that often the means to an end do not matter. An example might be whether to drink out of a green or a brown cup. In these cases, choice can occur without deliberation. Nevertheless, apart from happiness, every end is also an instance of or means to another end.[73] Consequently, such ends are subject to deliberation. The means to any particular end may be determined or unimportant. But the end itself is not the only means to or instance of happiness. Therefore, although choice can result from the knowledge

71. Thomas, *De Malo*, q. 16, art. 4, resp. (Leonine, 23.299). For the example of writing, see Idem, *Sententia Ethicorum*, lib. 3, lect. 7 (Leonine, 47.1.140).

72. Thomas, *De virtutibus*, q. 2, art. 12, ad 14 (Marietti ed., 2.788); Idem, *S.T.*, I-II, q. 74, art. 7, ad 4. But see also the apparently wider use of "deliberatio" in Idem, *S.T.*, art. 10, resp.; Idem, *De Malo*, q. 7, art. 5, resp. (Leonine, 23.172–73).

73. In addition to the texts cited above, see Guy Durand, "Les notions de fin intermédiare et de fin secondaire dans la Tradition thomiste," *Science et ésprit* 21 (1969): 371–402.

of a determinate means to a particular end, the end itself is not determined and can be subject to deliberation as itself a means. But deliberation need not immediately precede many choices. In the context of a particular act, the end is not subject to deliberation.

If choice is not immediately preceded by an act of deliberation, what intellectual act corresponds to choice? Although Thomas thinks that an intellectual judgment is required for choice, he does not think that this judgment itself belongs to deliberation.[74] Although deliberation is about means to or instances of the end rather than the end itself, the final judgment about the means seems to be the same judgment of choice that Thomas so carefully distinguishes from the judgments of conscience and of synderesis.[75] In the cases mentioned above, there is no need for deliberation to arrive at such a judgment, although there is a need for a practical syllogism that concludes in the judgment of choice. Thomas's appropriation of Nemesius's distinction between this judgment and deliberation allows him to separate choice from deliberation more clearly than Aristotle did.

Thomas, with his introduction of consent, adds to the Aristotelian account an act of the will that is posterior to deliberation but in some way prior to choice. Thomas states that consent is the "application of the appetitive movement to the determination of deliberation."[76] Why is an additional act needed? Sometimes deliberation shows that there are many pleasing means to an end. One example might be that of helping a poor person by teaching him or by giving him money that one has earned. The good agent might consent to both means, whereas he would not consent to an illicit means such as giving stolen money. Although the agent might consent to many incompatible means to or instances of an end, he will choose only one such at a time.

Choice and consent are not always distinct acts even though the words always have distinct meanings.[77] Thomas argues that they can

74. Thomas, *S.T.*, I-II, q. 14, art. 4, ad 2.

75. Westberg, *Right Practical Reason*, 167–69.

76. "motus appetitivus applicatur ad id quod ex consilio iudicatum est"; Thomas, *S.T.*, I-II, q. 15, art. 3, resp.

77. Thomas, *S.T.*, I-II, q. 15, art. 3, ad 3.

be the same if there is only one means to or instance of an end. For example, the only licit means of helping a pauper might be to teach him. We understand choice and consent as distinct in this case, but in reality there is one act of the will. Similarly, choice and consent are distinct only by reason when an agent chooses without deliberation.

Up until this discussion of consent, Thomas's description of the act is basically Aristotelian in its focus on simple willing, deliberation, and choice. His discussion of these three stages of the act corresponds to his commentary on Aristotle's description of them. Nevertheless, Thomas gives a more detailed approach by adding the acts of intention and consent. Although Gauthier argues that these acts are philosophically insignificant, they play an important if subordinate role in Thomas's theory. Their subordinate role can be clearly seen in the fact that Thomas argues that these acts do not always signify really distinct acts. For instance, the intention to achieve an end through a means need not be a separate movement from the actual choice of the end. The means to or instance of the end is willed only insofar as the end is willed. Indeed, the clearest instance of a distinction between intention and choice is when the agent intends an end but cannot find a determined means to choose. Although such a situation shows that intention is distinct from choice, it does not indicate that the two are always distinct movements. Similarly, consent is often distinct from choice only in reason. The acts improve the basic Aristotelian picture by accounting for descriptions that are needed for a full account but are not covered by the threefold division between simple willing, deliberation, and consent.

Whereas the addition of intention and consent improves and clarifies the Aristotelian description of an act's structure, Thomas's addition of command and use extends the description of the act to include an element of the act that Aristotle does not address, namely its execution. Whereas Alan Donagan argues that Thomas's addition of an extra act of the will to cover execution is superfluous, Daniel Westberg shows that it is needed to connect choice with the actual bodily movement, and Stephen Brock argues that it explains how an immanent act of the will can have effects on other powers.[78] For Thomas, the execution of the acts occurs when the will uses the soul's other powers.[79] This "use" has its roots in Augustine's distinction between *uti* and *frui* and ultimately Stoicism, but it is used here in a more technical sense. *Use* is an act of the will insofar as the will moves other powers or even other acts of the will.[80] Use both names a distinct stage of the act and also the will's use of the intellect and itself in the human act's other stages. Use, as the appetitive stage of the executed act, is preceded by command *(imperium)*, which is an act of the intellect by which the execution of the act is ordered.[81] Thomas emphasizes that this command of the intellect is naturally prior even though it is not always temporally prior.[82] Command and use may be simultaneous, but command is prior to use because the execution of the act follows the will's ordering.

The executed or commanded acts may themselves be other acts of the intellect and will, or even complete acts.[83] Nevertheless, there is a unity between the command and the commanded act that is like the unity of matter and form, or the unity of a house.[84] The act has parts. If someone chooses to walk to church and commands the act, this act may include parts such as putting on shoes, opening the door, and walking in a particular direction. Nevertheless, as a human act it is one.

In summary, Thomas explains the structure of the act in a thematic fashion from the willing of the end, the choice of the means, and the execution of the act. The first two sections of this exposition more or

78. Westberg, *Right Practical Reason*, 175–83; Stephen L. Brock, "What Is the Use of *Usus* in Aquinas' Philosophy of Action?" in *Moral and Political Philosophies of the Middle Ages,* Proceedings of the Ninth International Congress of Medieval Philosophy, Ottowa 17–22 August 1992, ed. B. Carlos Bazán, Eduardo Andujár, and Léonard G. Sbrocchi, 3 vols. (New York: Legas, 1995), 2.654–64.

79. Thomas, *S.T.,* I-II, q. 16, art. 2.

80. Thomas, *S.T.,* I-II, q. 16, art. 4, ad 3.

81. Thomas, *S.T.,* I-II, q. 17, art. 1.

82. Thomas, *S.T.,* I-II, q. 17, art. 3, resp. et ad 3.

83. Thomas, *S.T.,* I-II, q. 17, art. 5–6.

84. Thomas, *S.T.,* I-II, q. 17, art. 4.

less follow Aristotle's discussion of the act, but Thomas adds or clarifies Aristotle's basic schema by adding intention and consent as separate acts. The third section of the exposition, which is involves the execution of the act, is an advance over the Aristotelian treatment. Thomas's addition of command, use, and enjoyment reflects the influence of non-Aristotelian sources, but is used to address the needs of an Aristotelian account.

Thomas differs from Aristotle not only by adding stages but also by explicitly stating that the stages are distinct acts of two separate powers, namely the intellect and the will. For instance, Thomas in large part accepts Aristotle's description of choice as deliberative desire, but he also mentions the need for a special judgment of choice. The addition of extra volitional and intellectual acts makes his action theory not only more complicated but also more sophisticated. Nevertheless, this more sophisticated schema should not distract us from Thomas's frequent emphasis on the acts of simple willing and choice.[85]

John Duns Scotus and William of Ockham

Scotus and Ockham do not give such complicated accounts of an act's structure. Part of the difference may be in that they do not explicitly address the topic at length in the way that Thomas does in the *Prima Secundae* and to some extent in his commentary on Aristotle' *Ethics*. They also do not attempt to integrate the patristic sources into the Aristotelian structure in the way that Thomas does. Nevertheless, they assume the basic Aristotelian division between willing or at least intention, deliberation, and choice, although they do not always integrate this threefold division into their discussions of the will's acts.

In particular, Scotus often mentions the will's acts without making

---

85. It seems to me that this emphasis on choice as the free act is rejected by Stump, *Aquinas*, 294–300.

explicit reference to the Aristotelian stages. Scotus's understanding of the will's acts is much simpler than that of Thomas.[86] He first makes a division between "to will" *(velle)* and "to will against" *(nolle)*. Then he distinguishes between two kinds of willing: (1) conditional willing or the will of complacency, and (2) efficacious willing. This division between kinds of willing also seems to apply in some way to willing against, although Scotus does not develop the point.[87] Scotus more often uses this distinction between kinds of acts than he uses the Aristotelian scheme, and we shall see that he describes Aristotelian choice in the context of these distinctions.

What is the distinction between "to will" *(velle)* and "to will against" *(nolle)*? When the will pursues a fitting object, then it "wills," and when it flees or recoils from an unfitting object it "wills against."[88] "To will against" is not the same as "not to will" *(non velle)*, since "willing against" is just as much of an act as willing itself is. "Willing against" depends on willing because willing against a good implies some order to a good that is willed.[89] For instance, someone can will against justice, but only because he wills another good such as money. Consequently, willing is in a way prior to willing against. In chapter 1, we have already seen how Scotus thinks that we cannot will against happiness, even though we are free to "not will" happiness. For Scotus, we can never will any evil as such, or will against any good. We will everything under the formality of the good *(sub ratione boni)*.[90]

---

86. This point is made by Hieronymus de Montefortino, *Summa Theologica Ioannis Duns Scoti*, I-II, q. 15, art.1, 4; q. 16, art. 4; q. 17, art. 3 (Rome: Sallustiana, 1902), 159–61, 162–63, 165, 168–70. For Scotus's understanding of the different acts, see especially Minges, *Ioannis Duns Scoti doctrina*, 1.353–66.

87. William of Alnwick, *Additiones Magnae* 2, d. 22, n. 2 (Wadding ed., 11.1.361).

88. Scotus, *Ord.* 2, d. 6, q. 2, n. 34 (Vat., 8.39); Idem, *Ord.* 4, d. 4, p. 2, q. 1, n. 69 (Vat., 11.244); Idem, *Ord.* 4, d. 49, q. 5, n. 2 (Wadding ed., 10.423); Idem, *Ord.* 4, d. 49, q. 10, n. 8 (Wadding ed., 10.513). This last text, published by Wadding with the *Ordinatio*, seems to be taken from a *reportatio* of Scotus's Parisian lectures. See the Vatican editors, Vat., 1.27*–28*.

89. Scotus, *Lect.*, 2, d. 6, q. 2, n. 24 (Vat., 18.376–77); Idem, *Ord.*, d. 6, q. 2, nn. 35–36 (Vat., 8.40–41).

90. Scotus, *Collatio* 4, n. 6 (Wadding ed., 3.355).

He writes, "Just as with respect to an apprehended evil [*malum*] I am not able to elicit [any] act of the will except 'willing against' [*nolle*], so with respect to the good [I am not able to elicit any of the will] except 'to will' [*velle*]."⁹¹

Scotus divides the act of willing only into two acts, namely conditional willing and efficacious willing. Scotus claims, "I say that volition is twofold: one is efficacious, which is in respect to an end through means ordered to the attainment of that end; the other is simple or conditional, which is in respect to some end, not in executing the means for achieving that end, but that end is simply desired, and it would will to tend to this end if it were able, and if the object were itself present [*secundum se praesens*]."⁹² Conditional willing resembles Aristotle's description of "*boulesis*" in that it applies to impossible objects. Nevertheless, conditional willing seems to differ from "*boulesis*" because it can be meritorious or demeritorious. This inefficacious willing is not merely about what is in itself impossible, such as a creature's wishing to be equal to God, but it also about what is impossible for the agent, or in a particular situation. For instance, someone might want to fornicate but lack the opportunity.⁹³ Such an agent sins and deserves punishment even if he knows that the end is impossible for him to attain.

What is the relationship between these two kinds of willing and choice? According to Scotus, the word "choice" is equivocal, since it includes these two different kinds of acts, namely efficacious and inefficacious acts of the will. The first kind of choice more or less resembles Aristotle's understanding of choice. With respect to this

---

91. "sicut circa malum ostensum non possum elicere actum voluntatis nisi *nolle*, ita nec circa bonum nisi *velle*"; Scotus, *R. P.*, 4, d. 49, q. 9, n. 10 (Wadding ed., 11.2.913).

92. "dico quod duplex est volitio: Una est efficax, quae est respectu finis per media ordinata ad illum finem consequendum; alia est simplex seu conditionalis, quae est respectu alicujus finis non exequendo media ad illum finem consequendum, sed simpliciter appetitur finis ille, ut vellet tendere in ipsum si posset, et si objectum esset secundum se praesens"; Scotus, *Ord.* 4, d. 49, q. 10, nn. 12–13 (Wadding ed., 10.539). Cf. William of Alnwick, *Additiones Magnae* 1, d. 47, q. 2, nn. 1–2 (Wadding ed., 11.1.237).

93. Scotus *Ord.* 4, d. 49, q. 10, nn. 12–13 (Wadding ed., 10.539).

second kind, Scotus states that it is taken "for an act of the will following the full apprehension of the intellect, in which way it is said that someone sins from choice when there is no passion disturbing the intellect, nor [is there] ignorance."[94] This kind of choice makes it possible for an agent not only to be responsible for some acts that are impossible for him to carry out, but even for some acts that he knows are impossible for him. Consequently, this kind of choice does not fall under Aristotle's narrower description of choice. This less proper notion of choice is important for understanding the angels' first sin.[95] Since the angels suffered no intellectual failings, they could choose to be God's equals only when "choice" is understood in this sense. The angels knew that they could never be God's equals, but nevertheless they chose to be so. The angel's choice is a clear example of how an object can be known to be impossible and yet be chosen. The other case is that of someone who wishes to fornicate even though he knows that such fornication is impossible. Scotus explicitly states that such willing can be described as a kind of choice for which the agent is responsible.

Although Scotus wants to attribute choice and responsibility to these cases that Aristotle does not consider, he states that choice has another meaning if taken in its more proper sense, namely as "an efficacious will following a practical syllogism."[96] Such choice is of a means to an end, and this means is found through deliberation or at least through a practical syllogism.[97] "Choice" in this stricter meaning corresponds fairly closely to Aristotle's description of choice *(prohairesis)*. Following Aristotle, Scotus argues that this kind of choice can never be of the impossible, since the agent does not construct

94. "pro actu voluntatis consequente plenam apprehensionem intellectus, quo modo dicitur quis peccare ex electione quando non est passio perturbans intellectum, nec ignorantia"; Scotus, *Ord.* 2, d. 6, q. 1 (Vat., 8.29). See also Idem, *Collatio* 4 (Wadding ed., 3.355–56).

95. Scotus, *Ord.* 2, d. 6, q. 1, nn. 15–16 (Vat., 8.30).

96. "volitio efficax consequens syllogismum practicum"; Scotus, *Ord.* 2, d. 6, q. 1, n. 15 (Vat., 8.30).

97. Scotus, *Ord.* 3, d. 33, q. un., nn. 55–56 (Vat., 10.167–68); Idem, *Ord.* 4, d. 49, q. 10, n. 13 (Wadding ed., 10.539).

practical syllogisms concerning what is impossible. In order to reason about how to attain a goal, the goal must be regarded as possible. Consequently, the two kinds of choice seem to correspond to the distinction between efficacious and merely conditional willing. Scotus seems to describe this merely conditional willing as in some sense "choice" because it can be meritorious or sinful, and the agent is responsible for it.

Scotus gives an arguably Aristotelian account for one act of the will, namely efficacious willing, and a non-Aristotelian account for a different act of the will, namely conditional willing. But he calls both "choice." The word *choice* is used equivocally in these two instances. This distinction between two meanings of *choice* makes it difficult to compare Scotus with Thomas. Like Thomas, Scotus accounts for cases in which choice does not require deliberation. But although Thomas thought that sometimes choice follows deliberation and sometimes it does not, in both instances "choice" has the same signification. For Thomas, there is only one kind of choice, which is in some way separable from deliberation. Scotus's distinction between two kinds of choice allows him to hold that choice in the strictest sense always requires both deliberation and a practical syllogism even though agents can also be said to choose when they do not deliberate.

Although Scotus gives a more complicated account of choice than Thomas does, he does not share Thomas's enthusiasm for multiplying the stages of one act. Scotus does not think that consent, use, and enjoyment are themselves acts, and he does not give them much of a role in his description of action. Scotus seems to identify consent with conditional willing or choice.[98] There are only a few discussions of these acts, and these discussions do not give a comprehensive account. Use *(uti)* also seems to be a kind of choice, although Scotus is unclear. Unlike Thomas, Scotus seems to reserve enjoyment *(frui)* for the will's rest in the ultimate end.[99] Enjoyment is an act of the will inasmuch as the last end is willed through the love of friend-

---

98. Scotus, *Ord.* 4, d. 4, p. 2, q. 1 (Vat., 11.244).
99. Scotus, *Ord.* 1, d. 1, p.1, q.1, n. 15 (Vat., 2.9–10).

ship.[100] It is not a separate stage of the human act, but rather a distinct and complete act.

Although he considers them only in passing, Scotus gives a clearer account of intention and command. He carefully distinguishes between intention and use.[101] Intention is about the end, whereas use is about the means. Since choice is also about the means, it could be that the relationship between intention and use is like that between intention and choice. But the "use" of a means may imply a successful choice; therefore it might be the same as efficacious willing. Scotus mentions that intention is a wider term that can be loosely applied to any sort of "to tend to another from itself."[102] In contrast to Thomas, who thinks that intention is an act of the will, Scotus claims that intention taken in a narrower sense belongs to the whole faculty of free choice *(liberum arbitrium),* including the intellect and the will.[103] In this text Scotus applies his position that the known object is a partial cause of the will's act to his discussion of the power to which intention belongs. Nevertheless, since the free willing belongs more to the will than to the intellect, it follows that intention belongs more to the will than to the intellect.

How is intention distinct from use or choice? Scotus thinks that the act denoted by intention and use can be the same even though the words have different meanings.[104] Sometimes the act of willing the end is the same as that of willing the means. When the two acts are distinct, then intention and use are distinct. But even when the two acts are really distinct, in some way they form one act in the sense that the use is like the matter of the intention. Scotus writes that intention is "formally that act by which it tends to the end, and mate-

100. Scotus, *Ord.* 4, d. 49, q. 5, n. 2 (Wadding ed., 10.523).

101. Scotus, *Ord.* 2, d. 38, q. un., nn. 8–12 (Vat., 8.450–53); Idem, *Lectura,* d. 38, q. un., nn. 7–11 (Vat., 19.372–74).

102. "in aliud tendere ex se"; Scotus, *Ord.* 2, d. 38, q. un., n. 11 (Vat., 8.451).

103. Scotus, *Lect.* 2, d. 38, q. un., n. 12 (Vat., 19.374); Idem, *Ord.* 2, d. 38, q. un., nn. 11–12 (Vat., 8.451–52).

104. Scotus, *Ord.* 2, d. 38, q. un., n. 12 (Vat., 8.452); Idem, *Lectura* 2, d. 38, q. un., n. 12 (Vat., 19.374).

rially the act of use by which it refers another to that end."[105] Even in this case the distinction between intention and use is not between two independent acts, but the act of use or choice materially belongs to intention.

Scotus's distinction between intention and willing the means is more clearly brought out in his discussion of a minister's intention in baptizing and saying Mass.[106] Although the act of intention ceases, a virtual intention is sufficient for the validity of the sacrament. For example, a priest who forgets about the ends for which he is pouring the water during baptism or saying words over the host does not cease to intend virtually baptismal regeneration or the sacrifice of the Mass and transubstantiation. Similarly, someone who walks on a pilgrimage to Santiago does not cease to intend virtually the end of his pilgrimage even though he does not think of it when he is choosing particular means, such as walking. The virtual intention only ceases when the agent chooses an incompatible end. The distinction between intending the end and willing the means in this context seems to be to some extent between stages of the same act, such as saying Mass or walking to Santiago. On the other hand, there is also a sense in which intending the end seems to be distinct from the different acts that make up the way in which the act is achieved. In this passage, Scotus contrasts intention not with choice or use but rather with command *(imperium)*. Nevertheless, this discussion might shed some light on Scotus's understanding of the relationship between intention and choice, since the contrast is between intention and willing the means.

Unlike Thomas, Scotus thinks that command properly belongs to the will.[107] This usage was traditional.[108] For Scotus, the will influ-

---

105. "formaliter actum illum quo tendit in finem, et materialiter actum utendi quo refert aliud in illum finem"; Scotus, *Ord.* 2, d. 38, q. un., n. 12 (Vat., 8.452).

106. Scotus, *Ord.* 4, d. 6, p. 3, q. 2, nn. 138–50 (Vat., 11.336–40).

107. Scotus, *Ord.* 2, d. 33, nn. 44–45 (Vat., 10.162–63); *Ord.* 4, d. 14, q. 2, nn. 9–10 (Wadding ed., 9.40).

108. For the Franciscans, see Kent, *Virtues of the Will*, 66–68, 126–29. For Giles and Thomas, see Eardley, "Thomas Aquinas and Giles of Rome," 855–57. For general is-

ences the other powers by commanding them. Consequently, both use and command seem to be acts of the will that involve the act's execution. Scotus does not explicitly address the difference between use and command. In his discussion of intention, Scotus mentions that whereas intention is about the end, use is about the means. In this context use does not seem distinct from choice in its strictest meaning, although it also seems to connote the exercise of the act through the will's causal influence on the other powers. However, on this reading use does not seem entirely distinct from what he describes as command. They both seem to be two acts of the will that are distinct from choice only in that they connote the exercise of the soul's other powers.

Whereas Thomas discusses the stages of an act by combining patristic accounts of the will's stages with his reading of Aristotle and his own philosophical insight, Scotus focuses more simply on two sets of distinctions, one between two acts of the will, namely to will and to will against, and another between two kinds of willing, namely conditional and efficacious. Although Scotus himself relates only choice to these acts, the other stages must correspond to them or somehow involve them. But the nature of this relationship is unclear. One problem is that there are two kinds of choice. If we take "choice" in the strict sense, then choice requires deliberation. The structure of the act would then seem to be as follows: (1) knowledge of the end, (2) intention of the end, (3) deliberation concerning the means, (4) choice of the conclusion of a practical syllogism. A fifth stage could be added with respect to the will's command of the other powers and its use of them in the execution of the act, although it is hard to distinguish use and command from choice. This structure occurs whenever efficacious willing requires deliberation about means to an end. On this account, intention might be distinct from choice before deliberation occurs, but the choice of the means materially belongs to the intention of the end.

---

sues, see Roland J. Teske, "The Will as King over the Powers of the Soul: Uses and Sources of an Image in the Thirteenth Century," *Vivarium* 32 (1994): 62–71.

Choice in the wider sense does not require a kind of choice that follows deliberation or syllogistic reasoning. There are two kinds of acts that might fall under this category. First, some agents do not need to deliberate in order to efficaciously will. For instance, Christ does not reason discursively when performing meritorious acts.[109] Second, some agents can will and intend even if they are unable to deliberate concerning a means because the end is impossible. Examples of such merely conditional willing include the first sin of the angels and the would-be fornicator.

Properly speaking, choice only applies to that efficacious willing that follows deliberation and requires a practical syllogism. Unlike Thomas, Scotus seems to think that deliberation is connected with the practical syllogism at least to the extent that everyone who forms a practical syllogism must also have deliberated. He is unclear about whether deliberation has its own kind of reasoning that is distinct from that of the practical syllogism.

In general, Scotus's description of deliberation follows the broad Aristotelian outline. Nevertheless, Scotus is distinctive in that he does not think that all human action corresponds to such stages. There are clear theological reasons for his alternative accounts, such as the need to account for Christ's meritorious acts and the angels' sin. Nevertheless, he also wishes to account for such ordinary acts as willing to do what one cannot. If such an act is bad, then the act is sinful, even if there is no deliberation and the choice is different in kind from that choice which follows deliberation. If "choice" is taken in the strictest sense, then Aristotle's description of choice is more or less correct. But such a description does not apply to Christ, the angels, or even humans who will to do what they cannot do. Scotus gives moral value to these acts by stating that they are instances of a different kind of choice.

In contrast with Scotus, Ockham clearly lays out his understanding of an act through the different stages, but he does so in only one text, which is his discussion of praxis.[110] Although he discusses Sco-

---

109. Scotus, *Lect.* 3, d. 18, n. 41 (Vat., 21.12).
110. Ockham, *Ord.*, 1, prol., q. 10 (OTh, 1.285–87). For a discussion, see Holopainen, *Foundations of Ethics*, 38–61, 64–65.

tus's understanding of praxis, he does not mention Scotus's description of the different kinds of choice. Ockham states that everyone or almost everyone agrees about the basic stages of praxis, and that the disagreement between authors concerning praxis is merely a disagreement of usage concerning which parts of the process should be described as praxis. The six stages are (1) the presentation of the end by the intellect, (2) the willing of the end, (3) deliberation, (4) judgment, (5) choice, and (6) execution. In many respects, his description of the stages resembles Scotus's description of the process that leads to Aristotelian choice. The most obvious difference is that Scotus does not distinguish between the third and fourth stages.

The six different stages involve interaction between the intellect and the will. The first two stages are the intellect's presentation of the end and the willing of the end. For instance, a sick person has this first practical principle, namely "health should be acquired." The sick person then wills health once he has formed this judgment. The next step, namely deliberation, belongs to the intellect. The fourth, namely judgment, also belongs to the intellect. What is the difference between these third and fourth steps? Ockham illustrate this distinction with the example of a sick person:

Deliberation or inquiry of the intellect follows that willing by which someone inquires into that which is better able to attain this health, that is, whether through walking, or through a drink, or through a poultice [cocturam], or through some other way. And a judgment [sententia] follows after this deliberation or inquiry, by which it is judged determinately that health is better attained through this determined way or that determined way. And the choice of the will follows or can follow that judgment or dictate, by which he determinately wills to walk or to take the drink, and so with the others.[111]

111. "Istam autem volitionem sequitur consilium intellectus vel inquisitio qua inquirit per quid potest melius attingere istam sanitatem, utrum scilicet per ambulationem vel per potionem vel cocturam vel aliquam aliam viam. Et post istud consilium vel inquisitionem sequitur sententia qua determinate sentiatur quod sanitas melius attingitur per istam viam determinate vel per aliam determinate. Et istam sententiam vel dictamen sequitur electio voluntatis vel sequi potest qua determinate vult

Unlike Scotus, Ockham distinguishes between deliberation and the judgment that immediately precedes choice. Both are distinct acts of the intellect that fall between the willing of the end and the choice of the means. Through deliberating, the agent discovers whether there are means to the desired end. Then the agent judges which way is best.

It is important that for Ockham there is not a necessary connection between deliberation and the judgment *(sententia)* or dictate *(dictamen)* that precedes choice, or between this preceding judgment and the choice itself. Ockham notes that judgment "follows or can follow" deliberation. His qualification seems to be necessary because often there may not be a best way, or perhaps even any way to achieve the end. When a judgment is made, the will "follows or can follow" the judgment by an act of choice. Here the qualification seems to be based on the will's freedom. As we have seen in the previous chapter, Ockham thinks that the intellect can always reject that which is presented to it by the intellect.

Is deliberation a necessary condition for choice? Although he does not discuss the connection between deliberation *(consilium)* and choice here at length, in his passage on the first sin of the angels he does discuss whether thinking something over *(deliberatio)* is necessary for a meritorious or a demeritorious act. According to Ockham, there are two kinds of thinking over.[112] First, there is an investigation that takes place over time. Second, there is "perfect knowledge or assent with respect to a practical principle or a conclusion."[113] The first kind of thinking over is unnecessary for either a meritorious or a demeritorious act. The second kind of thinking over is necessary for a

---

ambulare vel accipere potionem, et sic de aliis"; Ockham, *Ord.,* 1, prol., q. 10 (OTh, 1.286–87). "Coctura" might instead mean "cooked food" or "cauterization." Following Holopainen, I translate *sententia* as "judgment." Although this "sententia" in many respects corresponds to Thomas's "iudicium" in "iudicium electionis," the translation of both as "judgment" should not mask the difference in Latin.

112. Ockham, Quod 2, q. 6 (OTh, 9.139).

113. "perfecta cognitio sive assensus respectu principii practici vel conclusionis"; Ockham, Quod 2, q. 6 (OTh, 9.139).

meritorious act but not for a demeritorious act. This kind of thinking over can occur in an instant. Nevertheless, a sinful act can occur suddenly without any thinking over if someone is obligated to do what he does not. For instance, someone who unthinkingly hates God still sins if he is obliged to love God.

Although meritorious acts and consequently choices require thinking over but not some sort of investigation, do they still require some sort of practical syllogism? First, Ockham argues that practical syllogisms with present-tense propositions can be known even in an instant of time.[114] For instance, the angels can know in an instant that God is the highest good and creator, and therefore that he should be loved. Nevertheless, Ockham interestingly states that even meritorious acts do not require practical syllogisms.[115] Therefore, meritorious acts require a thinking over that does not necessarily take the form of a practical syllogism. He does not give a reason for this position, but it indicates that for him the judgment that choice follows is not always the conclusion of a practical syllogism.

Ockham's brief discussion gives a clearer description of the distinctions between deliberation, the practical syllogism, and choice than is given by Thomas or Scotus. For Ockham, although deliberation takes time, a practical syllogism can be understood in an instant. Consequently, the practical syllogism is distinct from deliberative inquiry. Moreover, some choice can be made without any practical syllogism.

From the first step of simple apprehension through the fifth step, which is choice, each act clearly belongs to either the will or to the intellect. Three stages of an act belong to the intellect, namely the apprehension of the end, deliberation, and judgment concerning the best means. There are two acts of the will, namely volition and choice. Ockham is unclear about whether the execution of the act, which follows choice, belongs to the intellect or the will. He states that the act's execution follows choice "if there is not some impediment." In an-

---

114. Ockham, Quod 2, q. 6 (OTh, 9.140).
115. Ockham Quod 2, q. 6 (OTh, 9.141).

other text, Ockham states that command is merely willing something without an impediment.[116] The difference between commanding and willing without commanding depends not on the will itself but rather on exterior obstacles. For Ockham, the act's execution is relatively unimportant. Although the word *praxis* in a wide sense applies to the execution of the act and anything under the will's control, the word first applies merely to acts of the will, such as volition and choice.[117] The execution of the act is important only because the act was chosen by the will.

Ockham's account is much simpler than that of Thomas or of Scotus. In contrast to Thomas, Ockham's account of an act's various stages is relatively uninfluenced by Augustinian and Stoic terms. Ockham does not think that enjoyment, intention, consent, command, and use are distinct stages, and he does not discuss in particular and at length intention, consent, and command. Although Ockham discusses enjoyment and use at length, they are not considered as stages of an act but rather acts themselves. For Ockham, use *(uti)* either more strictly means an act of the will that is distinct from enjoyment, or more strictly it is any act of the will.[118] Enjoyment is either the enjoyment of God as the ultimate end or any resting in a good.[119] Even taking the terms in a narrow sense, the enjoyment/use distinction is a distinction between kinds of loves and not between stages of an act. In contrast to Scotus, Ockham treats the term "choice" as univocal. Consequently, he does not need to distinguish between the way in which an agent arrives at distinct kinds of choice, or develop an alternative to the basically Aristotelian account.

---

116. Ockham, *Q. V.,* q. 7, art. 2 (OTh, 8.333–34); see also Idem, *Q. V.,* q. 7, art. 3 (OTh, 8.371–72).

117. Ockham, *Ord.* 1, prol., d. 1, q. 10 (OTh, 1.292–96). For Ockham's understanding of praxis, see Holopainen, *Foundations of Ethics,* 61–67; Freppert, *Basis of Morality,* 24–27.

118. Ockham, *Ord.* 1, d. 1, q. 1 (OTh, 1.373).

119. Ockham, *Ord.* 1, d. 1, q. 11 (OTh, 1.396–97); Idem, *Ord.* 1, d. 1, q. 6 (OTh, 1.506).

ADDITIONS AND CHANGES
TO ARISTOTLE

One of the more obvious differences between the different accounts is in the number of stages that are enumerated. By any plausible account, Thomas describes more than eight stages and he may give as many as twelve. In contrast, Ockham enumerates only six, and Scotus describes five or fewer. Thomas's account is arguably more complex than the others because it can account for a wider variety of acts and problems. Although Thomas follows Aristotle in primarily focusing on two appetitive acts, namely simple willing and choice, the addition of intention and consent makes it possible to account for intermediate appetitive acts between these two. Similarly, Thomas's addition of use and enjoyment more clearly describes the act's execution.

All three figures give a more sophisticated account of the relationship between deliberation and choice than Aristotle does. Aristotle himself unclearly described choice both as the central ethical act and as the product of deliberation. Thomas, Scotus, and Ockham focused on choice as the central act. Their motivation is largely the desire to account for choices in which there is no deliberation. But even though deliberation is unnecessary for every choice, there must be a cognitive element.

How is it possible to have choice without deliberation? Scotus accounts for the possibility of such choice by distinguishing between two different meanings of "choice." For Scotus, the judgment that precedes a choice is not clearly separate from the conclusion of a practical syllogism or the conclusion of deliberation. Strictly speaking, choice taken in the strictest sense must follow deliberation. On the other hand, Scotus states that there is a looser way in which choice applies to acts that do not fall under Aristotle's description.

Both Thomas and Ockham address the issue by distinguishing between the intellectual judgments that are followed by choice and those that belong to deliberation. Thomas describes this judgment, which he sometimes calls the judgment of choice *(iudicium electionis)*, as the conclusion of a practical syllogism and somehow the form of the choice itself. The judgment of choice seems to be related to the will's act as form is related to matter. This close cooperation between the intellect and the will reflects Thomas's distinction between the known object's role as the final or formal cause of the act, and the will's role as the efficient cause.

Thomas's separation of the judgment of choice from deliberation seems plausible as an attempt to account for instances in which there is only one means to an end, or when the means are insignificant. On the other hand, since Thomas argues that an object's indeterminacy is rooted in the ability to deliberate between different instances of and means to an end, there may be a way in which this separation of choice from deliberation is difficult to reconcile with Thomas's description of such acts as free. But such indeterminacy probably results from the ability to have one end rather than another. Deliberation is about the means rather than the end. Consequently, if the means is obvious or insignificant, there is no need for deliberation to precede the choice of a means to an end. But every end apart from happiness can be considered as a means. Therefore, happiness is the only end that cannot be subject to deliberation.

The discussion of the stages of the act directly addresses the first two themes of this book, which involve the connection between natural inclination and willing, and a difference over the emphasis placed on the will's activity. Thomas's position reflects his wider emphasis on the continuity between natural inclination and free action. The willing of happiness is by nature. Freedom involves an ability to think about and choose means to and instances of this end that is willed by nature. Scotus and especially Ockham do not incorporate natural inclination into their understanding of an act's stages. According to Ockham, will's act of choice follows judgment (*sententia* or *dictamen*) as a really distinct and independent act. Moreover, Ockham's clear distinction between deliberation and the judgment that precedes choice allows him to explain how the same kind of choice exists with or without deliberation. Deliberation is a distinct step that is sometimes unnecessary. Scotus's connection of choice with a kind of deliberation made it necessary for him to hold that the word *choice* is used equivocally when it is applied to an act of the will that occurs without deliberation.

More broadly, Ockham more clearly distinguishes this judgment (*sententia* or *dictamen*) that precedes choice from the process that leads to it, which could either be a lone practical syllogism or a more complicated deliberation. Furthermore, Ockham states that this judgment can exist even without a practical syllogism. In general, Thomas seems to think that the judgment of choice *(iudicium electionis)* must be a conclusion of a fully practical syllogism. Although in his clearest discussion of the issue he states that such choice can occur without deliberation, he makes many remarks that are at least in tension with this position. Ockham's explicitness and greater clarity may result from his simpler account of the interaction between the will. First the intellect shows the object to the will, and then the will can elicit an entirely separate act.

The different views of an act's stages also reflects this book's third major theme, which involves the difference over understanding mental causation. Ockham and Scotus emphasize the overriding importance of the will's causal influence by arguing for the will's ability to elicit acts that are more clearly separate from intellectual acts. Thomas's understanding of the different kinds of mutual causality exercised by the intellect and the will perhaps requires a more complicated account. As we saw in chapter 1, both Scotus and Ockham think of the intellect as involving an efficient cause of the act that is subordinate to the efficient causality of the will. Their discussion of an act's stages seems to be a discussion of similar and distinct causal influences. The intellect and the will act in separate stages. In contrast, Thomas's account of choice in particular shows how the intellect and the will have acts that cannot be separated. Insofar as choice is a judgment, it is an act of the intellect. In this respect, choice is specified by the known object. The possible distinct judgments of choice correspond to the liberty of specification. In contrast, the material aspect of choice is an act of the will that is specified by the judgment of choice. This freedom of this will act corresponds to the liberty of exercise. Since these two kinds of freedom belong to the same act of free choice, Thomas cannot hold that there is first a judgment of choice and then a later will act of choice. In contrast, since Scotus and Ockham root freedom in the will's ability to act freely and principally, they think that the act of choice consists entirely in the will's ability to choose or not choose the object that is presented to it by the intellect.

4

EVALUATION AND SPECIFICATION
OF THE ACT

Thomas, Scotus, and Ockham all evaluate an act in terms of its object, end, and circumstances, although these three figures differ in their understanding and application of these terms. Their language has roots in ancient philosophy and the patristic tradition, and also in a particularly medieval interest in individual acts. In particular, the increasing importance of the Sacrament of Penance made it necessary for theologians to consider how to evaluate and describe such acts.[1]

The distinction between the object, the circumstances, and the end has three principal sources, namely (1) the rhetorical literature about circumstances, (2) debates over whether some acts are evil even if they are directed to a good end, and (3) the development of the new Latin term "*obiectum.*" Thirteenth-century discussions of an act's circumstances are in part based on lists of what confessors thought that they should ask about penitent's acts. The most popular list of seven circumstances comes mostly from Boethius although it is usually attributed to Cicero. This list does have its source in Cicero's *De inventione* and more remotely in a Greek rhetorical tradition concerning

1. For auricular confession, see John Mahoney, *The Making of Moral Theology: A Study in the Roman Catholic Tradition* (Oxford: Clarendon Press, 1987), 1–22.

what should be included in narratives of particular events.[2] The same circumstances are enumerated in slightly different mnemonic verses, such as the following verse that Thomas cites: *"Quis, quid, ubi, quibus auxiliis, cur, quomodo, quando."*[3] This mnemonic gives a list of the seven features that are relevant to an act's morality, which are in English: (1) the agent, (2) what is done, (3) where it is done, (4) what instrument is used, (5) why it is done, (6) how it is done, and (7) when it is done.

Although the list of seven circumstances is taken from the rhetorical tradition, it also corresponds in large part to Aristotle's description in the *Nicomachean Ethics* of what an agent must know about an act for the act to be voluntary.[4] According to Thomas, there are two main differences between the Ciceronian list and Aristotle's list.[5] First, Aristotle distinguishes between two aspects of circumstance (2) what is done *(quid)*, namely between the act's genus *(quid)* and the act's matter or object *(circa quid)*. Second, Aristotle combines circumstances (3) where *(ubi)* and (7) when *(quando)* into one circumstance, namely in which *(in quo)*. Thomas is also exposed to Nemesius's much expanded list, which is based on that of Aristotle.[6]

The Fourth Lateran Council (1215) states that confessors should consider an act's circumstances, and there seems to be no clearly delineated difference between an act's circumstances and any morally relevant features.[7] The lists of circumstance and the use of the term in a moral context existed before the more technical later usage, which is for indicating those features of an act that can be morally relevant even though they do not change the act's kind. Thomas's teacher

2. D. W. Roberts Jr., "A Note on the Classical Origin of 'Circumstances' in the Medieval Confessional," *Studies in Philology* 43 (1946): 6–14.

3. Thomas, *S.T.*, I-II, q. 7, art. 3, resp.

4. Aristotle, *Nicomachean Ethics* 3.1.1111a3–7.

5. Thomas, *S.T.*, I-II, q. 7, art. 3; Idem, 4 *Sent.*, d. 16, q. 3, art. 1, nn. 159–60 (Moos ed., 796–97); Idem, *Sententiae Ethicorum*, lib. 3, lect. 3 (Leonine, 47.1.126). See Joseph Pilsner, *The Specification of Human Actions in St. Thomas Aquinas* (Oxford: Oxford University Press, 2006), 176–80.

6. Emil Dobler, *Syrichen Quellen*, 174–88.

7. Robertson, "Classical Origin," 6; Stanley B. Cunningham, *Reclaiming Moral Agency: The Moral Philosophy of Albert the Great* (Washington, D.C.: The Catholic University of America Press, 2008), 128.

Albert the Great is one of the first to discuss moral circumstances at length as a distinct category.[8] For Thomas and Albert, circumstances are like the properties or accidents of a human act. This new usage posed a problem for two of the circumstances in the traditional lists, namely what *(quid)* and why *(cur)*. Albert the Great notes that the reason or end of an act is more significant than the other circumstances.[9] Thomas states that the end is a circumstance only when it is joined to the act.[10] The good that characterizes an act as such is not a circumstance. Similarly, the circumstance "what" is not the necessary feature of the act itself, namely the matter or the object, but an additional feature. For instance, washing is not a circumstance of pouring water even though it is a "what," but cooling and heating are instances of the circumstance "what."

A second historical source of later terminology concerning the act's end is the twelfth-century dispute over whether some acts are intrinsically evil.[11] Peter Abelard was widely interpreted as holding the

8. Cunningham, *Reclaiming Moral Agency,* 129–38.

9. Cunningham, *Reclaiming Moral Agency,* 138–41.

10. Thomas, *S.T.,* I-II, q. 7, art. 3, ad 3.

11. See Lottin, *Psychologie et morale,* 4.1.354–98; Tobias Hoffmann, "Moral Action as Human Action: End and Object in Aquinas in Comparison with Abelard, Lombard, Albert and Duns Scotus," *The Thomist* 67 (2003): 75–80. For Abelard, see especially John Marenbon, *The Philosophy of Peter Abelard* (Cambridge: Cambridge University Press, 1997), 251–64; William E. Mann, "Ethics," in *The Cambridge Companion to Abelard,* ed. Jeffrey Brouwer and Kevin Guilfoy (Cambridge: Cambridge University Press, 2004), 279–304. For a representative passage, see Peter Abelard, *Scito teipsum,* ed. Rainer M. Ilgner, Corpus Christianorum, Continuatio Mediaevalis 190 (Turnhout: Brepols, 2001), 1–24. For the wider history, see D. E. Luscombe, *The School of Peter Abelard,* Cambridge Studies in Medieval Life and Thought, Second Series 14 (Cambridge: Cambridge University Press, 1969), 261–80; Marcia L. Colish, *Peter Lombard,* Brill's Studies in Intellectual History 41 (Leiden: Brill, 1994), 2.471–516. For the general importance of the discussion, see Servais Pinckaers, *Ce qu'on ne peut jamais faire: La question des actes intrinsèquement mauvais: Histoire et discussion,* Étude d'éthique Chrétienne 19 (Fribourg: Éditions universitaires; Paris: Cerf, 1986). John Dedek argues that the notion of an "intrinsically evil" act is fully developed only in the fourteenth century with Durandus of Saint Pourçain. Dedek strangely reserves this term for purely physical acts, and he does not concentrate on the importance of the moral object and the different uses of the term "matter." As will be shown, Thomas and Scotus were not largely concerned with the human act's natural species, but with its charac-

view that acts are good or bad merely on account of their intention or end. Peter Lombard attacks this view in his *Sentences*. Although Lombard admits that the end is important, he argues that some acts, such as fornication and blasphemy, are intrinsically evil, such that they remain evil even when they are ordered to good ends. Consequently, such acts have their moral characterization apart from the end. Later theologians disagree over the exact relationship between the end and the act itself, but all agree with Lombard that at least some acts can be characterized as evil independently of their end. The distinction focuses attention on a distinct kind of end that is chosen by the agent, namely the *finis operantis*, and not the end that is intrinsic to the act, namely the *finis operis*.[12] This *finis operantis* is the same as or at least an instance of the circumstance "why" *(cur)*. Debates over the difference between the act and the end are concerned with difference between the act and that end which is the *finis operantis*.

The third important terminological development is the use of the term "object" to indicate that which specifies the act or at least principally contributes to its specification.[13] This use of the Latin *"obiectum"* is a thirteenth-century innovation that seems to follow upon the nearly contemporary use of the term to indicate something that corresponds to a power. For instance, in the likely first usage of "object," color is the object of the sense power of sight, and sound is the object of the sense power of hearing. In the second usage, the object of the act corresponds in some way to the power of willing or choice. For instance, the object of an act of theft might be "another's thing" or "taking another's thing without permission." Although the object in this moral sense seems to correspond to the circumstance "what" *(quid)*, it is different from a moral circumstance strictly speaking because it indicates an essential feature of the act. In thirteenth-century discus-

---

ter as a human act. But for his otherwise helpful accounts, see John Dedek, "Intrinsically Evil Acts: An Historical Study of the Mind of St. Thomas," *The Thomist* 43 (1979): 385–413; Idem, "Intrinsically Evil Acts: The Emergence of a Doctrine," *Recherches de théologie ancienne et médiévale* 50 (1983): 191–225.

12. Lottin, *Psychologie et morale*, 4.2.489–517.

13. Dewan, "Obiectum."

sions, the generically or per se evil act is evil on account of its object, and is evil even if the agent has a good end in willing the object.

The object of the moral act is distinct not only from the object of a power, but also from the object of a natural act, or an act considered according to its natural species. From the early thirteenth century until Ockham, theologians generally distinguished between the interior act, the exterior act, and the act's natural species.[14] The *interior act* is the act of the will itself in eliciting the activity of other powers. The *exterior act* is the executed, commanded, or elicited act. The interior and exterior acts are both moral acts that differ insofar as the will differs from those powers that it moves. For instance, someone who attempts adultery but meets with rejection has committed the interior act of adultery, whereas the successful adulterer has committed both the interior and the exterior act. Although the interior and the exterior acts are both moral acts, a human act can also be considered as belonging to a natural species. For instance, adultery and the marital act are the same acts when considered as species of natural or physical acts, even though they are very different moral acts. Even though they have the same natural object, the moral objects are different.

The distinction between the exterior act and the natural species of the act is used by many medieval thinkers to show how the numerically same natural act can belong to two different species of exterior acts. For example, both Bonaventure and Albert mention the standard example of someone who walks to church first for God but then for vainglory. They both think that there are two interior and two exterior acts even though there is only one natural act. There is some difference in vocabulary. Albert states that there are two moral actions even though there is one action naturally *(naturaliter)*.[15] In contrast, Bonaventure states that there are two acts in the genus of morals *(in genere moris)* even though there is one act in the genus of nature *(in*

---

14. Thomas M. Osborne Jr., "The Separation of the Interior and Exterior Acts in Scotus and Ockham," *Mediaeval Studies* 69 (2007): 111–39.

15. "in tali actione sunt duae actiones, licet una sit naturaliter"; Albert, 2 *Sent.*, d. 40, art. 5, ad 5, in *Opera Omnia*, 38 vols., ed. Borgnet (Paris: Vivès, 1890–1899), 27.636–37.

genere naturae).[16] But the distinction is the same. Thomas and Scotus retain this traditional threefold division between the interior act, the exterior act, and the natural act, but Ockham distinguishes primarily between the contingently virtuous or vicious act and the necessarily virtuous or vicious act. Moreover, he thinks that the exterior act can be described as a kind of act according to its natural species. These distinctions need to be kept in mind when distinguishing between the objects of the various acts.

We will see that although Thomas, Scotus, and Ockham all discuss the moral object, circumstances, and end of an act, they often understand these terms differently. Although differences in terminology often reflect more fundamental differences, we should keep in mind that their terminology reflects a variety of disparate historical sources and consequently is fluid and even imprecise.

THOMAS AQUINAS

According to Thomas, each human act has a fourfold human goodness.[17] The first goodness comes from the act's being as such.[18] Thomas shares the widely held medieval and Neoplatonic view that goodness is convertible with being. Since human acts exist, they are in some way good. Moreover, he considers the goodness at which natural acts aim.[19] For instance, the act of generation aims at the procreation of children. Consequently, adultery can be described as good insofar as it produces a child, although it is bad from the perspective of the rational agent. This first kind of goodness is "generic" goodness. Even a sin is good in this respect. This generic characteristic of the act is prior to its presence

16. "licet illa actio una sit in genere naturae, non est tamen una in genere moris"; Bonaventure, 2 *Sent.*, d. 41, art. 1, q. 1, ad 4 (*Opera*, 2.938). For comparisons of Thomas with Bonaventure, see Johannes Gründel, *Die Lehre von der menschlichen Handlung im Mittelalter,* Beiträge zur Geschichte der Philosophie und Theologie des Mittelalters 39.5 (Münster: Aschendorff, 1963), 552–68, 580–646.

17. Thomas, *S.T.*, I-II, q. 18, art. 4, resp.

18. Thomas, *S.T.*, I-II, q. 18, art. 1; Idem, *De Malo*, q. 2, art. 4, resp. et ad 12 (Leonine, 23.39, 41).

19. Thomas Aquinas, *S.T.*, I-II, q. 1, art. 3, ad 3; q. 18, art. 5; q. 24, art. 4, resp.

in a properly human species. Specific goodness comes from the object and accidental goodness comes from the circumstances. The end gives a goodness that differs insofar as the end is an object or a circumstance.

What is the object? When discussing the act's specification, Thomas most often states that acts are specified by their object.[20] Nevertheless, Thomas also states that the end, circumstances, and matter specify human acts.[21] The characteristics of an object and their relationship to these other features of an act are unclear. As if to complicate matters, Thomas sometimes states that the object is an end, or that circumstances are part of the object. Consequently, to understand Thomas's account of the act's specification, it is important to be clear both on what an object is and how it is related to ends and circumstances.

Thomas often gives examples to illustrate what the object is, but the examples seem disparate.[22] An object can be the thing itself, but it can also be a human action. How can a thing be the object of the act? In the *De Malo*, Thomas states that the object of theft is "another's thing" *(res aliena).*[23] Similarly, a related object of sacrilege could be the sacred thing that belongs to another. The two different things are distinct objects that specify different acts. This object that is a thing seems to be the same as the "matter concerning which" *(materia circa quam).*[24] The *materia circa quam* differs from the circumstance "concerning which" *(circa quid)* because it is essential to the act.[25] For instance, in the *Secunda Secundae* Thomas states that money is the object or matter of liberality, which is a virtue by which someone gives

20. Pilsner, *Specification of Human Actions*, 71.

21. Pilsner, *Specification of Human Actions*, 1–7, passim.

22. Pilsner, *Specification of Human Actions*, 73–91.

23. Thomas, *De Malo*, q. 2, art. 7, ad 8 (Leonine, 23.51).

24. Thomas, 2 *Sent.*, d. 36, q. 1, art. 5, ad 5 (Mandonnet ed., 2.936); Idem, *De Veritate*, q. 20, art. 3, ad 3 (Leonine, 22.2.579); Idem, *S.T.*, I-II, q. 18, art. 2, ad 2; Ibid., q. 73, art. 3, ad 1. See the Salmanticenses, *Cursus Theologicus*, tract. 11, disp. 3, dub. 1, nn. 11–12, in *Cursus Theologicus*, 20 vols. (Paris: Palmé, 1870–1883), 6.68–69. For detailed discussions, see Pilsner, *Specification of Acts*, 144–53; Stephen L. Brock, "*Veritatis Splendor* #78: St. Thomas and (Not Merely) Physical Objects of Moral Acts," *Nova et Vetera*, English Edition 6 (2008): 1–62.

25. Thomas, *S.T.*, I-II, q. 7, art. 3, ad 3.

out of his riches.[26] Furthermore, he states that the matter or object specifies sexual sins.[27] For example, the matter or object of adultery is someone else's wife.

Thomas also sometimes states that the object of an act is the very action done or an effect of the action. For instance, in the *Prima Secundae*, Thomas states that theft is "taking someone else's thing" *(suscipere aliena)*.[28] In this passage, the act of theft is specified not merely by the object but also by the act of taking. In many passages Thomas states that the exterior act is the object of the interior act.[29] Consequently, some cases in which actions are objects may be cases in which an exterior act is an object of an interior act. Moreover, different actions concerning the same thing can specify different acts. For instance, one and the same thing can be an object of robbery or burglary depending on whether the item is stolen openly or secretly.[30]

Although the moral object can be a thing, it involves or presupposes an order of reason.[31] Consequently, the thing by itself consid-

---

26. Thomas, *S.T.*, II-II, q. 117, art. 3, resp.   27. Thomas, *S.T.*, II-II, q. 154, art. 1.

28. Thomas, *S.T.*, I-II, q. 20, art. 1, ad 1.

29. Thomas, *2 Sent.*, d. 40, q. 1, art. 3, sol. (Mandonnet ed., 2.1017); Idem, *De Malo*, q. 2, art. 4, resp., ad 3, ad 8 (Leonine, 23.36–37). Pilsner, *Specification of Acts*, 80–81.

30. Thomas, *S.T.*, II-II., q. 66, art. 3–4.

31. Pilsner, *Specification of Acts*, 85. This connection between physical acts and the order of reason is discussed especially in John Finnis, "Object and Intention in Moral Judgments according to St. Thomas Aquinas," in *Finalité et intentionalité: Doctrine Thomiste et perspectives modernes*, Actes du Colloque de Louvain-la-Neuve et Louvain 21–23 Mai 1990, ed. J. Follon and James McEvoy (Paris: Vrin/Leuven: Peeters, 1992), 127–48; Carlos Steel, "Natural Ends and Moral Ends according to Thomas Aquinas," in *Finalité et Intentionalité*, 113–26; Martin Rhonheimer, "Intentional Actions and the Meaning of Object: A Reply to Richard McCormick," *The Thomist* 59 (1995): 279–311; Idem, "The Perspective of the Acting Person and the Nature of Practical Reason: The 'Object of the Human Act' in the Thomistic Anthropology of Action," *Nova et Vetera*, English Edition, 2 (2004): 461–516; John Finnis, Germain Grisez, and Joseph Boyle, "'Direct' and 'Indirect': A Reply to Critics of Our Action Theory," *The Thomist* 65 (2001): 1–44; Steven J. Jensen, "A Defence of Physicalism," *The Thomist* 61 (1997): 377–404; Ibid., "A Long Discussion of Steven A. Long's Interpretation of the Moral Species," *The Thomist* 67 (2003): 623–34; Steven Long, "A Brief Disquisition Regarding the Nature of the Object of the Moral Act according to Thomas Aquinas," *The Thomist* 67 (2003): 45–71; Lawrence Dewan, "St. Thomas, Rhonheimer, and the Object of the Human Act," *Nova et Vetera*, English Edition, 6 (2008): 63–112.

ered apart from its reasonable possession is always or at least almost always insufficient to specify an act. For instance, the object of theft is "someone else's thing," which indicates that the object is not specified just by the stolen object but also by the fact that the stolen object belongs to someone.[32] Moreover, the same thing will further specify different acts if it is taken secretly or by force, or even if it is taken with permission.[33] If it is a sacred object that is wrongfully taken, then the act will be sacrilege. Different kinds of features make the act reasonable or unreasonable, and the different kinds of reasonableness or unreasonableness specify the object. The object of the act is not just the thing itself but also involves the way in which the object is acted upon by the agent.

What features of a thing make it possible for the same thing to serve as the object of different acts? More generally, if different acts are specified by their objects, then how can the same thing serve as the object for different acts? Thomas distinguishes between the thing itself and the formal aspect *(ratio)* of the thing.[34] Different acts can have the same thing as an object, materially speaking, but under a different formal aspect *(ratio)*. For instance, the same woman can be the object of both the marital act and adultery.[35] The difference is in whether she is one's own wife or another's wife. Similarly, money can pertain to different acts and virtues of liberality, justice, or magnificence.[36] The different formal aspects of the same object make it possible for the same thing to be different objects of different acts.

The role of reason in the determination of the object also helps to explain why acts may be the same formally even though they are materially distinct.[37] For example, murder might involve poison or a gun.

32. Thomas, *S.T.*, I-II, q. 18, art. 2, resp.

33. Thomas, *S.T.*, II-II, q. 66, art. 3, resp. et ad 1. Pilsner, *Specification of Acts*, 85.

34. Thomas, *De Malo*, q. 2, art. 4 (Leonine, 23.37–42); Ibid., q. 9, art. 2, ad 10; Idem, *S.T.*, q. 25, art. 1. For additional texts and a discussion, see Pilsner, *Specification of Acts*, 101–12.

35. Thomas, *S.T.*, II-II, q. 154, art. 1.

36. Thomas, *S.T.*, II-II, q. 117, art. 3, resp. et ad 1.

37. Thomas, *S.T.*, I-II, q. 72, art. 6, resp. See Jacobus Ramirez, *De vitiis et peccatis: In I-II Summae Theologiae Divi Thomae Expositio (QQ. LXXI–LXXXV)*, ed. Victor

More interestingly, an omission might belong to the same species as a commission. For example, a miser might sin by taking money from someone else. The act would clearly be avarice. But a miser might also sin by keeping money when he should give it to others. Materially the acts are distinct. Formally, they are both acts of avarice. Similarly, gluttony could be a sin of commission, as when someone overeats, or a sin of omission, as when someone eats during an obligatory fast. Thomas states that in such cases "the negation, even if it properly is not in the species, is however constituted in the species through the reduction to some affirmation which it follows."[38] The failure to act is voluntary insofar as someone is able to perform the task and bound to follow it. The sin must be voluntary insofar as it consists in a contrary willing or at least the cause or occasion of the omission is in some way under the will's power.[39] For example, a helmsman is bound to steer, and so he is responsible for a shipwreck caused by his negligence.[40] Such negligence can sometimes be a sin that is caused by an ignorance concerning something that the agent is bound to know.[41] For example, a glutton, since he is bound to know when he should fast, sins through not observing a fast of which he is ignorant.

An object has a formal aspect insofar as it is related per se to an active principle.[42] For instance, the yellowness or redness of the rose has a per se relation to sight and an incidental (*per accidens*) rela-

Rodriquez, Edicion de las Obras Completas de Santiago Ramirez 8, 2 vols. (Madrid: Instiuto de Filosofia "Luis Vives," 1990), 1.126–28. For Thomas's understanding of voluntary omissions, see especially G. E. M. Anscombe, "Sin," in *Faith in a Hard Ground: Essays on Religion, Philosophy and Ethics*, ed. Marty Geach and Luke Gormally (Exeter, U.K.: Imprint Academic, 2008), 127–38; Barnwell, *Negligent Omissions*, 97–132.

38. "negatio, etsi proprie non sit in specie, consituitur tamen in specie per reductionem ad aliquam affirmationem quam sequitur"; Thomas, *S.T.*, I-II, q. 72, art. 7, ad 3.

39. Thomas, *S.T.*, q. 71, art. 5; Idem, *De Malo*, q. 2, art. 1 (Leonine, 23.27–31). Ramirez, *De vitiis et peccatis*, 1.75–79. For a similar point, see Ockham, *Rep.* 3, q. 11 (OTh, 6.373).

40. Thomas, *S.T.*, I-II, q. 6, art. 3, resp.; Idem, *S.T.*, I-II, q. 71, art. 5, ad 3; Idem, *2 Sent.*, d. 35, art. 3 (Mandonnet ed., 2.904–7); Idem, *De Malo*, q. 2, art. 1, ad 2 (Leonine, 23.30). Ramirez, *De actibus humanis*, 33–36.

41. Among the many passages, see Thomas, *S.T.*, I-II, q. 76, art. 2–3. Ramirez, *De vitiis et peccatis*, 1.407–42.

42. Thomas, *S.T.*, I-II, q. 18, art. 5; Ibid., *De Malo*, q. 2, art. 4, resp. (Leonine, 23.39–40). I am particularly indebted to discussions with Steven Jensen on this point.

tion to smell. Consequently, yellowness and redness as different formal aspects differentiate acts of sight, but they are irrelevant to acts of smelling. In general, color is a formal aspect that distinguishes acts of sight from other sense acts. For instance, a rose is an object of sight as colored, whereas it is an object of smell insofar as it is fragrant. With respect to the senses, the difference between color and smell is a difference between formal aspects of the object. There is a per se relation between the smell and the color of the rose and the powers of smell and sight. In contrast, color and smell are only incidentally *(per accidens)* related to the intellect, which considers the object under the common formal aspect of being or truth. Consequently, when a rose is known, smell and color are not or need not be part of the rose's formal object. Since human acts proceed from the intellect and the will, their objects have a per se relation to reason. For example, the same woman can be the object of marriage or adultery precisely because of the way in which she is known: as one's own wife or another's wife.

In addition to the distinction between the formal and the material consideration of the object, Thomas also distinguishes between the formal and the material objects of faith and hope. These distinctions can be confusing because faith, hope, and even charity all have the same object materially speaking, which is God.[43] Nevertheless, faith and hope both have principal objects formally speaking that can be divided into formal and material objects.[44] The formal object makes the act concerning the material object virtuous. For example, the principal material object of faith is the thing believed, whereas the principal formal object of faith is the first truth by which it is believed. Believing in God is not a virtue unless the agent believes by means of God's truthfulness. Similarly, the primary material object of hope is beatitude, whereas the primary formal object of hope is the divine help. Hoping in beatitude apart from divine help is vicious. The difference between the formal and the material objects is important for understanding the nature of these virtues, but they are both differences in

---

43. Thomas, *S.T.,* I-II, q. 62, art. 1, 3; Ibid., II-II, q. 17, art. 6.

44. Thomas, *De Spe,* art. 1 (Marietti ed., 2.803–6); Idem, *S.T.,* II-II, q. 1, art. 1; Ibid., q. 5, art. 4; Ibid., q. 17, art. 2

the object formally speaking. Materially speaking, both faith and hope have the same object, namely God. Consequently, the difference between the material and formal object is not the difference between the object materially speaking and the formal ratio. For instance, faith has the following object or objects: (1) the thing believed (material object), (2) first truth (formal object), and (3) God (object materially speaking). Similarly, hope has the following object or objects: (1) beatitude (material object), (2) divine help (formal object), and (3) God (object materially speaking). Thomas also thinks that these virtues have a variety of secondary objects.[45]

In general, Thomas states that circumstances increase or decrease an act's goodness but do not affect the act's species. However, Thomas's discussion of circumstances is complicated by the fact that he adheres to the traditional list of seven circumstances while at the same time he recognizes that this list includes items that in some cases are part of the object's formal characteristic and in other cases are irrelevant to its evaluation.[46] Consequently, Thomas distinguishes between and provides examples of different kinds of circumstances:

Nothing prevents that which is considered as an object according to one condition from being considered as a circumstance according to another, which sometimes gives species to the sin, and sometimes not, just as "another's thing" is the proper object of theft giving it a species. Now too "another's thing" can be of a greater quantity, and this circumstance does not give the species but aggravates it only; and yet "another's thing" might be a sacred item, and this circumstance constitutes a new species of sin; and still it can be a white or black "another's thing," and this circumstance will be indifferent from the part of the object, neither aggravating it nor constituting the species. Similarly it should be said of the end that the proximate end is the same as the object, and we should speak of it as the object; however, the remote end is taken as a circumstance.[47]

45. See also *De Spe*, art. 4, resp. (Marietti ed., 2.810–11).

46. Thomas, *De Malo*, q. 2, art. 7 (Leonine, 23.50–51). Pilsner, *Specification of Acts*, 172–98; Dobil, *Syrische Quellen*, 174–88; Thomas Nisters, *Akzidentien der Praxis: Thomas von Aquins Lehre von dem Umständen menschlichen Handelns* (Freiburg/München: Karl Abler, 1992).

47. "nichil prohibet id quod consideratur ut obiectum secundum unam conditionem

In this passage Thomas mentions that theft becomes sacrilege when the object is sacred. In the *Prima Secundae* he makes the same point with respect to the circumstance of place. If theft occurs in a holy place, then there is a new species of act, namely sacrilege. Both when the item is sacred or the place is sacred, what ordinarily are circumstances become parts of the act's object.[48] When Thomas discusses circumstances other than the end, such specifying circumstances are described as the object's conditions.[49] But in two other kinds of acts the circumstances are accidental and not essential to the act. First, many circumstances are irrelevant to the act's goodness or malice. Just as the location of theft usually does not make the theft worse, so the color of the stolen object generally does not make it worse. Second, the example of a greater or lesser quantity shows that sometimes circumstances do change the value of an act, as when a stolen item is worth much more.[50] But such circumstances do not change the act's species. This last kind of circumstance is the only kind involved in discussions of an act's circumstantial goodness or malice.

The above passage from the *De Malo* significantly distinguishes between the circumstance "why" *(cur)* or the remote end from the other circumstances. Whereas the remote end is a circumstance, the proximate end is not just a condition of the object but is described as the object. What is the distinction between the proximate end and the remote end? Aristotle discusses a case in which someone steals in order to commit adultery.[51] When intending and choosing to steal,

---

considerari ut circumstantiam secundum aliam, que quandoque dat speciem peccato, quandoque non. Sicut res aliena est proprium obiectum furti dans sibi speciem; potest etiam res aliena esse magne quantitatis, et hec circumstantia non dat speciem set aggrauat tantum; potest etiam res aliena esse sacra, et hec circumstantia consitutet novam speciem peccati; potest etiam esse res aliena alba uel nigra, et hec erit circumstantia ex parte obiecti indifferens, nec aggravans nec speciem constituens. Similiter dicendum est de fine, quod finis proximus est idem quod obiectum, et similiter dicendum est de eo sicut et de obiecto; finis autem remotus ponitur ut circumstantia"; Thomas, *De Malo*, q. 2, art. 7, ad 8 (Leonine, 23.51).

48. Steven J. Jensen, " Do Circumstances Give Species?" *The Thomist* 70 (2006): 1–26.

49. Thomas, *S.T.*, I-II, q. 18, art. 10; q. 7, art. 4, ad 3; q. 18, art. 5, ad 4.

50. Thomas, *S.T.*, I-II, q. 18, art. 3, 11.

51. Aristotle, *Nicomachean Ethics* 5.2.1130a24–27; Thomas, *S.T.*, I-II, q. 18, art. 4,

the theft is the proximate end and the adultery is the remote end. Although adultery is itself an act, in this case it is also a remote end or circumstance of the theft. Similarly, someone who gives alms out of vainglory has almsgiving as the proximate end or object and vainglory as the remote end or circumstance of the end.

Thomas states that the end as a circumstance is the same as the *finis operantis*, or end of the agent, and that the *finis operis*, or end of the work, is the object or a condition of the object.[52] The difference is between the end-directedness of the act itself and further ends to which the agent directs the act. For instance, almsgiving on its own is directed to relieving someone in need. But the agent can direct it to a further end such as vainglory. In general, Thomas uses the terms "proximate end" and "remote end" rather than the traditional pair of "*finis operis*" and "*finis operantis*," although he uses the latter pair throughout his career.[53] The important point is that since the object is itself an end, there need to be terms that distinguish the end that is the object from that which is a circumstance.

Thomas is distinctive in his emphasis on the role of the end in human action.[54] In many passages Thomas states that a human act is specified by the end.[55] This specifying end is the proximate rather

---

obj. 3 et ad 3; q. 18, art. 7; q. 11, art. 1, ad 2; Idem, *De Caritate*, art. 3, resp. (Marietti ed., 2.761).

52. Thomas, 4 *Sent.*, d. 16, q. 3, art. 1 (Moos ed., 4.796). I follow Salmanticenses, *C.T.*, tract. 11, disp. 5, dub. 1, n. 1 (6.99). For the different kinds of end, see especially Reginald Garrigou-Lagrange, *De Beatitudine: Commentarius in Summam Theologicam St. Thomae I-II qq. 1–54* (Turin: Berruti, 1951), 35–36; Guy Durand, "Les notions de fin intermédiaire et de fin secondaire."

53. See, for instance, Thomas, 2 *Sent.*, d. 1, q. 2, art. 1 (Mandonnet ed., 2.45–47); Idem, *S.T.*, II-II, q. 141, art. 6, ad 1.

54. Servais Pinckaers, "Le rôle de la fin dans l'action morale selon saint Thomas," *Revue des sciences philosophiques et théologiques* 45 (1961): 393–412.

55. Thomas, 2 *Sent.*, d. 40 art. 1 (Mandonnet ed., 2.1011); Idem, *De Virtutibus*, q. 1, art. 2, ad 3 (Marietti ed., 2.712); Ibid., q. 2, art. 3 (Marietti ed., 2.760–62); Idem, *S.T.*, I-II, q. 1, art. 3; Ibid., I-II, q. 18, art. 6. For a discussion, see Garrigou-Lagrange, *De Beatitudine*, 40–43; Iacobus Ramirez, *De hominis beatitudine*, 5 vols. (Madrid, Consejo Superior de Investigaciones Científicas, Instituto Francisco Suárez, 1942), 1.251–78; Pilsner, *Specification of Acts*, 46–69.

than the remote end.[56] This view in part is based on his understanding of the way in which natural movement is specified, namely by the term of the motion. Nevertheless, human action is distinctive because the human will is a self-moving power whose object is the end. According to Thomas, the end is both the act's principle and its term. As a self-mover, an agent moves himself to one end rather than another. The agent's powers are also moved by the will to the end, since the end is the act's term.

The distinction between the interior and exterior acts sheds light on the end's object. Thomas states that the object of the interior act is the end whereas the matter is the exterior act's object.[57] What is the relationship between the end and the matter? Part of the answer can be found in the way in which Thomas describes the exterior and interior acts as one. He states that they are diverse in the genus of nature but one act in the genus of morals.[58] Furthermore, the interior act is like the form, whereas the exterior act is like the matter.[59] For instance, theft can be considered as taking another's thing and it has its own disorder as a completed act. Nevertheless, the intention of theft as an end is prior to any execution, and the means are chosen simply insofar as they are ordered to this end. The exterior object or matter of the act is the will's end. The difference between the matter and the end is in the way of looking at the object. Thomas writes that "the object, even if it is the matter *circa quam* which the act has as a term, has however the characteristic [*ratio*] of an end, according to which the intention of the agent is brought to it."[60] In another text, Thomas states that the

56. Thomas, 2 *Sent.*, d. 38, q. 1, art. 1 (Mandonnet ed., 2.969; Idem, *De Malo*, q. 4, art. 4, ad 9 (Leonine, 23.41); Ibid., q. 6, ad 9 (Leonine, 23.49); Idem, *S.T.*, I-II, q. 60, art. 1, ad 3; Ibid, II-II, q. 11, art. 1, ad 2; Ibid., II-II, q. 111, art. 3, ad 3. See Pilsner, *Specification of Acts*, 133–40.

57. Thomas, *S.T.*, I-II, q. 18, art. 6; Ibid., I-II, q. 20, art. 2–3. David Gallagher, "Aquinas on Moral Action: Interior and Exterior Acts," *Proceedings of the American Catholic Philosophical Association* 64 (1990): 118–29.

58. Thomas, *S.T.*, I-II, q. 17, art. 4; Idem, *S.T.*, I-II, q. 20, art. 3, ad 1.

59. Thomas, *S.T.*, I-II, q. 18, art. 6; Idem, *S.T.*, I-II, q. 72, art. 6.

60. "obiectum, etsi sit materia circa quam terminatur actus, habet tamen rationem finis, secundum quod intentio agentis fertur in ipsum"; Thomas, *S.T.*, q. 73, art. 3, ad 1. Cf. Idem, *S.T.*, I-II, q. 19, art. 2, ad 1.

same object has two different aspects *(rationes)* when compared to the interior act and the exterior act.[61] With respect to the exterior act, the object is the matter *circa quam*. With respect to the interior act, the object is an end. The same object is both matter and proximate end. The fact that the one object has different characteristics as matter and end helps to explain the way in which the exterior act can be the object of the interior act. Thomas writes that "the exterior act is the object of the will, inasmuch as it is presented to the will by reason as a certain good which is apprehended and ordered through reason."[62] In this and other passages Thomas explains that an exterior act is an object to the extent that it can be apprehended as good.[63] The features that make the act good also make it able to be willed as an object and end of an interior act.

Although Thomas often states that the species of an act is taken from the proximate end, he also states more generally that ends are like forms to the matter that is chosen in an act. The remote end or *finis operantis* is often more formal than that proximate end that gives the act its species. This remote end can itself be a separate act, or it can be an end that causes the choice of another act as a means to it.[64] An instance of the first is someone who steals in order to fornicate or commit adultery. Thomas argues that although the person materially is a thief, formally he is a fornicator or adulterer and intemperate. Although the adultery or fornication is a separate act with its own proximate end, it also serves as the remote end of an act whereby theft is chosen as a means to the adultery. The adultery or fornication affects the act of theft in the way that form affects matter.

There are many cases in which the act of one habit is commanded by that of another.[65] For instance, acts of hypocrisy might be directed

61. Thomas, *S.T.*, I-II, q. 72, art. 4, ad 2.

62. "actus exterior est obiectum voluntatis, inquantum proponitur voluntati a ratione ut quoddam bonum apprehensum et ordinatum per rationem"; Thomas, *S.T.*, I-II, q. 20, art. 1, ad 1.

63. Thomas, 2 *Sent.*, d. 40, q. 1, art. 3, resp. (Mandonnet ed., 2.1017); Idem, *De Malo*, q. 2, art. 4, ad 1, 3 (Leonine, 23.37).

64. Thomas, *S.T.*, I-II, q. 7, art. 4, ad 2.

65. Thomas, *De Malo*, q. 8, art. 1, ad 14 (Leonine, 23.196); Idem, *S.T.*, I-II, q. 7, art. 3, ad 3.

to different bad ends such as vainglory or avarice.[66] Moreover, the virtues of justice and charity are each general in such a way that they can command to their own ends acts that belong to other virtues.[67] Some acts are good only insofar as they are ordered by another virtue. For instance, martyrdom is good when ordered to the ends given by faith and justice.[68] Patience is good when ordered to the love of God.[69] Nevertheless, even the object of patience is in itself reasonable.[70]

Thomas maintains both that an act's species comes from the proximate end and also that the remote end in some way characterizes the act. The two theses are possible because the two kinds of ends are responsible for specification in different ways.[71] The species from the proximate end or object is more essential. It gives the act its basic species. In contrast, the species from the remote end is accidental and does not do away with the other kind of specification. But this accidental specification is also more formal because the proximate end in some way receives the form given by the more remote end.

Thomas's characterization of the human act is made by using the traditional terminology of object, circumstance, and end, but his understanding of the relationship between these terms is complex. First, even though he accepts Cicero's list of seven circumstances, he thinks that the list includes items that in many cases are conditions of the object or joined to the object, such as the matter, the end, and even other circumstances insofar as they affect the way in which an object is grasped as reasonable. Moreover, Thomas's understanding of the interior and exterior acts allows for a complicated interaction between the matter and the end. The matter of an act can be described as the exterior object, which in turn can be the end that specifies an interior act. Second, although he divides the object from the circumstance of the end, the object itself can also be characterized as a proximate end, which is distinct from the circumstance of the end,

---

66. Thomas, *S.T.*, II-II, q. 111, art. 3, ad 3. See Pilsner, *Specification of Acts*, 219–21.

67. Thomas, *S.T.*, II-II, q. 58, art. 6. See Pilsner, *Specification of Acts*, 230–33.

68. Thomas, *S.T.*, II-II, q. 124, art. 2.   69. Thomas, *S.T.*, II-II, q. 136, art. 3.

70. Thomas, *S.T.*, II-II, q. 136, art. 1.

71. Salmanticenses, *Cursus Theologicus*, tract. 11, disp. 6, dub. 4, nn. 69–76 (vol. 6, *Cursus Theologicus*, 155–58). See also Pilsner, *Specification of Acts*, 222–27.

which is more remote. Third, he states that even the remote end gives a formal character to the act, although it gives only an accidental species to it. The simplicity of the threefold division between object, end, and circumstances disguises Thomas's description of the complex relationships between them.

JOHN DUNS SCOTUS

John Duns Scotus gives a simpler account of the distinction between the object, the circumstances, and the end. He not only provides a briefer account of what they are, but he also does not blur the distinctions between them in the way that Thomas does. The object gives the act a generic goodness, and then the circumstances, and most especially the end, determine the act to a given specific goodness. But Scotus's simplicity gives rise to problems with his account of the relationship between the object and the act's specification. He seems to depend on a plainer understanding of what an object is, but this account of the object is insufficient for distinguishing between many kinds of act even on a more generic level.

According to Scotus, the generic goodness of an act comes from the object.[72] Before considering whether the end or the other circumstances are good, we can first consider whether the act is the kind of act that can reasonably be done.[73] Right judgment concerning the act's object requires knowledge of the agent, the power by which the agent acts, and the quidditative nature *(ratio)* of the act, or what the act is. For in-

72. For Scotus on moral goodness, see Richard Cross, "Duns Scotus on Goodness, Justice and What God Can Do," *Journal of Theological Studies* 48 (1997): 48–76; Williams, "The Unmitigated Scotus"; Idem, "A Most Methodical Lover"; Idem, "From Metaethics to Action Theory," 335–42; Mary Elizabeth Ingham, "Duns Scotus, Morality and Happiness," 173–95; Dreyer and Ingham, *Philosophical Vision*, 173–200; Allan B. Wolter, "The Unshredded Scotus"; Hoffmann, "Moral Action as Human Action," 89–92.

73. Scotus, *Quod* 18, nn. [3]8–[8]23 (Alluntis ed., 632–41); Idem, *Ord.* 2, d. 7, nn. 28–39, (Vat., 8.88–93); Idem, *Lect.* 2, d. 40, q. un., nn. 6–9 (Vat., 19.390–91); Idem, *Ord.* 2, d. 40, q. un., nn. 6–11 (Vat., 8.468–70). For a summary of various texts, see Minges, *Ioannis Duns Scoti doctrina*, 2.391–400; Idem, "Bedeutung von Objekt, Umständen und Zweck für die Sittlichkeit eines Aktes nach Duns Scotus," *Philosophisches Jahrbuch* 19 (1906): 338–47.

stance, consider the differences between eating a stone, eating grass, and eating ham. If we know what a human is and we know something about human nutrition and eating, then we can judge that it is suitable for him to eat ham. Since human nutritive powers differ from those of grazing animals, we know that grass is unsuitable for humans and consequently that humans cannot reasonably eat grass. Similarly, a stone is nutritional neither for humans nor for grazing animals. Unlike other animals, humans can make an intellectual judgment concerning the suitability of the object and act accordingly.

Scotus generally states that an act's first goodness comes from the object, although in *Ord.* 2, d. 40, he argues that the first goodness comes from the will because the will is the efficient cause of any moral act.[74] In this passage he states that any natural act is good if it is appropriate in respect to its efficient cause, object, end, and form. The connection to Aristotle's four causes is plain. Only the material cause is missing. But the object is the material cause because, as we have seen, the object is also described as an object's matter. Moreover, in the early *Lectura* Scotus mentions that the act's greatest goodness does not come "from the circumstance of object or matter" as if they are the same.[75]

An act is the kind of thing that is blameworthy or praiseworthy because it is efficiently caused by the will. But the object still more clearly puts the act more firmly into a moral category, although the act cannot be more fully evaluated until it is placed in the species. Consequently, the first goodness of the act comes from the will in the sense that the efficient cause makes it the kind of act that is freely chosen, and therefore can be morally good or bad. But the first goodness comes from the object if we are looking more carefully at the distinction between different kinds of free acts. Goodness from the efficient cause is common to both good and bad human acts. Goodness from the object is present only in good acts and some bad acts.

---

74. Scotus, *Ord.* 2, d. 40, q. un., n. 9 (Vat., 8.469). For the reconciliation of this passage with others, see Hugh MacCaghwell, *Conciliationes,* Quod 19, con. 6 (Wadding ed., 12.572).

75. Scotus, *Lect.* 2, d. 40, q. un., n. 9 (Vat., 19.391).

Scotus most often states that the first goodness is that generic goodness that comes from the object.[76] This presupposes that the act was freely willed and consequently does not directly contradict his statement that a prior goodness comes from the will. The difference between the two positions seems to be that in most passages he presupposes that the act has been freely chosen, and consequently he does not need to mention the will's causality. This use of "generic goodness" to indicate the goodness that comes from the object has its roots in the early thirteenth century. Thomas Aquinas attests to the usage of generic goodness or evil for what he describes as specific goodness or evil, although he also develops his own distinctive view that goodness and badness essentially distinguish human acts.[77] In contrast, Scotus thinks that the act's specific goodness comes from further determination by the circumstances, and most especially by the end. The object shows a potentiality to be determined to a good act. But the determination must be done by additional features. According to him, the object really puts the act in a genus rather than a species. At least some circumstances are needed to distinguish between acts that belong to different species.

Scotus's distinctive view might be confusing because in many contexts his description of moral objects resembles that of Thomas. For example, Scotus states that almsgiving has its characteristic features from the object. There is no obvious difference between Thomas and Scotus on this point. But unlike Thomas, Scotus thinks that almsgiving lacks specific goodness. The act must be further determined by circumstances. For instance, giving alms is morally good when it is given (1) from one's own money, (2) to a poor person in need, (3) in a place that is appropriate, and (4) for the love of God.[78] The most principle circumstance is the fourth, which is the end. Here Scotus mentions God as a morally good end and not as loved through the supernatural virtue of charity. The key point here is that for Scotus the

76. Scotus, *Ord.* 2, d. 7, n. 29 (Vat., 8.89); Idem, *Quod* 18, n. [6]14 (Alluntis ed., 637).

77. Thomas, *S.T.*, I-II, q. 18, art. 2, resp. For the context, see Ramirez, *De actibus humanis*, 527–42.

78. Scotus, *Ord.* 2, d. 7, q. un., n. 32 (Vat., 8.90).

almsgiving's intrinsic end is unimportant. There must be another end willed by the agent, which in this case happens to be God.

Scotus does think that it is possible for there to be no extrinsic end that is willed, but in such cases the act will not be morally good since it is missing the specific goodness that primarily comes from the end. There are two ways in which the circumstance that comes from the end might be missing.[79] First, there may be no end at all. Second, there might be a contrary end. For instance, almsgiving could be morally good, evil, or indifferent. It is good when the end is God. Giving alms out of vainglory or another bad end makes the almsgiving evil. These ends are incompatible with doing it for God. Third, the almsgiving might be performed without any thought for the further purpose, or at least without thought for a morally good or bad further purpose. In such a case, goodness or badness from the circumstance of the end is missing, and the act is indifferent. The mere generic goodness of the object is insufficient to make the act good unless it is joined by a goodness that comes from the end. Otherwise, the act is bad or indifferent.

On Scotus's account there is a sharp division between the end and the object. Although some acts such as eating have ends that are fixed by nature, this end is not sufficient for the moral characterization of the act.[80] An act is good only when the agent intends a separate end that is due to the act according to right reason. An act is better when better circumstances and especially better ends are willed by the agent.[81] For example, going to church can be good when the agent goes out of obedience, or to worship God, or to edify one's neighbor. The act is even better if he goes for all three reasons, since each end adds its own further goodness.

Although the end is the most principal circumstance, an act must have other good circumstances in order for the act to be good. Scotus

79. Scotus, *Ord.* 2, d. 7, q. un., nn. 35, 37 (Vat., 8.91–92); Idem, *Quod* 18, nn. 7[20] (Alluntis ed., 639–40). Cf. Idem, *Ord.* 2, d. 7, n. 77 (Vat., 8.112).

80. Scotus, *Lect.* 2, d. 40, q. un., n. 9 (Vat., 19.391). This example is taken from the Franciscan tradition, which has its roots in John of Rupella. See Lottin, *Psychologie et morale*, 2.469–70.

81. Scotus, *Quod* 18, n. [8]22 (Alluntis ed., 641).

does not develop the traditional list of circumstances, but he does establish an order of importance for four.[82] As we have seen, the end is first. After the end comes the way in which something is done. Other "formal" circumstances might also be placed here. The less important circumstances are extrinsic to the act, namely time and then place. It is not evident to me why Scotus places time and place in this order, but the schema is clearly (1) the end, (2) the mode and perhaps other intrinsic circumstances, (3) the time, and (4) the place. Scotus also does not mention whether at times a lower placed circumstance might be higher than another one, but it seems that it would be, as in the case of someone who commits sacrilege by stealing in church. But it might also be the case that the place would be part of the object.

The circumstance and indeed the object are morally significant insofar as they show a consonance or dissonance with the right reason of a freely acting agent. The human act as opposed to a merely animal act is distinctive not only in that the act is chosen by the will, but also because the human intellectually judges that the act is reasonable.[83] The object and circumstances can make the act morally good only if they are dictated by right reason. Loving God is good merely on account of its object.[84] The reason is that no circumstances can make such an act evil since there is no way in which loving God can be done too much or incorrectly. Similarly, hating God is intrinsically repugnant to reason, since it is opposed to this act. Other acts are indifferent in their genus or even in their species, since it is the circumstances that make them good or bad.

Whereas Thomas argues that many acts are good on account of their object unless made bad by their circumstances, Scotus thinks that, apart from loving God, acts must be made good by the circumstances as well as the object. Circumstances are not only a sufficient

---

82. Scotus Quod 18, n. [6]15 (Alluntis ed., 637–38); Idem, *Ord.* 2, d. 40, q. un., n. 10 (Vat., 8.470).

83. Scotus, *Ord.* 1, d. 17, p. 1, qq. 1–2, nn. 92–97 (Vat., 5.184–88); Idem, Quod 18, [3]9–[4]12 (Alluntis ed., 632–35).

84. Scotus, *Ord.* 4, d. 26, q. un, nn. 3–4 (Wadding ed., 9.575–76); Idem, *R. P.* 4, d. 28, q. un., n. 6 (Wadding ed., 11.2.787); Idem, *Ord.*, prol., pars 5, qq. 1–2. n. 362 (Vat., 1.234–35).

condition for an act's badness, but they are a necessary condition for its goodness. For instance, even a normally virtuous act such as penance is good only on account of its circumstances. Judas's act of penance was not distinct as an act of penance from that of Peter or other justified sinners, but it lacked the good end. Scotus writes:

Not every act of penance suffices for the removal of sin … but it is necessary that the act be ordered, and most of all from the circumstance of the end, which is first among the circumstances of the moral act. However, Judas did not do penance with this circumstance, that is, from the love of God.[85]

The difference between Peter's penance and that of Judas is in the end rather than in the object. Similarly, Scotus thinks that attrition, which is roughly an imperfect sorrow for sin without grace, is the same species of movement as contrition, which is the perfect sorrow for sin that is accompanied by grace.[86] The difference between Judas's attrition and one that removes sin is whether there are additional good circumstances. Similarly, good attrition itself becomes contrition when God gives charity to the agent. There is no real change in the will's movement.

Scotus gives two arguments for his position that aside from hating God, no act is good merely on account of its object. The first argument is that God can command and make good any act that does not involve hating God.[87] The commandment to love God is true simply through its own terms. Therefore, this commandment can never be false. But God could alter any commandment that is not necessarily connected to it. For instance, the fifth commandment states "Thou shall not kill." Even if we assume that the person to be killed is innocent and useful to the political community, it does not follow that such killing is always wrong. In chapter 2, we have seen how Scotus

85. "non quicumque actus poenitendi sufficit ad deletionem peccati … sed oportet quod sit actus ordinatus, et maxime ex circumstantia finis, quae prima est inter circumstantias actus moralis; Judas autem non poenituit cum ista circumstantia, id est, ex dilectione Dei"; Scotus, *Ord.* 4, d. 14, q. 1, n. 19 (Wadding ed., 9.26). Cf. Idem, *R. P.* 4, d. 14, q. 1, n. 15 (Wadding ed., 11.2.710).

86. Scotus, *Ord.* 4, d. 14, q. 2, nn. 14–15 (Wadding ed., 11.2.710).

87. Scotus, *Ord.* 3, d. 38, q. un., nn. 17–18 (Vat., 10.299–300); Ibid., 3, d. 37, q. un. n. 13 (Vat., 10.276–77); Idem, *Lect.* 3, d. 38, q. un., n. 12 (Vat., 21.357–58).

thinks that God can dispense with those precepts that belong to the second table. For instance, God commanded Abraham to kill Isaac, and that Abraham's killing would have been meritorious. In one passage, Scotus describes "prohibited" and "nonprohibited" as circumstances of the act.[88] Consequently, the object of the meritorious killing and the murder is the same. The only difference is in the circumstance of whether it is prohibited by God.

The second argument for the position that only hating God is bad on account of its object is based on Scotus's thesis that certain words name generically evil acts only because they signify something other than the act itself.[89] Such acts are not evil merely on account of their objects, apart from these other features. Scotus develops this position in his attempt to reconcile the belief that only hating God is evil on account of its object with the traditional and Aristotelian position that many acts, such as adultery, theft, and lying, are evil in themselves. In his discussion of lying, Scotus states that these acts have names that signify both the act and its deformity. For example, "theft" signifies not just taking something, which is the act, but taking something that belongs to someone else against both his will and that of a superior authority *(dominus)*. "Adultery" signifies not only the natural act of coming together but also the defect that at least one party is married to someone else. These additional factors are all circumstances, and yet they make the act one of adultery. Similarly, "lying" is not evil on account of its object, but rather on account of the additional circumstances that make the act bad, such as intending to deceive. It is unclear how in this passage Scotus wishes to distinguish between the natural act and the moral act.

What is the relationship between these two arguments for the position that intrinsically evil acts (other than hating God) are not evil on account of their objects? The second argument is that these acts are bad not just on account of their natural kind but rather on account of further circumstances. But Scotus is unclear about why some of

88. Scotus, *Ord.* 3, d. 37, q. un., n. 13 (Vat., 10.277).

89. Scotus, *Ord.* 3, d. 38, q. un., nn. 19–21 (Vat., 10.300–302); Idem, *Lect.* 3, d. 38, n. 14 (Vat., 21.358).

these circumstances do not belong to the act's object. For instance, "belonging to another" seems to be a circumstance of theft and not part of the object, and the act signified by the word "adultery" is just natural copulation. Consider Scotus's argument that God could make any act (apart from loving God and associated acts) evil by his command. The existence or absence of such a command is itself a circumstance. Similarly, it would follow that apart from the hatred of God and those acts that are necessarily connected with it, God could make it such that any generically evil act, such as theft or adultery, is good. Although this argument establishes the point that only one kind of act is generically evil on account of its object, it does not shed light on the difference between objects and other kinds of circumstances. The one circumstance or feature that seems most important for an act's goodness or badness, namely that of being prohibited or commanded by God, is necessarily connected with those acts that are intrinsically good or evil on account of their object, namely loving and hating God.

A discussion that seemingly comes from Scotus's Parisian lectures poses a difficulty for these texts.[90] Scotus states that acts against the Ten Commandments are not bad because they are prohibited, but prohibited because they are bad. He adds that they can be known to be bad apart from any revelation. In this text, adultery and theft are evil on account of the natural law, and God's prohibition of them is a result of their already being evil. How can this passage be reconciled with his other passages? First, it may simply be that although Scotus thinks that God can dispense with the natural law, he also thinks that certain objects can be bad prior to a prohibition by God simply because they are in violation of the natural law. In this sense, "natural law" would be understood in the wider way. Second, Scotus may be making a remark in passing that conflicts with views expressed elsewhere. Third, the text may not be an adequate witness to Scotus's own views.

In general, Scotus holds that the object is insufficient for determining an act's goodness or badness. Often the circumstances seem more important for identifying an act. Moreover, Scotus often states that

90. William of Alnwick, *Additiones Magnae* 2, d. 22, n. 3 (Wadding ed., 11.1.361).

one and the same formal aspect of an object can belong to several different acts. Consequently, objects do not always specify acts. The clearest instances are given by the theological virtues.

Whereas Thomas states that the theological virtues have the same object materially considered, namely God, he states that the objects differ formally. In contrast, Scotus denies that there is any formal difference in the object.[91] They are theological virtues because they each immediately have God as their object. The difference between faith and charity is not a difference between objects, but instead a difference between the way in which the intellect obtains the object by faith and the will obtains it by love. Similarly, hope and love differ insofar as there is a difference between the two different inclinations of the will. By the *affectio commodi,* the agent loves God for his own sake, whereas by the *affectio iustitiae* he loves God for himself. Acts with the same object can differ specifically on account of the power to which they belong. Acts can also differ specifically on account of their perfection.[92] For instance, by hope God is imperfectly loved in this life, whereas in heaven he will be loved by a kind of cleaving *(tensio).* Both hope and this cleaving have exactly the same object and belong to the same part of the will. The difference is merely one of perfection.

Scotus does not sharply distinguish between the objects of the exterior and interior acts. He does state that the exterior act can be considered as the object of the interior act of willing and that consequently in some way its suitability is based on that of the interior, but he does not develop the way in which the exterior act is an object.[93] In general, even though Scotus makes suggestive hints that could be developed, he describes the difference between the interior and the exterior acts as merely between the eliciting and commanding act of the will and the elicited and commanded acts. The distinction between

91. Scotus, *Ord.* 3, d. 31, nn. 22–23 (Vat., 10.124); Ibid., 3, d. 26, q. un., nn. 89–111 (Vat., 10.7–37).

92. Scotus, *Ord.* 3, d. 31, nn. 14–18 (Vat., 10.119–22); cf. Ibid., 3, d. 26, q. un., n. 33 (Vat., 10.13–14).

93. Scotus, Quod 18, art. 3, nn. [14]38–[15]40 (Alluntis ed., 649–51).

the interior and exterior act does not play as great a role in Scotus's thought as it does in that of Thomas.

Scotus's description of the object, end, and circumstances is in some respect simpler than that of Thomas in that he keeps the three elements separate. Scotus does not describe the end as a kind of moral object, or indicate ways in which circumstances are parts of the object. In some respects, Scotus's account shifts the importance away from the object. First, although the first goodness comes from the object, this first goodness is, except in the cases of loving or hating God, insufficient for determining an act's moral value. Circumstances not only vitiate an act with a good object, but they also are needed for an act with a good object to be good rather than indifferent. Second, acts that belong to different species often have the same object under the same formal aspect. The object neither ensures the goodness of an act nor does it always specify the act.

WILLIAM OF OCKHAM

Ockham's account of the object, end, and circumstances resembles that of Thomas rather than that of Scotus in that the same items are sometimes circumstances and at other times objects or at least parts of the object. Like Thomas, Ockham gives different accounts for different kinds of acts. But the central distinction is not between interior and exterior acts, but rather between exterior acts and those interior acts that are necessarily virtuous or vicious.

Ockham thinks that a specific difference in the objects requires a specific difference in acts.[94] There may be exceptions when the objects are related, but so long as there is a formal difference in the objects, there will be a difference in the acts.[95] He often uses examples from cognition in order to illustrate his points about the objects of volition. For example, he defends his position that distinct objects require distinct virtues by appealing to the way in which distinct kinds of proposition are known by distinct cognitive acts. Since there is a

94. Ockham, *Q. V.*, q. 7, art. 1 (OTh, 8.323–27).
95. Ockham, *Rep.* 2, q. 17 (OTh, 5.393–94).

formal difference between principles and conclusions, the principles and conclusions of the same science are known by specifically different acts.

Like Scotus, Ockham thinks that God is in one way the object of the three theological virtues and the corresponding acquired virtues with the same name.[96] The difference between a theological virtue such as faith and the acquired virtue of faith is that the theological virtue not only has God as its object, but it is also infused by God. But immediately and more importantly, Ockham thinks that the three theological virtues have diverse complex objects:

For the proximate object of faith is this complex: "everything revealed by God is true in the way in which it is revealed by God." The object of hope [is] this complex: "future happiness will be conferred on a man on account of merits." The object of charity is this complex: "God and everything that God wills to be loved by me through charity." But then there is a doubt about the object of hope, since God and not a creature is at least a partial object: it can be said that the object of hope is this complex: "the divine vision and enjoyment will be conferred on a man on account of merits."[97]

Although God is an object of the theological virtues, Ockham does not think that God himself is immediately their whole object. The remark about hope shows that the inclusion of God in the object can be problematic. Nevertheless, in each case the object of the theological virtue indicates or can indicate how God is attained through the human act.

Ockham uses examples taken from cognition in order to show how different acts can have the same object.[98] First, he follows previous thinkers such as Scotus in distinguishing between the abstractive knowledge of an absent object and the intuitive knowledge of a pres-

96. Ockham, *Rep.* 3, q. 9 (OTh, 6.279–82); Idem, *Q. V.*, q. 7, art. 2 (OTh, 8.338).

97. "Nam obiectum proximum fidei est hoc complexum: 'omne revelatum a Deo est verum eo modo quo revelatur a Deo'. Obiectum spei, hoc complexum 'futura beatitudo est homini conferenda propter merita'. Obiectum caritatis est hoc complexum 'Deus et omne quod Deus vult diligi a me caritative'. Sed tunc dubium est de obiecto spei, quia videtur quod Deus sit saltem partiale obiectum et non creatura: potest dici quod hoc complexum sit obiectum spei 'visio et fruitio divina est homini conferenda propter merita'"; Ockham, *Rep.* 3, q. 9 (OTh, 6.283–84).

98. Ockham, *Q. V.*, q. 7, art. 1 (OTh, 8.326).

ent object. He along with others holds that such knowledge is specifically distinct even though the difference depends only on the absence or presence of the object to the knower and not a difference in the object itself. Second, he points out that the same proposition, such as "Socrates is bald," can be doubted or known. Doubt and knowledge are specifically distinct acts even when they have the same object. Therefore, the act cannot be entirely specified by the object.

Ockham's description of circumstances is confusing because, like Thomas, he sees that many circumstances affect the species of an act. Ockham also resembles Thomas in making the end an object that specifies the will's act.[99] But Ockham's emphasis on a necessarily virtuous will-act is distinctive.[100] Since Ockham thinks that the exterior act is merely the natural act, he also thinks that such exterior acts are contingently virtuous or vicious. They are said to be virtuous or vicious merely by extrinsic denomination, since the goodness or badness comes from another act. Ultimately, since there cannot be an infinite series of contingently virtuous acts, each contingently virtuous or vicious act can be traced back to an act of the will that is necessarily virtuous or vicious, and can said to be so by intrinsic denomination. Such an act must belong to the will. The moral value of such an act cannot be separated from it unless God decides to change the moral value of this kind of act.

The same exterior act can be virtuous or vicious depending on whether the act is caused by a virtuous or a vicious act of the will.[101] Ockham gives a different description of someone who while walking to church changes from doing so for a good end to a bad one, such as from worshiping God to vainglory. Previous thinkers describe such walking as one according to the species of nature but as two exterior acts. Ockham thinks that there is only the exterior act of walking and

99. Ockham, *Rep.* 3, q. 11 (OTh, 6.380–81). Freppert, *Basis of Morality*, 68–76.

100. Ockham, Quod 3, q. 14 (OTh, 9.255); Idem, *Q. V.*, q. 7, art. 1 (OTh, 8.327–28). Freppert, *Basis of Morality*, 53–60; Holopainen, *Foundations of Ethics*, 103–10.

101. Ockham, *Rep.* 3, q. 11 (OTh, 6.359–62); Idem, Quod 3, q. 14 (OTh, 9.253–56). For Ockham's understanding of exterior and interior acts, see Ockham, Quod 1, q. 20 (OTh, 9.101): Idem, Quod 3, q. 16 (OTh, 9.266); Idem, *Rep.* 3, q. 3, qm 11 (OTh, 6.383). For a discussion, see Osborne, "Separation of Interior and Exterior Acts," 129–39.

the two interior acts. He makes no distinction between the exterior act and the act according to the species of nature. Consequently, in such a case the numerically identical exterior act of walking is first good and then bad. Since the exterior act is virtuous or vicious only by extrinsic denomination, its moral value changes when the interior act changes. But the interior act that is good or bad by intrinsic denomination is necessarily so and consequently cannot change in value.

The interior act carries all the moral weight in Ockham's theory. Every feature that affects an act's moral value becomes part of the will's object, at least when an act of the will is necessarily virtuous or vicious.[102] Consequently, Ockham differs sharply from Thomas and Scotus in his inclusion of all the circumstances as part of this interior act's moral object, and in his description of right reason as either a circumstance or a partial object. When Ockham distinguishes between the object and morally relevant circumstances, he is describing an exterior act. For instance, the act of praying has the prayer's words as the object, whereas eating has food and walking has the path or road by which one walks. Each of these objects specifies the exterior act, which remains the same even when the agent's intention changes.

The interior act also has a common object. For instance, someone who wills to pray has the exterior act as the common object of his will. Nevertheless, although the end is a circumstance of the exterior act, it is the principal object of the interior act. Someone who prays for God's honor has God's honor as the principal object of his prayer. This principal object is more important than the common object. The other morally relevant circumstances are secondary objects. Ockham does not give a list of these secondary objects, but he mentions the example of someone who prays according to right reason, on Sunday, and in a church. It is helpful to contrast the exterior and interior acts with this example. The exterior act would have the words as the object and the following circumstances: God's honor (end), on Sunday (time), in church (place), and right reason. The interior act would have a principal object, namely God's honor, a common object, namely the exterior act of praying, and the following secondary par-

102. Ockham, Quod 3, q. 16 (OTh, 9.266–67).

tial objects: on Sunday, in church, and according to right reason. The circumstance of the end becomes the principal partial object of the interior act. The other circumstances are secondary partial objects. The exterior act of praying is the common object. The interior act seems to have no morally relevant circumstances. If such features are morally relevant, then they are secondary partial objects.

Ockham differs from his predecessors in his description of right reason as a circumstance of a contingently virtuous exterior act and as a secondary partial object of a necessarily virtuous interior act.[103] The reason for this description is that the reasonableness of an act is essential to its moral value. In order for an act to be virtuous, the agent must not only have habitual prudence, but he must actually judge that the act should be done. Moreover, Ockham attacks Scotus's view that right reason is merely a cause of the virtuous act because Ockham thinks that the causal relationship is a natural feature that could not affect the act's morality.[104] If an act of the will is necessarily virtuous, then it must conform to right reason. The inclusion of right reason as a secondary partial object means that this conformity is part of the act's description as willed. The relationship is not merely causal.

What does it mean for right reason to be a secondary partial object? For Ockham, right reason is part of the object insofar as the dictative judgment is. His theory has the interesting consequence that continence, temperance, and heroic virtue differ because each state has a correspondingly different judgment about what should be done. For instance, Ockham writes:

For the right reason which is the object of continence dictates that the will must flee those irregular pleasures which are now present [*inhaerentes*] when it should and as it is should etc. Right reason which is the object of the

---

103. Ockham, *Q.V.*, q. 7,, art. 4 (OTh, 8.393–95); Idem, *Q.V.*, q. 8 (OTh, 8.425–27). David W. Clark, "William of Ockham on Right Reason," *Speculum* 48 (1973): 15–20; Freppert, *Basis of Morality*, 50–55; Holopainen, *Foundations of Ethics*, 115–30; Osborne, "Ockham as a Divine-Command Theorist," 2–11.

104. Ockham, *Q. V.*, q. 7, art. 4 (OTh, 8.380–83); Idem, *Q. V.*, q. 8 (OTh, 8.414–15). Erwin Iserloh, *Gnade und Eucharistie in der Philosophischen Theologie des Wilhelm von Ockhams* (Wiesbaden: Franz Steiner, 1956), 57–59.

aforesaid temperance dictates that not only must it flee those irregular pleasures which are actually present [*inhaerentes*], but every occasion of such, for instance that a man not see pleasurable things, nor touch the beautiful, nor hear filthy things, and such concerning other occasions.[105]

Similarly, Ockham thinks that the right reason of the heroic dictates that something should be done that exceeds the ordinary. Consequently, although Scotus thinks that the different grades of virtue and vice are distinct according to degree (with the exception of extraordinarily depraved habits), Ockham thinks that they are specifically distinct.[106]

Ockham's expansion of what belongs to the intrinsically virtuous act's object makes it difficult to compare him with his predecessors over whether certain acts are always bad on account of their object. Although Ockham thinks that no exterior act is necessarily bad, this view is unsurprising since he thinks that the exterior act is indistinct from the natural act. Moreover, Ockham goes farther than Scotus in his belief that God could change the moral value of not only every act directed to one's neighbor, but even of loving and hating God.[107] According to Ockham, hating God could be made virtuous if God commanded such hate. Like Scotus, Ockham thinks that certain words such as "adultery" and "murder" always signify bad acts because they signify not just the act itself but also connote the act's badness.[108] Consequently, in some respects Ockham even more than Scotus thinks that no act by itself is necessarily bad apart from a divine command. He usually states that acts are necessarily bad so long as the divine prohibition of them is assumed. Nevertheless, Ockham

105. "Nam recta ratio quae est obiectum continentiae dictat quod voluntas debet fugere concupiscentias pravas iam inhaerentes quando oportet et ut oportet etc. Recta autem ratio quae est obiectum praedictae temperantiae dictat quod non tantum debet fugere concupiscentias pravas actualiter inhaerentes sed omnes occasiones talium, puta quod homo non videat delectabilia, pulcra non tangat, nec audiat turpia colloquia, et sic de aliis occasionibus"; Ockham, *Q. V.*, q. 6, art. 10 (OTh, 8.274–75).

106. Scotus, *Ord.* 3, d. 34, q. un. (Vat., 10.214).

107. Ockham, *Rep.* 2, q. 15 (OTh, 5.353).

108. Ockham, *Rep.* 2, q. 15 (OTh, 5.352–53); Idem, *Rep.* 4, q. 16 (OTh, 7.352). See Thomas M. Osborne, "Ockham as a Divine-Command Theorist," 12–16; Pinckaers, *Ce qu'on ne peut jamais faire*, 43–50.

does not describe these elements that make the act bad as mere circumstances. For Ockham, the conformity and also apparently the lack of conformity is a secondary object of the interior act. So there is a way in which these necessarily bad acts are bad on account of their object. But Ockham can hold this view because he has expanded the object to include anything that would make the act necessarily bad.

In general, Ockham's focus on the necessarily virtuous act causes him to give more weight to circumstances as specifying an act, and to make more distinctions between different species of action. Not only does he distinguish between the different grades of virtue on account of the way in which right reason is a partial object, but he also uses circumstances to distinguish between the moral virtue of a pagan and that of a Christian.[109] Since the Christian principally has God as his end and is concerned with following God's command, a Christian's act of temperance has a different object from that of a pagan.

In many respect, Ockham's account of the object and circumstances is simpler than that of his predecessors. Ockham replaces the traditional threefold division between exterior act, interior act, and natural act with a twofold division between an exterior act and an interior act that is moral by intrinsic denomination. Interior acts that are not moral by intrinsic denomination share the same moral characteristics as exterior acts. Since Ockham simplifies the act's structure, he gives a simpler account of the object. The exterior act's object is like the natural object and is moral only by extrinsic denomination. In contrast, the necessarily virtuous act's object includes anything that is relevant to the act's morality, including what are normally described as circumstances.

When it comes to the most fundamental unit of the moral act for Ockham, namely the necessarily virtuous or vicious act, there are no circumstances. The circumstance of the end is the principal partial object, and the other circumstances are secondary partial objects. For Ockham, there is a way in which the circumstances either have less or more moral importance than they have in Thomas or especially Scotus. They are less important because they cease to be circumstances

109. Ockham, Q. V., q. 7, art. 4 (OTh, 8.403): Idem, Rep. 4, qq. 3–4 (OTh, 7.58).

precisely when they have moral weight. They are more important because when they are relevant they become part of the object and consequently more than just circumstances.

OBJECT, END, CIRCUMSTANCES

The differences between Thomas, Scotus, and Ockham are made especially clear in their understanding of (1) the way in which goodness comes from the object, (2) the relationship between the object and the end, (3) the nature of circumstances, and (4) the way in which an object or circumstances is constituted by the order of reason. First, Thomas thinks that the primary goodness comes from the object because it places the act in a moral species. Consequently, an act with a good object will be good unless it is vitiated by the circumstances or the end. Thomas describes this goodness from the object as "specific," although he states that it corresponds to the "generic goodness" of many contemporaries. In contrast, Scotus thinks that the goodness from the object is generic in the sense that it must be further determined by circumstances in order for the act to be good. Someone who wills a good object such as almsgiving for its own sake does not perform a good act. Ockham's view resembles that of Thomas in that at least for every necessarily good act the goodness comes from the object. But since such objects include much of what Scotus and even Thomas would number among the circumstances, his view amounts to a redefinition of what a moral object is.

Second, the different views of an object's goodness reflect a conflict over the relationship between the object and the end. All three thinkers draw an intrinsic connection between the goodness of an action and the end. For Scotus, the end is a distinct circumstance that must be willed in order for an act to be good even when the act's object is good. For Thomas and Ockham, the end is the object of the interior act. Thomas in some ways remains closer to the traditional discussion of the object because he states that the same object is both the proximate end of the interior act and the matter of the exterior act. Consequently, what is often considered to be an object or matter is also an end. The difference is in the way in which it is considered. When Thomas distinguishes between the object and the end, he is either making this distinction or another distinction between the object (proximate end) and the circumstance of the end (remote end). But for Ockham, the exterior act's object has no necessary moral value. The exterior act's object is itself not an end but must be ordered to an end by the agent. Only the necessarily virtuous or vicious act has the end as its principal, but not its only, object.

The disagreement over the role of the end is connected to larger differences over all of the circumstances. Thomas accepts the traditional list of seven circumstances but he makes some qualifications. The circumstance "what" must be distinguished from the "what" that is the act's matter, and the circumstance of the end must be distinguished from the proximate end, which is the interior act's object. With respect to the other circumstances, what is ordinarily a circumstance can be a condition of the object, such as a location in church might be part of sacrilege's object. Scotus more sharply separates the circumstance from the object because he needs the circumstances to make an act specifically good. Ockham seems to retain the distinction between circumstances and object with respect to the exterior act, but he states that any morally relevant circumstances are secondary partial objects of a necessarily virtuous interior act.

An underlying cause of the abovementioned differences is a disagreement over the way in which an object can be repugnant to the order of reason. For Thomas, many objects are inherently reasonable or unreasonable. For instance, adultery can never be reasonable, and almsgiving will be good unless a circumstance makes it unreasonable. In contrast, Scotus thinks that loving God is the only intrinsically fully reasonable object, and that hating God is the only intrinsically fully unreasonable object. Every act that is not necessarily related to these acts could be made good or bad by God's command. For Scotus, the divine command can be described as a circumstance of an act. Ockham extends the list of circumstances to include even right reason. According to Ockham, right reason is not only a cause of the good act, but also a circumstance of a contingently virtuous act and a secondary partial object of a necessarily virtuous act. For Ockham, any circumstance can become a secondary partial object of a necessarily virtuous act insofar as it conforms to right reason, and they become the same kind of objects of a necessarily vicious act if they violate right reason. Scotus and Ockham increasingly expand the list of circumstances to include morally relevant items that were described differently by earlier thinkers.

The issues discussed in this chapter most clearly illustrate the second and third themes of this book, namely the differences over the role of the will and a new kind of mental causation. With respect to the will's role, Thomas most of all bases the specification of the action on the order of reason. The object is determined by reason, and the act of the will is specified by the object. Scotus separates the object from the end and focuses particularly on the agent's own end in willing the object. In some cases distinct acts can have exactly the same formal object presented by the intellect, as is the case with the theological virtues. The specific difference between these acts is based only on the way in which the object is willed. Ockham ultimately focuses almost entirely on interior acts of the will.

Ockham's focus on interior will acts may show a shift in thinking about human action. For Thomas, the interior and exterior acts are part of one human act much in the same way as one substance is composed of matter and form. Although Scotus thinks of the exterior act as having its own significance apart from the interior act, he like Thomas thinks of the exterior act as intrinsically moral. Ockham redescribes the exterior act in such a way that it becomes what Thomas and Scotus would describe as the natural species of an act. According to Ockham, the only intrinsically moral acts are interior in the sense that they cannot be observed by others, and they are acts of the will. Visible acts are only physical acts that have their value insofar as they are efficiently caused by the inner acts of the will.

5

INDIFFERENT, GOOD, AND MERITORIOUS ACTS

Medieval discussions of how acts are characterized are ultimately ordered to considerations about how such acts should be evaluated. Thomas, Scotus, and Ockham not only have different ways of understanding an act's object and circumstances, but they also disagree about the different kinds of goodness and badness indicated by these features. The three kinds of goodness that belong to acts are natural goodness, moral goodness, and supernatural merit.

The distinction between natural goodness and the other two kinds of goodness is a distinction between the goodness of acts in general and the goodness that belongs to distinctively human acts. An act has natural goodness because it is a natural act, whereas it has the other kinds of goodness insofar as the distinctively human act corresponds to right reason. In chapter 4, we have seen that Thomas and Scotus distinguish between (1) the act's natural species, (2) the interior act, and (3) the exterior act. Different kinds of acts are good in different ways. An act's natural species is the basis of its natural goodness. Rendering the marriage debt and adultery can both belong to the same natural species, namely human reproduction. The act is naturally good on account of the act's being, or more particularly in the way in the act attains its natural end, which is the production of a healthy child. In contrast, both interior and exterior acts can have moral goodness and an additional goodness that is merit.

Natural goodness is "natural" in the way that the natural is distinct from the rational. Moral goodness can be described as a different kind of natural goodness, if by "natural" we do not mean "natural" as distinct from "rational," but instead as distinct from what God out of his own graciousness adds to nature. The goodness of merit is natural in neither way. An act is meritorious insofar as it somehow directs or is directed to a supernatural reward or demeritorious insofar as God will punish it and it earns the weakening or withdrawal of God's favor and gifts. Merit and demerit do not consist in an act's mere moral goodness or badness, although, at least in the order that God has established, moral goodness is a necessary condition for merit.

First, we will consider the distinction between the kinds of acts to which goodness can accrue, namely the act in its natural species, the interior act, and the exterior act. In particular, there is disagreement over the way in which the exterior act's moral worth and merit can be connected with that of the interior act. Second, we will examine more narrowly moral goodness and badness, as well as the question of whether acts can be morally indifferent. Third, we will consider the way in which moral goodness is related to merit, and whether agents who have charity can perform morally good acts that are indifferent to merit. The first point is especially connected to the question of how the goodness of free human acts is connected with natural inclination. All three points reflect disagreements over the explanatory power of the human and even divine will, and over how acts are caused.

NATURAL AND MORAL GOODNESS

Medieval thinkers thought successful murder deserves a worse punishment than merely attempted murder. Similarly, martyrdom merits a special reward that the mere readiness to be martyred does not. They agree that the completion of an act affects the worth of the whole act, although they differ in their explanations of how it does.[1] Debates over

1. Osborne, "Interior and Exterior Acts," 111–22.

the difference between mere choice and an act's completion occur in discussions over the connection between the interior and the exterior act. There is disagreement both over whether the exterior act has its own moral worth and also over what the exterior act is. The first disagreement is partially based on the second disagreement.

What is the exterior act? In chapter 4, we have seen that for Thomas the exterior act has its own object, which can also be considered as the act's matter, or as the proximate end and object of the interior act. The interior and exterior act are distinct in their natural species, although they form together one human act.[2] The interior act belongs to the intellect and the will, whereas the exterior act primarily belongs to other moving powers insofar as they are commanded by the intellect and used by the will. The interior act can involve every stage of the act up to command and choice, whereas the exterior act follows the intellect's command, and consists in the will's use *(uti)*. The interior and exterior act together are parts of one human act. Sometimes the interior act's willing of the end has the same moral goodness as the exterior act that is willed.[3] For instance, when someone picks up a stick to remove an obstacle in another's path, the exterior act of picking up the stick has the same moral goodness as willing to move the obstruction. At other times the interior act is affected by the goodness or badness of the exterior act. For instance, if someone gives alms for the sake of penance, then the act has goodness not only from willing the penance, but also from the almsgiving itself. Similarly, if someone steals in order to give alms, then the interior act of almsgiving is vitiated by the badness of the exterior act that is chosen as a means.[4]

Which act is prior with respect to the whole act's moral goodness? Thomas states that interior and exterior acts each have a different kind of priority.[5] Since the interior act's moral worth depends upon

2. Thomas, *S.T.*, I-II, q. 20, art. 3, ad 1; q. 17, art. 4. Gallagher, "Interior and Exterior Acts"; Jensen, *Good and Evil Acts,* 73–131; McInerny, *Aquinas on Human Action,* 82–86, 98–101; Idem, *Ethica Thomistica: The Moral Philosophy of Thomas Aquinas,* rev. ed. (Washington, D.C.: The Catholic University of America Press, 1997), 81–83.

3. Thomas, *S.T.*, I-II, q. 20, art. 3.   4. Thomas, *S.T.*, I-II, q. 20, art. 2.
5. Thomas, *S.T.*, I-II, q. 20, art. 1.

the reasonableness of the exterior act's object and circumstance, the exterior act has a priority in the order of reason. It also has a priority in that the exterior object must first be apprehended by reason as good in order for there to be an interior act. But the exterior act has goodness only insofar as the human act proceeds from the interior act of the will. Consequently, the interior act's goodness is prior with respect to the act's execution.

The exterior act is intrinsically moral. Its species includes its goodness or badness.[6] The exterior act is not merely the act of a human power according to its natural species, but insofar as it is commanded by an interior act. For instance, the same act of walking to church may continue when the agent has a good or a bad intention. This act of walking is not the exterior act, but rather one natural act. The exterior acts of walking are specified and distinct in the way that the interior acts are. The walking to church with a good intention has as an exterior act the exercise of the powers of local movement used in walking, but merely insofar as these powers are moved by the interior act of willing a good end. Once the interior act of walking changes, there is a new exterior act even though the physical act of walking remains exactly the same.

The exterior act adds to the interior act's essential goodness or malice in two different manners, namely insofar as it affects the act of willing and also insofar as the exterior act has its own moral worth.[7] According to the first manner, the exterior act can affect the act's worth in three different ways. First, it can increase the number of interior acts. For instance, someone who wants to steal something might be frustrated in his first attempt, and this frustration might lead to a second attempt and consequently a second interior act of theft. Second, the length of the act might increase. Someone who in passing consents to an unintentionally unsuccessful adultery is less involved in the act than someone who spends several hours in the complete act. Third, the completion of the act can make the willing more intense. Someone

6. Thomas, *S.T.*, I-II, q. 20, art. 6; Idem, 2 *Sent.*, d. 40, q. 1, art. 4 (Madonnet ed., 2.1019–21).

7. Thomas, *S.T.*, I-II, q. 20, art. 4; Idem, 2 *Sent.*, d. 40, q. 1, art. 3 (Mandonnet ed., 2.1015–19).

who successfully completes adultery enjoys it more and is somehow able to more completely will it than someone who briefly consents and is frustrated. In all three instances, the exterior act adds to the act's goodness or malice only insofar as it adds to that of the interior act.

According to the second manner, the exterior act has goodness insofar as its object and circumstances are the term and end of the interior act. The exterior act is needed to complete the act. Thomas suggests two ways in which the exterior act on its own contributes to the act's goodness. First, if someone does not wish to complete the act, then the act is to some extent involuntary and consequently it loses some of its goodness or badness. Second, there may be some way in which the exterior act involves a secondary or accidental goodness or badness. This second point is not expressed in the *Prima Secundae,* in which Thomas merely states that if the act's incompletion is entirely involuntary, it does not add to the punishment or reward.[8] However, in his early *Sentence Commentary* and in the *De Malo,* Thomas follows a long-standing tradition in holding that the exterior act also has a distinct moral value insofar as the successful completion of an act earns an "accidental" reward or punishment.[9]

Scotus clearly argues not only that the exterior act is intrinsically good or bad, but also that it has a moral goodness or badness that is distinct from that of the interior act.[10] He resembles Thomas in his account of the exterior act as an act of a human power that is under the will's control. Although the interior act is immediately an act of the will, the exterior act belongs immediately to another power. Because the exterior act ultimately is caused by the will, the exterior act is an intrinsically moral act and distinct from the act in its natural species.

He distinguishes sharply between the natural goodness of the act and moral goodness, which is necessarily connected to right reason. Scotus writes that "the moral goodness of an act is from an aggregation of everything appropriate for the act, not absolutely from the

8. Thomas, *S.T.,* I-II, q. 20, art. 4, resp.

9. Thomas, 2 *Sent.,* d. 40, q. 1, art. 3, sol. (Mandonnet ed., 2.1017); Idem, *De Malo,* q. 2, art. 2, ad 8 (Leonine, 23.34).

10. Osborne, "Interior and Exterior Acts," 122–29.

act's nature, but those things which are appropriate for it according to right reason."[11] Correctness in the interior act causes a corresponding correctness in the exterior act.[12] The connection to right reason ensures that the same act cannot change its moral value. Scotus notes that both the exterior and the interior act cannot change from correct to incorrect, since the human act is not something that remains apart from the willing in accordance to or against right reason. Scotus makes a similar point in his discussions of the way in which someone who avoids one mortal sin is capable of avoiding all mortal sin.[13] If someone wills to avoid sin, he is incapable of sinning at the same time. He retains his ability to sin only because he can sin by committing a different act in the future. Scotus assumes that numerically the same human act cannot be first good and then bad.

Scotus also defends the thesis that the exterior act has its own moral worth even apart from its effect on the interior act. By attributing a greater moral worth to the exterior act than Thomas does, Scotus follows a widespread medieval and Franciscan tradition. In his explicit discussion of the exterior act's moral value, Scotus is not concerned with whether the exterior act affects the interior act's intensity or duration, or whether it causes a new interior act. These issues involve the way in which the exterior act changes the interior act. But he wishes to isolate the exterior act's moral worth.[14] His position rests on two theses. First, he defends the position that an act is imputable not only if it is immediately elicited by the will, but also if it is elicited by powers that themselves are commanded by the will.[15] Since an act must be imputable to the agent in order for it to have moral value, he must hold that the exterior act is itself imputable. Second, he defends the position that

---

11. "bonitas actus moralis est ex aggregatione omnium convenientium actui, non absolute ex natura actus, sed quae conveniunt ei secundum recta rationem"; Scotus, 2 *Sent.*, d. 40, q. un., n. 8 (Vat., 8.469).

12. Scotus, Quod 18, art. 3, n. [16] 42 (Alluntis ed., 652–53).

13. Scotus, *Ord.* 2, d. 28, q. un., n. 17 (Vat., 8.297–98); Idem, *Lect.* 2, d. 28, q. un., n. 16 (Vat., 19.278). Cf. Franciscus Lychetus, *Commentarius in Quod* 18, n. 21 (Wadding ed., 12.488–89).

14. Scotus, Quod 18, n. [2] 5 (Alluntis ed., 631–32).

15. Scotus, Quod 18, art. 2, nn. [10] 26–29 (Alluntis ed., 644–46).

an exterior act has its own conformity or lack of conformity with right reason.[16] Since moral goodness consists in conformity to right reason, the exterior act would lack such goodness if it were incapable of such conformity, or if its conformity were the same as that of the interior act.

Although Ockham argues directly against Scotus's position that the exterior act has its own moral worth, their differences are difficult to evaluate because Ockham gives a different account of what an exterior act is.[17] We have seen already in chapter 4 that Ockham does not distinguish between the exterior act and the act in its natural species. Ockham's rejection of Scotus's position that the exterior act has its own moral worth depends upon this new description of what the exterior act is. Whereas previous thinkers had stated that someone who changes his intention while walking to church performs two exterior acts, Ockham states that there is only one exterior act even though there are two different interior acts. He holds this view because the exterior act is merely the natural act. Consequently, numerically the same exterior act can be good and bad at different times. This ability to be good or bad at different times is a kind of indifference to moral goodness.

Ockham not only gives a new description of what the exterior act is, but he also adds to the class of interior acts. Whereas previous thinkers had generally called commanded acts such as thinking exterior acts, Ockham describes them as interior acts.[18] For Ockham, an interior act seems to belong to the "interior" as opposed to the "exterior" powers. For instance, walking is an exterior act because it belongs to an exterior power rather than because it is commanded or elicited by the will. All exterior acts and some interior acts are good merely by extrinsic denomination. Any attribution of moral worth to them is also about the intrinsically moral act from which they proceed. Consequently, no exterior act has its own moral worth.

Thomas gives the most complicated account of what acts can have

16. Scotus, Quod 18, art. 3, n. [12] 32 (Alluntis ed., 647).

17. Ockham, Quod 1, q. 20 (OTh, 9.99–106). Cf. Idem, *Rep.* 3, q. 11 (OTh, 6.370–71, 375–80). For discussions, see Holopainen, *Foundations of Ethics*, 20–22; Osborne, "Interior and Exterior Acts," 129–38.

18. Ockham, *Rep.* 4, q. 16 (OTh, 7.358–59); Idem, *Q. V.* 7, art. 1 (OTh, 8.328).

moral value. For Thomas, the exterior act as well as the interior act is essentially good or bad. Although they are distinct physical acts, they are both parts of one human act. Both the interior and exterior acts contribute in different ways to the whole act's goodness or badness. Scotus not only thinks that the exterior act is a moral act, but he also states that it has its own moral worth. He argues for this position by stating that the exterior act has its own conformity to right reason. This argument seems to separate the interior act from the exterior act more than Thomas would allow. In contrast, Ockham partially resembles Thomas in stating that the exterior act's moral worth comes from that of the interior act. However, Ockham departs from both Thomas and Scotus by holding that the exterior act is a physical act, and that numerically the same exterior act can change from good to bad. Ockham's new account of the exterior act will also be important for his description of indifferent acts.

Morally Good, Bad, and Indifferent

One of the most significant differences between medieval thinkers concerning the value of acts is over whether there are some acts that are neither morally good nor bad, but indifferent. Many early Scholastics up to the time of Bonaventure did not carefully distinguish in their arguments between indifference with respect to moral goodness and indifference with respect to merit.[19] But at least since the time of Thomas Aquinas, the distinction was widely recognized.

Although Thomas and Scotus disagree over whether there are morally indifferent individual acts, they more or less agree over the importance of the issue for a proper understanding of the connection between the act's value and deliberation.[20] In contrast, Ockham's ap-

---

19. Bonaventure, 2 *Sent.*, d. 41, art. 1, q. 3 (*Opera*, 2.942–46). For the general background, see Lottin, *Psychologie et morale*, 2.469–82.

20. For a comparison of Thomas with Scotus, see especially Leo Elders, "La théorie Scotiste de l'acte indifférant et sa critique par Cajetan," in *Regnum Hominis et Regnum Dei*, Acta Quarti Congressus Scotistici Internationalis Patavii 24–29 septembris 1976, ed. Camille Bérubé (Rome: Societas Internationalis Scotistica, 1978), Studia Scholastico-Scotistica 7, 2.207–14; Klaus Hedwig, "Actus indifferens: Über die Theorie

proach presupposes at least one of Scotus's conclusions as a premise, namely that there are indifferent acts of the will. Consequently, it is best to first consider the disagreements between Thomas and Scotus before treating Ockham's position separately.

Both Thomas and Scotus agree that whereas some objects are themselves good or bad, others are indifferent. Consequently, certain kinds of acts are morally indifferent. For instance, Thomas notes that the object of almsgiving is itself reasonable, whereas the object of theft, which is taking another's property, is in itself against reason.[21] In the absence of bad circumstances, almsgiving is good, and theft is always bad. However, "picking up a stick" by itself is neither reasonable nor unreasonable. As a kind of act, picking up a stick is indifferent.

The fundamental disagreement between Scotus and Thomas is over the existence of particular morally indifferent acts. Thomas argues that although some kinds of acts may be morally neutral, no individual acts can be.[22] The reason for this position is that any individual act is chosen with morally relevant circumstances, and most importantly for an end that is either reasonable or not. For instance, no one picks up a stick for its own sake. Someone might do so in order to beat an innocent person. In such a case, the act is bad. Or someone might pick up a stick to illustrate the example of an act that is indifferent in kind. In such a case, the act can be good if it is not vitiated by other circumstances. Thomas's position presupposes that every human act is chosen for an end, and that at least this end is reasonable or unreasonable.

Scotus argues that many particular acts are morally indifferent. One of his principal arguments is based on his view that someone can act without deliberating concerning a morally relevant end. He makes this argument both in the early *Lectura* and in his later Paris lectures, although he does not explicitly use it in the *Ordinatio*. In the *Lectura*, he writes that "if someone, after acquiring virtue, elicits an act which

---

des indifferenten Handelns bei Thomas von Aquin und Duns Scotus," *Philosophisches Jahrbuch* 95 (1988): 120–31.

21. Thomas, 2 *Sent.*, d. 40, q. 1, art. 5 (Mandonnet ed., 2.1022–28); Idem, *De Malo*, q. 2, art. 5 (Leonine, 23.42–45); Idem, *S.T.*, I-II, q. 18, art. 8. See Lottin, *Psychologie et morale*, 2.482–88.

22. In addition to the texts cited above, see Thomas, *S.T.*, I-II, q. 18, art. 9.

is the kind that can be moral, but he does not elicit it by syllogizing from a moral principle, namely from the end, then [the act] is neither morally good nor bad."[23] The virtuous person would then perform an act that is neither virtuous nor vicious. It is not clear whether Scotus wishes to say here that such an act is performed for no end at all, or whether it is for an end that is not a moral principle. Since he does seem to think that an act such as almsgiving can be chosen without any end, he may think that in such cases the moral object is chosen for its own sake apart from any circumstance of the end.[24] Similarly, in a record of the Parisian lectures, he mentions that the just person can perform a morally indifferent but normally just act if he acts immediately and without deliberation, as when suddenly giving alms to a needy person.[25] In both texts, the agent seems to choose an object without choosing or intending any end, or at least any further end.

In the *Ordinatio*, Scotus gives two different arguments for the existence of particular morally indifferent acts. One argument addresses the acts of an agent who has already acquired virtue, whereas the other argument addresses the acts of an agent who is in the process of developing virtue. Scotus states that an already virtuous person can perform morally indifferent acts because the virtue might not be put to use: "it does not seem necessary that the will—having virtue—always necessarily uses virtue, but only when there occurs a passion so vehement that it would subvert reason unless it [the will] uses virtue."[26] This argument is similar to the argument in the *Lectura* and the Parisian lectures, since it assumes that even a virtuous person might choose a virtuous act apart from virtue. But in this text it is not explained how the virtuous person does so, although very possibly Scotus is thinking of the

23. "si aliquis post virtutem genitam elicit actum qui natus est esse moralis, non tamen elicit syllogizando ex principio morali, scilicet ex fine, non est bonus moraliter nec malus"; Scotus, *Lect.* 2, d. 41, q. un., n. 10 (Vat., 19.396).

24. Scotus, *Ord.* 2, d. 7, q. un., nn. 35, 37 (Vat., 8.91–92); Idem, Quod 18, nn. 7[20] (Alluntis ed., 639–40). Cf. Idem, *Ord.* 2, d. 7, n. 77 (Vat., 8.112).

25. *Additiones Magnae* 2, d. 41, q. un., n. 2 (Wadding ed., 11.1.408).

26. "quia non videtur necessitas quod voluntas—habens virtutem—semper utatur ea necessario, sed tantum quando occurit passio ita vehemens quod subvertat rationem nisi utatur virtute"; Scotus, *Ord.* 2, d. 41, q. un., n. 8 (Vat., 8.475).

case that the other texts mention, which is that of someone who does not deliberate about a morally good end.

An interesting consequence of Scotus's argument is the thesis that an already virtuous agent will be unable to perform a morally indifferent act when he is faced with a strong passion. Scotus's argument assumes that the will is not only free with respect to its choice, but there usually is no conditional necessity for it to perform a good act if it wishes to stay virtuous. However, when faced with passion, it seems necessary to choose well in order to avoid sin. This necessity is not an absolute necessity, since such necessity is incompatible with willing. Scotus seems to mean that the will has only two choices, namely (1) to give into passion, or (2) to use virtue. The first choice involves a morally bad act, whereas the second involves a morally good act. In such a case the agent is not free to elicit an indifferent act.

In the *Ordinatio*, Scotus's other argument for the existence of indifferent acts is concerned with the case of someone who is developing a virtue. Someone who acts out of vice performs bad acts. But anyone is free to choose the acts that are virtuous in kind. Nevertheless, Scotus argues that a virtuous habit is a necessary condition for virtuous action even though agents who are not yet virtuous can perform virtuous kinds of acts. He writes, "according to the Philosopher in Book II of the *Ethics*, the habit of justice is generated from just works, but they are not done justly; this [just] act is not morally good, since it is not from virtue."[27] The acts that lead to moral virtue are not morally bad, and yet they also lack a condition for moral goodness. Consequently, they must be morally indifferent.

These two arguments from the *Ordinatio*'s discussion of morally indifferent acts are brief and hard to relate to Scotus's wider views. In particular, it is hard to understand fully why Scotus argues that normally virtuous acts are indifferent if they are elicited without virtue. Although Scotus invokes Aristotle's authority, it is not clear how he intends to interpret the passage in this text. In a later report of Sco-

27. "secundum Philosophum II *Ethicorum*—habitus iustitiae generatur ex operibus iustis, non tamen iustis factis; iste actus non est bonus moraliter, quia non est ex virtute"; Scotus, *Ord.* 2, d. 41, q. un., n. 7 (Vat., 8.475).

tus's lectures, Scotus seems to interpret the same text of Aristotle as merely stating that some acts are neither just nor unjust, just as some individuals who are developing virtue are neither just nor unjust.[28] But in this passage of the *Ordinatio* Scotus clearly states that an act performed without virtue is indifferent.

In his commentary on Scotus's text, Francis Lychetus notes that Aristotle's text, along with Scotus's use of it, can be understood in two ways.[29] First, Scotus's use of it can be taken at face value, but then it seems to conflict with Scotus's position that moral goodness depends only on the conformity of the object and circumstances to right reason. Second, the statement can be reduced to an argument that a good act is not good unless it is performed deliberately in accordance with the circumstances that are required by right reason, such as the end. This second interpretation more closely corresponds to the text of the *Lectura* and an account of the Paris lectures, but it seems to conflict with at least a prima facie reading of the *Ordinatio*. Lychetus seems to favor the second reading. This second reading is more satisfying if one wishes to defend the passage as part of a system of Scotistic ethics. Nevertheless, the first prima facie reading is not only plausible but historically significant, since many later Scholastic theologians attributed to Scotus the view that an act must be produced by virtue in order for it to be morally good.[30]

This argument that virtue is a necessary condition for moral goodness contrasts sharply with Thomas's view of how virtues are acquired through morally good acts. Thomas admits that a just act is in some way not virtuous if it is performed without the virtue of justice.[31] He distinguishes between the act itself and the way in which it is performed. A virtuous and a vicious person can both perform a virtuous act, but only the virtuous person will perform it in a virtuous

---

28. *Additiones Magnae*, 2, d. 41, q. un., n. 2 (Wadding ed., 11.1.408).

29. Lychetus, *Commentarius in Ord.* 2, d. 41, nn. 2–3 (Wadding ed., 6.2.1035–36)

30. John Capreolus, 2 *Sent.*, d. 40, art. 2 (4.456); Thomas de Vio Cajetan, *In S.T.*, I-II, q. 18, art. 8, n. 2 (Leonine, 6.135); Franciscus Suarez, *De bonitate et malitiae humanorum actuum*, disp. 9, sect. 3, in *Opera Omnia*, 26 vols. (Paris: Vivès, 1856–1861), 4.420.

31. Thomas, 2 *Sent.*, d. 28, q. 1, art. 1, resp. et ad 4, 5 (Marietti ed., 2.719, 720); Idem, *De Virtute*, q. 1, art. 9, ad 13 (Marietti ed., 2.732); Idem, *S.T.*, q. 100, art. 9.

way, namely "promptly without doubt and pleasurably without difficulty."[32] For Thomas, virtue is then acquired through acts that are already good, even though through virtue they will be performed better.

Thomas directly contradicts the thesis that virtue is necessary for moral goodness by stating that virtue is important not for the substance of the act but for the way in which the act is performed. The later Scholastics who mention Scotus's position do so in order to neatly contrast Thomas and Scotus. One problem with this contrast is that in other passages Scotus himself makes the same point that Thomas does. For instance, in the *Ordinatio*'s discussion of habits, Scotus states that an act that is performed with acquired virtue could also be performed without virtue. The difference between the two acts is that an act performed from virtue is performed more easily and sweetly.[33] This description of what a virtue adds to the act resembles that of Thomas and is far from the position that virtue is a necessary condition for moral goodness. Similarly, in his earlier *Lectura*, Scotus states that a habit merely adds to an act's intensity and perfection. He assumes that the acts are already morally good even if they are performed without virtue.[34] In general, Scotus does not seem to hold the position that a virtuous act is morally indifferent unless it comes from a virtue.

The *Ordinatio*'s two arguments for the existence of morally indifferent acts, based on the necessity of virtue for moral goodness, are strange in the context of his wider thought. Nevertheless, these arguments are important if we wish to consider Scotus's view at the time of his writing this section of the *Ordinatio*. In particular, the argument about the necessity of first acquiring moral virtue for performing morally good acts is significant for latter discussions of indifferent acts. Nevertheless, since these arguments are short and difficult to relate to Scotus's wider thought, it seems to me that Scotus's other arguments shed more light on the basic difference between Scotus and Thomas.

---

32. "prompte absque dubitatione et delectabiliter absque difficultate"; Thomas, *De Virtute*, q. 1, art. 9, ad 13 (Marietti ed., 2.732).

33. Scotus, *Ord.* 1, d. 17, p. 1, qq. 1–2, n. 179 (Vat., 5.224.) Cf. *Additiones Magnae* 1, d. 17, q. 2, n. 9 (Wadding ed., 11.1.97).

34. Scotus, *Lect.* 1, d. 17, p. 1, qq. 1–2, n. 80 (Vat., 17.206–7); Idem, *Lect.* 3, d. 23, q. un., n. 48 (Vat., 21.115–16).

In light of Scotus's other texts on morally indifferent acts, there are two issues that determine the difference between Thomas and Scotus. First, there is disagreement about the specification of the act. Scotus thinks that an act receives a moral species only when there is a circumstance of the end. In contrast, Thomas thinks that an act receives its moral species from its object, which is also an end even though it is not a circumstance. Second, there is disagreement over whether the agent must always choose a morally significant end. Thomas thinks that an end is always reasonable or not, and that even an act with a morally indifferent object will be good or bad on account of its further end or circumstances, or bad on account of the absence of a necessary end or circumstances. Any particular act is either reasonable or not. Scotus thinks that acts can be chosen without morally relevant ends, and even seems to think that an object can be chosen without an end. These disagreements over specification and the role of the end in practical reasoning entail a disagreement over whether acts can be indifferent.

Whereas Scotus and Thomas are more or less concerned with the same issue, Ockham's discussion of indifferent acts is new because his primary concern is with the relationship between contingently virtuous and necessarily virtuous acts. His approach results from his description of all exterior acts as contingently virtuous and only some interior acts as necessarily virtuous.

Since for Ockham the exterior act is contingently virtuous or vicious, the exterior act is indifferent in the sense that the same exterior act can be either good or bad depending on whether there is a good or a bad interior act. It is clear that if walking to church out of devotion and then out of vainglory both have "walking" as numerically the same exterior act, then the exterior act can in a way be described as morally indifferent.[35] Numerically the same act of walking is first good and then bad. Since the necessarily virtuous interior act has right reason as a partial object, no such act can become bad. The rightness of the act is included in its very specification. Therefore, no necessarily vicious act can become virtuous, since to be virtuous it

---

35. Ockham, *Q. V.*, q. 7, art. 4 (OTh, 8.385); Idem, *Rep.* 3, q. 11 (OTh, 6.382–83). See Holopainen, *Foundations of Ethics*, 108–10.

would have to have right reason as a partial object. The exterior act is in a sense indifferent to vice and virtue because the same act can be virtuous or vicious depending upon the interior act that causes it.

A more interesting question is whether some interior act can change moral value and be indifferent in the way that exterior acts are.[36] Ockham assumes that some interior acts are indifferent. For instance, an agent might love another person for his own sake and not for any further good or bad end. For Ockham, this act is an obvious example of an act that is morally indifferent in the way that was discussed by earlier thinkers such as Thomas and Scotus. Ockham's concern is whether such an act is indifferent in the way that exterior acts are indifferent. Since Ockham has previously argued that two acts of the will can probably naturally exist at the same time, he thinks that the indifferent interior act can become virtuous.[37] If the agent loves God and the neighbor for God's sake according to right reason and does not cease loving him with the previous act, then the once indifferent act of loving becomes virtuous by extrinsic denomination.

Ockham's discussion of the indifferent interior act also clarifies the issue that for Ockham the relationship between the interior and the exterior act is not entirely causal. Ockham does not hold that the extrinsically virtuous act of loving one's neighbor must be caused by the intrinsically virtuous loving, but merely that they be at the same time. Similarly, an exterior act of falling off a precipice is bad when it is commanded by a suicidal interior act, but it ceases being bad when the agent repents. Nevertheless, the act of falling does not become a good act. Rather, the falling is no longer a result of the will. The difference seems to be not that the interior act causes or intrinsically changes the exterior act of falling, but that the falling is entirely outside of the will's power.[38]

Consequently, Ockham both severs the causal connection between the two acts and establishes some new kind of connection, which apparently is merely through the agent who performs the act. First, since

36. Ockham, *Rep.* 3, q. 11 (OTh, 6.383–87); Idem, *Q. V.,* q. 7, art. 4 (OTh, 6.385–86).
37. Ockham, *Rep.* 3, q. 11 (OTh, 6.385–86). See the texts indicated on 385, note 1.
38. Ockham, Quod 3, q. 14 (OTh, 9.254).

the exterior act is only a physical act, its identity is independent from whatever interior acts might cause it. The same exterior act of walking has numerically the same identity when the interior act changes. Second, although the interior act does not causally influence the exterior act, it can affect the exterior act's moral value, at least by removing its worth. The same act of falling is bad while the agent is falling and no longer bad when the agent rejects his suicidal intention and repents. The repentance has no causal influence on the falling. But the exterior act of falling was bad only by intrinsic denomination, since it was traced back to a bad act of the will. Since it is no longer willed and in fact the agent repents of having willed it, this exterior act of falling is no longer bad.

In general, Ockham's discussion of the exterior act's indifference is not about whether the exterior act at any given time is indifferent to moral goodness, but rather over whether the moral goodness or badness changes. His main discussions of indifference do not touch on the traditional issue of whether there are particular morally indifferent acts. Nevertheless, in his discussion of whether some interior acts are morally indifferent in the way that exterior acts are, Ockham assumes that there are acts that are morally indifferent in the way that was under discussion by Thomas and Scotus. These indifferent individual acts are neither good nor bad either in themselves or through another act. Presumably, Ockham thinks that exterior acts can be indifferent if they are commanded by such indifferent interior acts, but he does not seem to address this point.

Merit, Demerit, and Indifference to Merit

From a theological perspective, an act's merit in the eyes of God is more important than its moral goodness. Although medieval thinkers use the word "merit" *(meritum)* more broadly in a political context, they think that it is more properly used to describe the way in which an act deserves some sort of reward from God. At least in the present order that God has established, a meritorious act must be both morally good and elicited by an agent who has the virtue of charity.

Even though all meritorious acts are good, not all good acts are meritorious. There is disagreement both over whether an agent with charity can elicit good acts that are not meritorious, and over whether there is some sort of intrinsic or necessary dependence of merit on moral goodness. Although Thomas thinks that no acts are indifferent to moral goodness, he does think that some morally good acts are indifferent to merit. Nevertheless, Scotus disagrees with him over whether an agent with charity can perform such an act. More widely, Thomas, Scotus, and Ockham disagree about the way in which charity is necessary for merit. Is the virtue of charity distinct from grace? Must meritorious acts be explicitly elicited by the virtue of charity? Could God by his absolute power deny merit to or even punish acts that are elicited by the infused virtue of charity?

All three figures are concerned to some extent with distinguishing between the order that God actually established and any possible order that God could establish. This distinction is often at least partially expressed as a distinction between God's ordained and absolute power, although for Scotus this absolute power has a more legal connotation and can indicate God's ability to make exceptions to the laws that govern the ordinary course of events.[39] In the context of merit and goodness, the discussion of God's power is about the nature of the connections between merit, certain kinds of acts, charity, and created grace. The issue of whether these connections are necessary or contingent is the same as the issue of whether these connections are the result of God's free decision to establish one set of relations rather than another.

Thomas thinks that only good acts could be meritorious, and that

---

39. Marilyn McCord Adams, *William Ockham*, 2.1186–1207; Klaus Bannach, *Die Lehre von der Doppelten Macht Gottes bei Wilhelm von Ockham: Problemgeschichtliche Voraussetzungen und Bedeutung* (Wiesbaden: Franz Steiner, 1975); William J. Courtenay, "The Dialectic of Omnipotence in the High and Late Middle Ages," in *Divine Omniscience and Omnipotence in Medieval Philosophy: Islamic, Jewish, and Christian Perspectives*, ed. Tamar Rudavsky (Dordrecht: Kluwer, 1985), 243–69; Idem, *Capacity and Volition: A History of the Distinction of Absolute and Ordained Power*, Quodlibet 8 (Bergamo: Pierluigi Lubrina, 1990), 115–26; Maurer, *The Philosophy of William of Ockham*, 254–65; Mary Ann Pernoud, "The Theory of *Potentia Dei* according to Aquinas, Scotus, and Ockham," *Antonianum* 47 (1972): 69–95.

this merit involves some sort of proportion or order even though there is no strict justice between humans and God. Merit in the strict sense is made possible by God's decision to give humans grace as a created quality that elevates human nature. The supernatural habit of charity flows from grace and causes morally good acts to be meritorious.

Thomas thinks that merit is one of the features that follow on the goodness of an action, as does its rectitude and its praiseworthiness. He writes that "a good or bad act has the nature of praiseworthiness or blameworthiness insofar as it is in the power of the will; the nature of rectitude and sin according to its order to an end; the nature of merit or demerit according to the retribution of justice due to another."[40] Even though these additional characteristics of an act involve relations between the act and others, these relations are based on the act's intrinsic characteristics. For instance, praiseworthiness or blameworthiness is made possible by the intrinsic goodness or badness of the act and its relation to the will's power.[41] Similarly, an act is sinful or right according to its order to the end, and this ordering presupposes the goodness or badness of an act.[42] Bad acts cannot be ordered to the end that should be the goal of a human act. Merit and demerit similarly depend on the goodness or badness of the act even though it also involves a relation to another.

The badness of an act not only entails a disorder with respect to the end, which is sin, but it also deserves punishment from God, who is both the ultimate end of human activity and the ruler of the universe and all creatures, including rational creatures. Moreover, merit in the widest sense presupposes an act's moral goodness and praiseworthiness, but consists from the way in which the act affects the relation-

40. "quandoque actus bonus vel malus habet rationem laudabilis vel culpabilis, secundum quod est in potestate voluntatis; rationem vero rectitudinis et peccati, secundum ordinem ad finem; rationem meriti et demeriti, secundum retributionem iustitiae ad alterum"; Thomas, *S.T.*, I-II, q. 21, art. 3. For a discussion of merit in Thomas Aquinas, see Joseph P. Wawrykow, *God's Grace and Human Action: "Merit" in the Theology of Thomas Aquinas* (Notre Dame, Ind.: University of Notre Dame Press, 1995). For the relationship between merit and the other ways in which an act may be good, see especially Theo G. Belmans, *Le sens objectif de l'agir humain: Pour relire la morale conjugale de Saint Thomas*, Studi Tomistici 8 (Vatican City: Libreria Editrice Vaticana, 1980), 108, 131.

41. Thomas, *S.T.*, I-II, q. 21, art. 2.   42. Thomas, *S.T.*, I-II, q. 21, art. 1.

ship of the agent to other individuals and to the whole community.[43] It presupposes goodness and an order of justice. Thomas thinks that since the agent and other agents are part of the community, any benefit or sin done to a member is also done to the whole community.

A rational agent's most important relationship is to God as his ultimate end.[44] Although bad acts do not harm God, they take away from the honor due to him, just as some offenses against the dead or those who are otherwise outside of one's ability to harm.[45] Moreover, since God is the ruler of the whole universe and most especially of rational creatures, any disorder or injustice among the parts or against the whole is also against God. Every bad act is disordered in this way, and consequently deserves punishment from God.

No morally good act by itself can be strictly meritorious, because justice does not strictly cover God's relation to humans.[46] God does not really owe humans anything. Nevertheless, although God does not strictly owe a reward to good actions, there is a way in which such rewards are congruous, since it seems appropriate that God reward humans for what good they do. More importantly, God raises human abilities and acts through grace. Charity is the infused virtue that accompanies sanctifying grace (*gratia gratum faciens*) and orders the agent correctly toward God. This sanctifying grace makes agents pleasing in God's sight and is connected in a special way to the Holy Spirit, who is uncreated grace. Good acts that are performed by charity have as their principle supernatural grace, which is from the Holy Spirit. Since such acts come from God, they can merit eternal life according to "condign" merit, which is merit in a strict sense. Such good acts have "congruous" merit insofar as they proceed from the human being and "condign" merit insofar as they come from God. In contrast, those good acts that are performed without charity can be described as meritorious only in a very loose sense, perhaps in the way that they have a "congruous" merit for a temporal reward.[47]

43. Thomas, *S.T.*, I-II, q. 21, art. 3.   44. Thomas, *S.T.*, I-II, q. 21, art. 4.
45. Thomas, *S.T.*, I-II, q. 114, art. 1, ad 2.   46. Thomas, *S.T.*, I-II, q. 114, art. 1, 3.
47. Thomas, 3 *Sent.*, d. 18, art. 2 (Marietti ed., 3.559); Idem, *De Potentia*, q. 6, art. 9, resp. (Marietti ed., 2.183).

Could God give eternal life to someone who does not have grace?[48] Thomas denies that any creature's action necessitates God's will, or that God can only make happy those who are raised by a supernatural quality. Merit is based on a divine order that God freely establishes.[49] Consequently, it is possible for God to give eternal life to someone who does not have grace. Nevertheless, with regard to merit, God could not make human acts and persons worthy of eternal life without establishing some proportion between these acts and the reward. Grace makes merit possible in two ways.[50] First, it removes sin, which makes someone displeasing to God. Second, it raises humans to a supernatural level. Both of these features are necessary for meriting eternal life not just on account of God's will to make them necessary, but on account of what it means to merit. In order for there to be a real worthiness on the part of the agent and his acts, the agent must have created grace.

Charity, which accompanies grace, is a necessary condition of merit.[51] According to Thomas, charity is the form of the virtues in such a way that it directs all of the virtues and their actions to God, who is the agent's last end.[52] Charity is supernatural not only on account of its cause but also on account of its object. Whereas through natural love an agent might love God as the source of connatural goods, through charity the Christian can love God as the source of supernatural goods.[53] The agent can directly perform a meritorious act through charity, or a good act can become meritorious when it is somehow referred to God through charity.[54] For instance, someone might direct

48. Capreolus, 1 *Sent.*, d. 17, q. 1, art. 2 (2.92); Francis Sylvester of Ferrara, *Commentaria in libros quatuor Contra gentiles*, 3, 147, n. 4 (Leonine, 14.437).

49. Thomas, *S.T.*, I-II, q. 5, art. 7; Idem, q. 114, art. 1. Wawrykow, *Grace and Human Action*, 184–89.

50. Thomas, *S.T.*, I-II, q. 109, art. 5; q. 114, art. 2; Idem, *SCG* 3, 147.

51. Thomas, 3 *Sent.*, d. 30, art. 5 (Moos ed., 3.963–65); Idem, *De Potentia*, q. 6, art. 9, resp. (Marietti ed., 2.83); Idem, *S.T.*, I-II, q. 114, art. 4.

52. Thomas, *De Veritate*, q. 14, art. 5 (Leonine, 22.2.450–54); Ibid, *De Malo*, q. 8, art. 2, resp. (Leonine, 23.200); Idem, *De Virtutibus*, q. 2, art. 3 (Marietti ed., 2.760–62); Idem, *S.T.*, II-II, q. 23, art. 7.

53. Thomas, *S.T.*, II-II, q. 26, art. 3, resp.; Idem, I-II, q. 109, art.3, ad 1. For a discussion of various texts, see Osborne, *Love of Self and Love of God*, 70–86.

54. Thomas, 2 *Sent.*, d. 40, q. 1, art. 5 (Mandonnet ed., 2.1022–28); Idem, *De Malo*,

almsgiving to God while actually thinking about God and loving God through charity. In this case, the almsgiving is actually referred to God. But someone who loves God through charity refers all of his acts to God, including those acts of almsgiving that are performed without any explicit thought of God. According to Thomas, such acts are virtually *(in virtute)* ordered to God and also meritorious. By charity, an agent in a lesser way refers even his venial sins to God, although venial sins, since they are bad, can never be meritorious.

An agent who possesses charity refers all of his acts to God as his last end. Since charity makes good acts meritorious, it must be the case that for someone with charity, no good act lacks merit. Moreover, since all human acts are either morally good or bad, and bad acts merit punishment, it follows that, for someone with charity, all acts deserve either reward or punishment. On Thomas's account, an agent with charity cannot perform an act that is indifferent to merit. Nevertheless, Thomas thinks that agents without charity can perform such acts.[55] The reason for his position is that agents who lack charity and even unbelievers can perform good acts.[56] However, these acts cannot be meritorious because they are not ordered to God through charity. But since these acts are good, they do not deserve punishment. Consequently, they are morally good but indifferent to merit.

How does charity refer acts to God? His explanations of this referral generally involve the way in which charity is the form of the other virtues and how it makes sure that the agent is rightly ordered to the

---

q. 2, art. 5, ad 7 (Leonine, 23.44–45). For more texts and a discussion, see Thomas M. Osborne Jr., "The Threefold Referral of Acts to the Ultimate End in Thomas Aquinas and His Commentators," *Angelicum* 85 (2008): 715–36; Idem, "Thomas Aquinas and John Duns Scotus on Individual Acts and the Ultimate End," in *Philosophy and Theology in the Long Middle Ages: A Tribute to Stephen F. Brown*, ed. Kent Emery, Russell L. Friedman, Andreas Speer, and Kent Emery Jr., Studien und Texte zu Geistesgeschichte des Mittelalters 105 (Leiden: Brill, 2011), 351–74.

55. Thomas Aquinas, 2 *Sent.*, d. 40, q. 1, art. 5, sol. (Mandonnet ed., 2.1026); d. 41, q. 1, art. 2, sol. et ad 2 (Mandonnet ed., 2.1037–39); Idem, *S.T.*, I-II, q. 114, art. 3; q. 10, art. 4, resp; Idem, *Super epistolam ad Romanos Lect.*, cap. 14, *Lect.* 3, n. 1141 (Marietti ed., 1.213); Idem, *Super epistolam ad Titum Lect.*, cap. 1, *Lect.* 3, n. 43 (Marietti ed., 2.310).

56. See Thomas M. Osborne Jr., "Unbelief and Sin in Thomas Aquinas and the Thomistic Tradition," *Nova et Vetera*, English Edition 8 (2010): 613–26.

last end. Thomas's position that every act is ordered to an ultimate end seems to rest on the view that charity somehow refers all of an agent's acts to God, even venial sins.[57] If every act is directed to an ultimate end, and agents who have charity have God as their ultimate end, it follows that every act performed by such agents is directed to God. Nevertheless, the distinction between the referral of good acts and venial sins is significant. Good acts are the kind of acts that could actually be referred to God, whereas venial sins can only be habitually referred. This habitual order is insufficient for merit. Similarly, someone who lacks charity may perform a good act that is only habitually ordered to his own happiness, which he understands and wills in an incorrect way.

On Thomas's view, it is important that all acts are directed to a last end that is in some way one, whether it is God as a supernatural last end or some other good or set of goods that are mistakenly regarded as instantiating happiness.[58] This point is an important part of his moral psychology. With respect to the moral and supernatural value of the act, this point is not always relevant.[59] The ultimate end is not always a remote end or circumstance of the act. Agents with charity perform venial sins that are bad even though they are habitually ordered to the supernatural last end. Similarly, agents who lack charity perform good acts that remain good although they might be habitually ordered to a bad last end.

According to Thomas, charity must be a supernatural habit that is distinct from, although dependent upon, created grace.[60] The virtue

57. Thomas Aquinas, *De Malo*, q. 7, art. 1, ad 4, 9; art. 2, ad 1 (Leonine, 23.159–60, 163); Idem, *S.T.*, I-II, q. 88, art. 1, ad 2; II-II, q. 24, art. 10, ad 2; Idem, *Super epistolam ad Colossenses Lect.*, cap. 3, *Lect.* 3, n. 170, in *Super episotlas S. Pauli Lect.*, 8th ed., ed. Raphael Cai, 2 vols. (Turin: Marietti, 1953), 2.157, q. 44, art. 4, ad 2. See especially Réginald Garrigou-Lagrange, "La fin ultime du péché venial: Et celle de l'acte imparfait, dit 'imperfection,'" *Revue Thomiste* 7 (1924), 314–17; Thomas Deman, "Péché," *Dictionnaire de théologie catholique*, 12.1, 237–44; A. J. McNicholl, "The Ultimate End of Venial Sin," *The Thomist* 2 (1940): 373–410; Osborne, "Threefold Referral," 719–20.

58. Thomas, *S.T.*, I-II, q. 1, art. 5–6. The most detailed discussion is Ramirez, *De beatitudine*, 1.316–65.

59. See especially the discussion of Banez in Osborne, "Threefold Referral," 732–36.

60. Thomas, 1 *Sent.*, d. 17, q. 1, art. 1 (Mandonnet ed., 1.391–97); Idem, *SCG* 3, 150 (Leonine, 14.442); Idem, *De Virtutibus*, q. 2, art. 1 (Marietti ed., 2.753–57); Idem, *S.T.*, II-II, q. 23, art. 2.

of charity needs to be supernatural because by it the agent can perform acts that exceed his natural abilities. It cannot be some sort of merely exterior mover, or the acts produced would not be free. Consequently, it is an interior habit by which an agent performs acts that are fully his own even if they exceed his unaided abilities. Since they are his own, they can be imputed to him. Since they are meritorious, they must be proportionate to God. In order to be so proportionate, they must exceed his natural abilities.[61]

Although sanctifying grace makes the agent pleasing to God, it is not by itself the producer of meritorious acts. Charity flows from grace, along with the other infused virtues that come from charity.[62] These infused virtues correspond to the acquired moral virtues, since the love of God carries with it an ability to act well even for a supernatural end in a way that is appropriate to the matter of all the different virtues. Not only do charity and the infused virtues come from grace, but they also work toward an increase in sanctifying grace and its other effects on human nature.

Thomas gives an account of merit that involves a variety of interacting elements, and he seems to think that these elements are necessary not merely on account of God's free decision, but because of the natures of merit and grace. In order for acts to be meritorious, the agent and his abilities must be elevated by grace. Otherwise, there is no proportion between the human act and the supernatural reward. Moreover, meritorious acts must proceed from habits that come from sanctifying grace, among which the most important is charity. God did not have to save humans or raise human nature. But given that there are acts that merit a heavenly reward, there also needs to be sanctifying grace and a separate habit to produce or at least refer meritorious acts to God, which is the virtue of charity.

Although Scotus, like Thomas, thinks that the virtue of charity is necessary for an act to be meritorious, his account of merit and chari-

---

61. Thomas, *S.T.*, I-II, q. 109, art. 5; Idem, 2 *Sent.*, d. 26, q. 1, art. 1, resp. (Mandonnet ed., 2.740–41).

62. Thomas, 2 *Sent.*, d. 26, q. 1, art. 4 (Mandonnet ed., 2.676–79); Idem, *De Veritate*, q. 27, art. 6 (Leonine, 22.3.813–14); Idem, *SCG* 3, 151–53 (Leonine, 24.444–48); Idem, *S.T.*, I-II, q. 110, art. 3.

ty is very different.[63] First, he gives a different account of how acts are meritorious. According to Scotus, an act is meritorious because it is accepted by God. In order for it to be accepted, it needs either to be actually ordered to God by charity or elicited by charity. Other good acts are not meritorious even if the agent has charity. Second, even though Scotus thinks that a supernatural habit is necessary for merit in the order that God has created, he thinks that it is appropriate but strictly speaking unnecessary according to the requirements of justice. Charity does not through its object raise the agent to a supernatural level. Moreover, Scotus does not distinguish between the habit of charity and created grace.

According to Scotus, a meritorious act is an act that is morally good and accepted by God as somehow worthy of eternal life.[64] In every meritorious act, there is a distinction between that which precedes merit and the merit itself. An act's substance or nature, its intensity, and its moral rectitude are all prior to merit. Only free human acts can be meritorious. In general, Scotus thinks that moral goodness is necessary for merit. Nevertheless, in one early text he states that God could make lifting a stick meritorious if the lifting is done for love.[65] This lifting of a stick is the typical act that is indifferent in kind or even indifferent because it is not deliberative. It is not clear whether in this passage Scotus wishes to say that such a meritorious act is morally indifferent, since he usually describes merit as an addition to previously existing natural and moral goodness. Scotus compares lifting the stick to the morally good sacrifices of the Old Law, which were once meritorious but now are not. Scotus does not suggest that lifting a stick remains morally indifferent even if it is performed out of chari-

63. Paul Vignaux, *Justification et prédestination au xive siècle* (Paris: Leroux, 1934), 9–41; Richard Cross, *Duns Scotus*, 103–7. For the appropriation of Scotus's views, see Werner Detloff, *Die Entwicklung der Akzeptations- und Verdienstlehre von Duns Scotus bis Luther: Mit Besonderer Berucksichtigung der Franziskanertheologen*, Beiträge zur Geschichte der Philosophie und Theologie des Mittelalters 40.2 (Münster: Aschendorff, 1963).

64. Scotus, *Ord.* 1, d. 17, pars 1, qq. 1–2, n. 142 (Vat., 5.207–8); Idem, *Ord.* 2, d. 40, q. un., n. 12 (Vat., 8.470–71).

65. Scotus, *Lect.* 1, d. 17, pars 1, q. un., n. 89 (Vat., 17.209).

ty. Perhaps if the lifting of a stick has a good end through charity, then the lifting of the stick would be morally good. The point of the example is to show the importance of charity for merit and to emphasize the ability of God to accept ordinarily indifferent acts as meritorious. Consequently, he does not in this passage explicitly state that some morally indifferent acts are meritorious, although he may think that God according to his absolute power could make such acts meritorious. He never suggests that God by his absolute power could establish an order in which morally bad acts are meritorious.

The merit itself consists in the act's acceptance by the divine will and its order to a reward.[66] This merit is in addition to God's normal pleasure with a morally good act. It consists in a twofold relation. First, there is a relation between the act and the accepting will. Second, there is a relation between the act and the reward. Both relations are freely established by God and are not necessitated by any quality of the act.

According to the present order, acts are meritorious if and only if they are themselves acts of charity, or they are morally good acts that are elicited by charity. Both natural and moral goodness are necessary but not sufficient conditions for merit.[67] Charity makes the act lovable by God. Scotus writes:

For the act to be meritorious, it does not suffice that it has charity present with it in the person, but beyond this it is required that the act be elicited according to the charity which is present in him. For God, who loves himself alone and for his own sake, can give some godlike form to a creature, who, having it [this form], is specially loved; and his work, to which it [the form, grace or charity] inclines, insofar as it is according to its inclination, is specially accepted.[68]

66. In addition to the text cited in the previous note, see Scotus, *Ord.* 1, d. 17, qq. 1–2, nn. 142–44 (Vat., 5.207–9); Idem, Quod 17, art. 2, n. [3] 6 (Alluntis ed., 613–14).

67. Scotus, *Ord.* 2, d. 7, q. un., n. 31 (Vat., 8.89).

68. "ad hoc quod actus sit meritorious, non sufficit quod habeat secum caritatem inexistentem personae, sed ultra hoc requiritur quod secundum inclinationem caritatis inexistentis actus eliciatur. Deus enim, qui se solum et propter seipsum diligit, potest aliquam formam deiformem dare creaturae, quam habens specialiter diligatur, et opus eius, ad quod ipsa inclinat, pro quanto sit secundum ipsius inclinationem, specialiter acceptetur"; Scotus, Quod 17, art. 2, n. [5] 12 (Alluntis ed., 616–17).

Agents are not bound to elicit every good act through charity. Actual referral occurs when an act is explicitly referred through a contemporaneous act of charity.[69] Virtual referral occurs when the act can be otherwise traced back to an act of charity. Otherwise, the referral is merely habitual and not meritorious. Scotus thinks that an agent who has charity at least habitually refers all of his good acts to God as his ultimate end. But a merely habitual ordering is insufficient for merit. Since habitually referred acts are morally good, they do not deserve punishment. Consequently, they are indifferent with respect to merit. Scotus thinks that even an agent who has charity can perform morally good acts that are indifferent to merit.[70]

Both Scotus and Thomas think that no merely human agent in this life can be always actually thinking about and loving God. Consequently, the other kinds of referral are significant for understanding a large number of human acts. There are three significant ways in which Scotus departs from Thomas in his understanding of referral.[71] The first disagreement is over what it means for an act to be virtually referred to God. Thomas thinks that the virtual referral of an act depends on the state of the agent. If an agent is ordered to God through charity, then all of his good acts will be directed to God either because they are actually directed to him, or because they are virtually (in virtute) directed through this order that is established by charity. Scotus thinks that an act is virtually referred only if the act can be traced back to actual thinking and loving. Consequently, Scotus thinks that many acts are only habitually referred to God. Such acts are morally good but indifferent with respect to merit. Since Scotus agrees with Thomas that merit requires virtual or actual referral, this disagreement over virtual referral entails the second disagreement, namely over whether someone with charity can perform good acts that are not meritorious. Since Scotus has a nar-

69. Scotus, *Ord.* 2, d. 41, q. un., nn. 10–14 (Vat., 8.476–78); Idem, *Lect.* 2, d. 41, q. un., nn. 12–13 (Vat., 19.396–97).

70. Scotus, *Ord.* 2, d. 41, q. un., nn. 15–16 (Vat., 8.478); Idem, *Lect.* 2, d. 41, q. un., n. 14 (Vat., 19.397); Idem, *Ord.* 3, d. 7, q. un., n. 39 (Vat., 8.92–93); Idem, Quod 17, art. 2, n. [5] 11 (Alluntis ed., 616).

71. Osborne, "Individual Acts and the Ultimate End"; Idem, "Threefold Referral," 724–26.

rower notion of what virtual referral is, he must restrict the number of meritorious acts. Their disagreement about whether acts can be indifferent to merit is based on a disagreement over what it means for an act to be virtually referred to God.

The third significant disagreement is that whereas Thomas thinks that all acts of one possessing charity are habitually ordered to God, Scotus thinks that venial sins are not in any way orderable to God, since they are repugnant to merit.[72] He uses the distinction between a contrary and a privative ordering in order to distinguish between mortal and venial sins.[73] Mortal sins have a contrary ordering since they destroy charity. In contrast, venial sins are privatively ordered, since they lack the order that they should have. Nevertheless, since mortal and venial sins are both bad with respect to moral goodness, they are both demeritorious.[74]

According to Scotus, the habit of charity is the same as created grace, if we understand grace in the sense of something by which God freely makes someone dear to him.[75] He thinks that if grace were a distinct light and root of the theological virtues, then there would be no reason why charity remains in heaven whereas faith and hope do not. In general, it is superfluous to distinguish between a separate habit of charity and grace, since charity makes someone acceptable to God and worthy of beatitude. Since the same good characteristics that belong to grace also belong to charity, the two cannot be separated.[76] A related argument is based on the fact that there is no such thing as "unformed" charity, just as there cannot be unformed grace. One is never present without the other. The words do differ connotatively, insofar as "charity" connotes a principle of action, and "grace" connotes the object by which someone is dear to God.[77] But there is no real distinction between the two.

72. Scotus, Quod 17, art. 2, n. [5] 10 (Alluntis ed., 616).
73. For the sins, see supra, note 66; for the contrary/privative distinction, see especially Scotus, *Ord.* 2, d. 7, q. un. nn. 36–39 (Vat., 8.91–93).
74. Scotus, *Ord.* 2, d. 27, q. un. n. 39 (Vat., 8.92–93).
75. Scotus, *Lect.* 2, d. 27, q. un. (Vat., 19.271–72).
76. Scotus, *Ord.* 2, d. 27, q. un., n. 8 (Vat., 8.286).
77. Scotus, *Ord.* 2, d. 27, q. un., n. 14 (Vat., 8.289).

Created grace or charity is necessary for a meritorious act neither according to strict justice nor according to God's absolute power.[78] Grace is necessary because God freely willed to make it so. However, God's free decision was not merely arbitrary. Although justice does not require the existence of created grace, it does somehow make the agent or act appropriately worthy.[79] Although Scotus denies that God has to justify by giving created grace, he thinks that such justification is reasonable, and perhaps that the reasonableness of this justification holds even independently from God's ordered power.

Scotus might be able to argue that charity is not strictly necessary for an act's merit because he denies that acts of charity are specifically distinct from those acts of naturally loving God that can be elicited without grace.[80] Whereas Thomas thinks that charity raises human abilities to a higher level, Scotus thinks that its intrinsic effect on the act is merely of degree.[81] Charity, like the other habits, increases the act's intensity and perfection. But it does not change the act. Although it does add merit, even this merit is rooted in the already existing goodness of the act. Charity does not merely add a determinate amount to an act's value, but it increases its value geometrically. A geometric increase is like doubling rather than adding "2." The value of the act is increased directly in proportion to the original amount of the act.

What is the difference between Thomas's view that God can save someone without grace or meritorious acts and Scotus's view that grace and merit are merely the result of God's decision to accept the acts? For Thomas, grace and charity are necessary for a meritorious act if there is going to be some intrinsic way in which the agent and his acts are proportioned to charity. God could save someone without such an intrinsic proportion, but this proportion itself does not depend on God's free decision. By their very nature, grace and charity

78. Scotus, *Ord.* 1, d. 17, pars 1, qq. 1–2, nn. 149, 160–64 (Vat., 5.210–11, 215–17); Idem, *Ord.* 4, d. 49, q. 6, n. 21.

79. Scotus, *Ord.* 1, d. 17, pars 1, qq. 1–2, nn. 130–33 (Vat., 5.203–4).

80. Scotus, Quod 16, art. 3, nn.[6] 13–[12] 29 (Alluntis ed., 617–25).

81. Scotus, *Ord.* 1, d. 17, q. 3, nn. 179–82 (Vat., 5.224–26); Idem, *Ord.* 3, d. 27, q. un., n. 63 (Vat., 10.77); Idem, *Lect.* 1, d. 17, n. 79–81 (Vat., 17.206–7); Idem, *Lect.* 3, d. 23, q. un., n. 48 (Vat., 21.115–16).

cause merit. In contrast, Scotus does not argue for the necessity of merit by considering any intrinsic features of grace or charity, such as their ability to raise the agent to a supernatural level, or the way in which charity enables the agent to perform a specifically distinct kind of act. Scotus thinks that the connection between morality, grace, and charity is extrinsic and established by God's free choice.

Many theologians, but most especially Petrus Aureoli, attacked Scotus's position that according to strict justice grace is insufficient and unnecessary for merit.[82] In response, Ockham defends Scotus's positions that someone could be saved without grace, that grace itself does not guarantee merit, and that grace is not a distinct thing from charity.[83] In doing so, he further makes the issue of merit into a discussion of God's will rather than a discussion of any intrinsic feature of the meritorious act.

Ockham wishes to defend the complete gratuity of salvation. Since, like Scotus, he thinks that acts of charity are specifically the same as acts of natural love, he must deny that charity is necessary for an act's merit.[84] Every act that is performed by charity could be performed without it, including even the love of God.[85] Charity is distinct from natural love both in its degree and its circumstances.[86] Since for Ockham circumstances are part of the intrinsically virtuous act's object, it is not clear how the two acts can belong to the same species even though their objects are distinct. Moreover, Ockham does not discuss what the different circumstances are. Nevertheless, he states that the distinction between an act of charity and an act of natural love is not between different species. Like Scotus, Ockham thinks that there is

---

82. Vignaux, *Prédestination et Justification*, 43–95; Dettloff, *Entwicklung der Akzeptations- und Verdiendstlehre*, 22–92.

83. Vignaux, *Prédestination et Justification*, 43–95; Iserloh, *Gnade und Eucharistie*, 44–133; Dettloff, *Entwicklung der Akzeptations- und Verdienstlehre*, 253–90; Adams, "Voluntarist or Naturalist?" 243–45; Eadem, *William Ockham*, 2.1257–97; Rega Wood, "Ockham's Repudiation of Pelagianism," in *The Cambridge Companion to Ockham*, 350–73.

84. Ockham, *Ord.* 1, d. 17, q. 2 (OTh, 4.472–73).

85. Ockham, *Q. V.*, q. 6, art. 11 (OTh, 8.319); Ibid., q. 4 (OTh, 8.139).

86. Ockham, *Q. V.*, q. 1, art. 2 (OTh, 8.20); Ibid., q. 6, art. 9 (OTh, 8.291).

no reason to distinguish between grace as a quality and the infused habit of charity.[87]

Ockham agrees with both Thomas and Scotus that, according to the order that God has established, meritorious acts must be accompanied by grace and consequently charity. Thomas and Ockham have different views on the nature of congruous merit. Thomas not only uses the term "congruous merit" in the context of the very loose sort of merit that can be attributed to acts that are performed without charity, but he also distinguishes between condign merit and congruous merit in the context of the same meritorious act. Insofar as an act comes from the agent's free choice, the act has a congruous merit. This congruous merit does not strictly deserve any reward from God since there is no proportion between God and the merely human agent. In contrast, insofar as an act comes from the grace of the Holy Spirit, it has condign merit. This condign merit is a result of the way in which God makes someone with grace into a sharer of the divine nature. For Thomas, when considering the two kinds of merit as belonging to the same act, the two kinds of merit are distinct insofar as the same act has distinct sources. In contrast, Ockham thinks that congruous and condign merit belong to two numerically different acts. An act has condign merit merely because God has decided to accept certain acts as meritorious. In contrast, congruous merit is a looser kind of merit that belongs to good acts that are performed without grace.[88] The distinction between condign and congruous merit is a distinction between different kinds of acts, and its basis is in God's will to accept one act as strictly meritorious rather than another.

Ockham agrees with Scotus that grace is important for merit simply on account of God's will to give it importance. Since grace is the same as charity, it follows that charity also has no intrinsic importance. Consequently, grace and charity are in this strict sense unnecessary for salvation.[89] In the context of making this argument for a

---

87. Ockham, *Rep.* 4, qq. 10–11 (OTh, 7.215).

88. Ockham, *Q. V.*, q. 6, art. 11 (OTh, 8.320).

89. Ockham, *Ord.* 1, d. 17, q. 1 (OTh, 3.445–46, 452–53); Idem, *Rep.* 3, q. 9, art. 1 (OTh, 6.279–81); Idem, *Q.V.*, q. 1 (OTh, 8.10–15); Idem, Quod 6, q. 1 (OTh, 9.585–89).

position like that of Scotus, Ockham also argues for the stronger thesis that an act's merit or detestability is a result of God's free decision and is not rooted in the act's nature.[90]

According to Ockham, by God's absolute power someone can be pleasing to God not only if he lacks charity or grace, but even if he has the contrary act of hating God. Ockham writes:

> The hatred of God is not worthy of eternal punishment from the nature of the thing [i.e., the act]. Therefore neither is the love of God worthy of eternal life from the nature of the thing [i.e., the act]. The assumption is proved, since God can remit every sin with respect to its guilt without any grace or infused charity, and consequently such hatred is not worthy of eternal punishment.[91]

Even though Ockham thinks that God could issue a command that would make an act of hatred for him morally good, in this text Ockham assumes the establishment of the present order, in which hating God is sinful. Since merit and demerit are not intrinsic properties of the acts, God could by his absolute power make any act meritorious or demeritorious, whether it is good or bad.[92] The relationship between an act's moral value and acceptance by God is contingent and a result of God's will. Ockham's view of the contingent relationship between an act's demerit and its sinfulness is connected with his view that there is no intrinsic repugnance between being a sinner and having eternal life.[93]

Ockham not only denies that by God's absolute power grace is a necessary condition for merit, but he also denies that it is a sufficient condition.[94] No habit, including the supernatural habit of charity, makes it necessary that God accept someone as pleasing to him and worthy of eternal life. Ockham is concerned with defending God's

---

90. Ockham, *Ord.* 1, d. 17 (OTh, 3.446–49).

91. "... odium Dei non est ex natura rei dignum poena aeterna. Igitur nec dilectio Dei ex natura rei est digna vita aeterna. Assumptum probatur, quia Deus potest remittere omne peccatum quoad culpam sine omni gratia vel caritate infusa, et per consequens tale odium non est dignum poena aeterna"; Ockham, *Q. V.,* q. 1. art. 2 (OTh, 8.18).

92. Ockham, *Ord.* 1, d. 17, q. 1 (OTh, 3.454).

93. Ockham, *Rep.* 4, qq. 304 (OTh, 7.47); Idem, *Rep.* 4, qq. 10–11 (OTh, 7.206–7, 209).

94. Ockham, Quod 6, q. 2 (OTh, 9.589–92).

freedom and the complete contingency of salvation. Even acts such as martyrdom are not by their nature acceptable to God.[95] Why would Ockham hold such a view? He must avoid Pelagianism, which is the view that someone could be saved by natural powers. If the same acts that are performed with grace can be performed without grace, it follows that if there were a necessary connection between any kind of act and merit, then this connection would hold whether there were grace or not. If martyrdom by its nature were meritorious, it would be meritorious whether or not it is elicited by an agent who has charity. Similarly, there is no reason why an act of charity itself should by itself require an ordering to a reward that is freely given by God. By his absolute power, God could order to hell someone who has the virtue of charity.[96] Ockham wishes to avoid any suggestion that God owes salvation to someone.

There is a similarity between Ockham's purely forensic view of merit and his view of moral goodness, in that Ockham thinks that God's will is ultimately responsible for the moral value of any act. Both merit and moral goodness are based on God's will. But there are also significant differences. First, Ockham is unclear about whether the divine will merely can trump other factors that determines an act's moral worth, or whether it is the only factor. Scholars disagree over whether Ockham thinks that acts have natural goodness, and whether this goodness might be relevant to their moral value.[97] Second, even though Ockham thinks that God could change the moral value of acts, he also thinks that the moral worth of many actions can be known through natural reason. His use of the traditional distinction between positive and non-positive moral science presupposes that some acts can be known to be good or bad not only apart from knowledge of the civil law and canon law, but even apart from the revelation of God's will.[98] In contrast, Ock-

---

95. Ockham, *Ord.* 1, d. 17, q. 1 (OTh, 3.451–53).

96. Ockham, *Q. V.*, q. 1, art. 2 (OTh, 8.22).

97. Marilyn McCord Adams, "Ockham on Will, Nature, and Morality," 248–49, 265; Eadem, "Structure of Ockham's Moral Theory," 5–6; Osborne, "Ockham as a Divine-Command Theorist," 6–11.

98. Ockham, Quod 2, q. 14 (OTh, 9.176–78).

ham's teaching on the necessity of grace for merit is based entirely on God's revelation of what he has freely chosen to establish. Aristotle, philosophers, and non-Christians generally know that certain acts are morally good or bad. Only Christians know about merit.

Ockham's view that an act's merit is only contingently related to its moral worth is new. Although Scotus's somewhat forensic account of merit prepared the way for Ockham's view, he never arrived at Ockham's more extreme positions. Whereas Scotus had considered moral evil as repugnant to merit, Ockham thinks that God could give someone an eternal reward for any sin. Ockham probably arrived at this view by strongly reacting against Aureoli's view that grace is necessarily connected with merit. The novelty of Ockham's views was apparent to his contemporaries. With respect to merit, an investigation of Ockham's views by a commission at the papal court was, among other issues, concerned with Ockham's views that (1) by God's absolute power an act elicited out of charity does not by its nature merit eternal life, and (2) God can forgive any sin without charity, or order someone with charity to hell.[99] Although such concerns do not establish that Ockham was in any way unorthodox, they do show that his views on merit invited suspicion on account of their novelty.

The disagreement among medieval thinkers is not over whether grace and charity are necessary for merit in the world that God has actually ordered, but rather over the range of possible orderings. There has been considerable scholarly disagreement over the different views of merit, and more particularly over whether Thomas's "*ordinatio*" theory, according to which God has ordained the necessity of merit through grace, is different from the "*acceptatio*" theory of later theologians such as Ockham and Scotus, according to which God has decided to make certain acts meritorious.[100] We have seen that

99. See especially articles 14–20, the opinions of the commission, and, in the list of places, numbers 1, 16–17, in Josef Koch, "Neue Aktenstücke zu dem gegen Wilhelm Ockham in Avignon geführten Prozess," in Josef Koch, *Kleine Schriften*, Raccolta di Studi e Testi 128, 2 vols. (Rome: Edizioni di Storia e Letteratura, 1973), 2.302–3, 312–24, 361. This article (275–365) was originally published in *Recherches de théologie ancienne et médiévale* 7 (1935): 350–80; 8 (1936): 168–97.

100. Otto Hermann Pesch, *Theologie der Rechtfertigung bei Martin Luther und*

Thomas, Scotus, and Ockham give three conflicting positions on the connection between merit, good works, and grace. These differences can be seen in their different answers to two questions. First, can God make sinful acts meritorious? Thomas and Scotus both think that it is impossible, whereas Ockham thinks that it is possible according to God's absolute power. Second, do charity and grace change an act and agent such that there is some intrinsic characteristic that makes the agent and act worthy of eternal beatitude? Whereas Ockham was alone in his answer to the first question, Thomas is alone in his answer to this second question. Both Scotus and Ockham think that the connection to charity and grace is merely the result of God's free decision. Merit is a further relation that is added to the act. Of the three, only Thomas thinks that grace and charity can make an act meritorious by virtue of some intrinsic characteristic of the agent and the act.

THE SHIFT TO THE INTERIOR ACT

Although Thomas and Scotus disagree about whether there are morally indifferent acts and the nature of the relationship between charity and merit, their disagreements to a large extent occur within a shared framework of what the act is. In contrast, even though Ockham often directly addresses Scotus's positions, Ockham's position of the goodness of acts belongs to a new framework.

With respect to an act's goodness, the most significant disagreements between Thomas and Scotus are over (1) whether there are particular morally indifferent acts, (2) whether agents with charity can perform good acts that are indifferent to merit, and (3) whether exterior acts have their own moral worth. The first difference is over the role of the end in choice and in moral goodness. According to Thomas, some acts are good or bad merely on account of their objects. Whereas Scotus describes this goodness as only generic and requiring the further goodness or badness of an end, Thomas thinks that the object's goodness or badness can in some instances sufficiently char-

---

Thomas von Aquin (Mainz: Matthias-Grünewald, 1967), 708–14, 773–84; Wawrykow, *God's Grace and Human Action*, 17–33, 188–89.

acterize as bad, and in some other instances even partially as good. Moreover, Thomas states that even though some kinds of acts may be morally indifferent, every particular act is chosen with an end and circumstances that make the act either good or bad. An act cannot be chosen without some morally relevant end. In contrast, Scotus thinks that many acts can be elicited without a good end. It is not that there is something contrary to the goodness of an end. It is simply that the act lacks such goodness. Scotus thinks that a morally relevant end is an additional factor that may or not be chosen by an agent.

The second disagreement, which is over merit, reflects a difference in thinking about how acts are directed to God. Thomas thinks that good acts are orderable to God in themselves in such a way that if the agent is rightly ordered to God through charity, then the act will be meritorious. Scotus thinks that an agent with charity may or may not choose to order his morally good act to God. On one level, the disagreement between Scotus and Thomas is over whether someone with charity can perform acts that are good but not meritorious. The underlying disagreement is over whether in order to be referred to God in a way significant for merit, the act must be at least traceable back to an act of actually thinking about and loving God.

Third, although Thomas and Scotus agree that exterior acts are necessarily virtuous or vicious, they disagree over the way in which the exterior act adds to the whole act's moral goodness. They both are part of a wider tradition according to which acts are good or bad only insofar as they are voluntary, and an act's completion, or the exterior act, adds to or subtracts from the act's moral worth. Thomas ultimately roots the exterior act's moral worth in that of the interior act, but he does so by showing how the exterior act can affect the interior act in different ways, and that the exterior act also determines an act of choice insofar as the exterior act is an object. For Thomas, the interior and exterior acts are one in a way that resembles the unity of form with matter. Scotus to some extent separates the interior and exterior acts, since he focuses on the way in which the exterior act has its own conformity or lack of conformity to right reason. Scotus, like Thomas, thinks that the exterior act is praiseworthy or blameworthy insofar as it is voluntary, but he thinks that even the commanded acts themselves are broadly imputable to the agent in a way that differs from how the interior act is imputable.

Even though they differ on these three points, Scotus and Thomas share the wider view that distinguishes sharply between the natural goodness of the act in its natural species, and both the moral goodness and the supernatural goodness that belong to the interior and the exterior act. In contrast, Ockham describes the exterior act as a physical act that has no intrinsic moral worth. Indeed, he does not discuss its natural goodness, perhaps because of his views on the roles of natural goodness and final causality in physical explanation. Ockham shifts the discussion of an act's value from the whole human act to an interior and intrinsically valuable act of the will. This focus is reflected in later medieval and modern thinkers.

Ockham's attention to human willing in the context of moral goodness is accompanied by a shift of focus to the divine will in the context of merit. Scotus to a large extent prepared the way for Ockham's separation of merit from the intrinsic value of the act. Nevertheless, although Scotus argues that grace is not according to God's absolute power necessary for merit, he never suggests that simply any act can be meritorious. There is an intrinsic connection between merit and moral goodness. Although Scotus partially prepares the way of an entirely forensic view of merit, he does not abandon the older view that merit must in some way be connected with moral goodness. In contrast, Ockham argues not only against the thesis that grace is a necessary condition of merit according to God's absolute power, but he also argues against the theses that grace is sufficient for merit, and that merit and sin are incompatible. Ockham's view of the role of the divine will in moral goodness is unclear, although he seems to ultimately root moral goodness in a command of the divine will. But Ockham's description of merit is entirely forensic, and it is part of the shift to an ethics that is concerned with the will more than with reason.

Conclusion

No one theme or historical narrative fully accounts for all the differences between the theories of action that are developed by Thomas, Scotus, and Ockham. Any one grand theory that would account for the differences would neglect the individual genius of each thinker and the particular historical circumstances in which that thinker worked.

Many differences can be explained in terms of their individual propensities, their interests, and their reasons for writing. Scotus's discussions often have an ad hoc character. Frequently his immediate concern seems to be only the question at hand in the particular quodlibetal discussion or lecture on the *Sentences*. For instance, he does not give one account of those components of an act that are mentioned by his contemporaries. He discusses any particular act only in the immediate context of its relation to one or two other acts, such as use, command, or intention. Consequently, it is hard to determine how to relate all these acts to each other or into one fully developed view of willing. Another example involves the role of moral virtue. When Scotus argues that some acts are morally indifferent, he assumes that moral virtue is a necessary condition for moral goodness. But this assumption seemingly conflicts with views that he expressed while discussing other topics. It is hard to give a fully systematic account of Scotus's moral psychology. In contrast, Ockham's texts on the subject are relatively clear and consistent with each other. But he wrote comparatively little on ethics and action theory.

Thomas's approach is distinctive not only for its quantity and systematic character, but also for the way in which he accounts for a variety of sources, and the complexity of his analyses. He is both more interested in moral psychology and more sophisticated in his development of it. For instance, his account of an act's stages carefully integrates the insights of John Damascene, Augustine, and previous Scholastics. The complexity of this account results both from the topic itself and from the way in which the topic was addressed by previous thinkers. Similarly, his careful delineation of the degrees of practical knowledge is not matched by similar fully developed accounts in either Scotus or Ockham. These two examples illustrate the wider problem with comparing Thomas with Scotus and Ockham. Not only is Thomas seemingly a deeper thinker and certainly a more prolific writer on action theory, but he also provides a complex systematic account. In contrast, Scotus develops issues in a variety of discussions that are difficult to compare with each other, and Ockham addresses many topics only in passing.

An additional problem with developing a uniform historical narrative is that there is no linear progression from Thomas to Ockham through Scotus. On some issues, Thomas and Ockham are closer to each other than either is to Scotus. For instance, both Thomas and Ockham think that the completion of an act is morally valuable because of some influence on the will. Another example is that both of them seem to think that choice is univocal. This lack of linear progression complicates attempts to describe the shift. Nevertheless, despite these and similar examples, Scotus's position often falls midway between that of Thomas and Ockham. For instance, whereas Thomas most often states that God cannot dispense from the natural law, and Ockham thinks that God could change it, Scotus thinks that God could change part but only part of the natural law. Similarly, Scotus's view on the will's inclinations seems to fall somewhere in between Thomas's position that the will has one inclination to happiness or the good in general and Ockham's view that the will can choose whatever object is presented to it by the intellect.

Some of the widespread historical narratives seem to me particularly unhelpful in the context of action theory.[1] For instance, it was once common to describe Thomas's work as the high point of Scholasticism, and the views of Scotus and Ockham as progressive instances of intellectual disintegration.[2] Although Thomas does seem to be a greater figure than Scotus or Ockham, I hope that this book has shown that their philosophical views are important in their own right.

There have also been attempts to reject the common interpretation of thirteenth-century thought as a conflict between Aristotelianism and Augustinianism.[3] Although opponents of this interpretation may overstate their case, it does seem to me that the distinction between Aristotelianism and Augustinianism is unhelpful for discussing Scotus and Ockham. Both claim to be basically Aristotelian. Moreover, although Thomas may be more Aristotelian than they are, he is also arguably the most Augustinian. Nevertheless, since Augustine seems to have strongly influenced the later medieval understanding of the will, there may be a way in which the increasing focus on the will in Scotus and in Ockham can be seen as partially Augustinian, even if only in inspiration.

The traditional historical dichotomy between intellectualism and voluntarism can be helpful if it is appropriately qualified. There are several problems with the common description of Thomas as an intellectualist and Scotus and Ockham as voluntarists. For instance, as we saw in chapter 1, Thomas emphasizes the importance of the will by stating that it is the only necessary and per se proximate efficient cause of the human act. He does not mention the known object's efficient causality. Since Scotus (in most texts) thinks that the known object is a partial efficient cause and Ockham has the same view concerning the act of understanding, there is at least one way in which the known object plays a more significant causal role in their theories

1. A critical assessment of the different approaches can be found in John Inglis, *Spheres of Philosophical Inquiry and the Historiography of Medieval Philosophy,* Brill's Studies in Intellectual History 81 (Leiden/Boston: Brill, 1998).

2. A criticism can be found in Kent, *Virtues of the Will,* 1–38.

3. Fernand van Steenberghen, *Aristotle in the West: The Origins of Latin Aristotelianism,* trans. Leonard Johnston (Louvain: Nauwelaerts, 1955); Kent, *Virtues of the Will,* 39–93.

than in that of Thomas. Similarly, Thomas's distinction between the liberties of specification and exercise allow him to give an account of the act's stages in which both the intellect and the will play a prominent role. In contrast, Ockham and Scotus separate the will and the intellect to such an extent that even though the intellect has a subordinate role, it has its own independent role in the action. An additional complicating feature is Ockham's belief that the intellect and the will are in themselves not really distinct. Although this view has roots in the Franciscan tradition, it does not seem necessarily connected with a particularly Franciscan voluntaristic account.

Nevertheless, characteristic differences that might point to a Franciscan "voluntarism" can be seen in the three areas that are were mentioned in the introduction, namely (1) the relationship between the will and nature, (2) the explanatory role of the will, and (3) the causation of separate exterior acts by interior acts. First, there are differences over the relationship between willing and nature. Thomas thinks that the rational appetite is distinct from the natural appetite in that the rational appetite follows intellectual knowledge and is not determined to any one particular good, even though it is determined to happiness. There is a continuum between the natural inclination of the will to the good in general and all natural inclinations. Although the will is different from other inclinations insofar as it is a rational appetite, its ends are given by nature. Moreover, the principles of practical reason are largely based on human natural inclination. Secondary principles determine and apply these basic principles. Natural inclination also plays a role in the stages of an act. The natural willing of known goods is a simple willing that precedes choice, which is the central act of the will. A good act is in conformity with reason insofar as it is in conformity with the natural law, which is based on the natural inclinations toward different kinds of goods. Acts that violate the natural law, and consequently natural inclination, can never be meritorious. The importance of nature and natural inclination is behind each feature of Thomas's action theory.

For Scotus, the will is free precisely because it has an inclination that is not natural and directed toward the agent's own good. Natural inclination is self-directed; the will's inclination to justice is not. Scotus denies that the will can choose just any good. The inclination to one's own happiness is moderated only by the inclination to the just. There is no third alternative. Freedom results not from the availability of any two arbitrarily selected objects, but from the two alternative goods that correspond to the two inclinations, namely the advantageous and the just. Since natural inclination is for the advantageous, it can conflict with the just and cannot by itself be the foundation of ethics. Practical reason is not based primarily on natural inclination, but rather on principles that are self-evident from the meaning of their terms. Natural inclination is irrelevant to the capacity for acts to be meritorious or demeritorious. Although Scotus thinks that the will does have a natural inclination, and that even its inclination to the advantageous is not entirely free of restraint, he sharply separates human action from the nonrational world. On this issue Scotus seems to rest somewhere between Thomas and Ockham, who seemingly thinks it evident that the will is free from natural direction and can choose any object whatsoever. Moreover, for Ockham the principles of moral reasoning ultimately are true because of God's free decision to make them so, even though the agent may not know about this ultimate source in God's will. Ockham seems to separate the moral from the natural.

Second, there is much disagreement over the explanatory role of the will. Thomas sometimes gives an explanatory role to reason that Ockham and Scotus would give to the will. For instance, Thomas states that the will by itself is a rational appetite that is determined to happiness or the good in general. The ability to freely choose is rooted not only in the ability of the will to move itself, but in reason's ability to consider different instantiations of and means to happiness. Thomas's understanding of practical reason is reflected in this view that the known good by itself is motivating, and that certain kinds of objects are intrinsically practical and capable of directing action. Similarly, he thinks that the goodness and badness of acts consists in a conformity of their object and circumstances with reason. There are no individual morally indifferent acts, since the human agent can only choose an act that has a morally relevant object or end. Although

Thomas thinks that an act's merit is based not only on reason but also on God's decision to accept certain acts as meritorious, he also holds that there is an intrinsic connection between merit and good acts that are accompanied by charity. Merit is not merely extrinsic to the act and a result of the divine will.

Scotus thinks that freedom results from the will's special inclination to the just, and consequently that it is rooted in the will rather than in the intellect. This freedom extends even to morally indifferent acts. An agent is free to choose an act without choosing any morally relevant end. Although Scotus does not give an account of morality that is entirely based on the divine will, he does argue that God's will ultimately can determine the goodness or badness of any act that does not itself have God as its object or lacks a necessary connection with an act that does. Scotus's account of merit allows for conditions on the part of the meritorious act, such as that it be good, but it ultimately places merit in a contingent relation to the divine will and that reward that God freely chooses to give. These different features of Scotus's theory indicate a stronger emphasis on the will than we find in Thomas. But this emphasis on the will is accompanied by a different description of what the will is. For Scotus, a mere intellectual appetite would not be free. The human and angelic wills are free precisely because they have two inclinations.

Ockham similarly seems to root freedom in the will, although he rejects Scotus's account of the will's different inclinations. Ockham seems simply to assume that the will is free to choose any possible action, even if it is not understood as pleasurable or otherwise good. There is no discussion of its natural inclination. He makes a brief appeal to experience, but he thinks that his notion of freedom is more obvious than any argument that he could give for it. His belief that this notion is obvious may reflect the later historical context in which he worked, but it may also reflect his personal proclivities. This notion of freedom is reflected in his understanding of practical reason, since he thinks that the final cause of any science is strictly speaking merely what the agent directs it toward. Similarly, he thinks that the will plays a separate role in the stages of the act such that it can accept or reject any object that is shown to it by the intellect. Although Ockham thinks that many acts can be known to be morally good or bad apart from the knowledge of God's will, he also thinks that the goodness or badness of any act is ultimately a result of God's will. Similarly, Ockham thinks that merit is entirely a result of God's choice. He extends the list of acts that God could make meritorious in order to include even sinful acts. His emphasis on the possibilities of human and divine freedom is far greater than that of Thomas and Scotus.

The third theme is an increasing tendency toward a dualistic view according to which the mind's causal structure can be described in terms that also apply to mechanistic causality in the physical world. The immaterial mind produces volitions that have physical acts as effects. The physical acts are human acts because they are caused by volitions, and they are physical only under a description. This tendency has been discussed as a modern innovation by some philosophers of mind, but it may have medieval roots in the views of Scotus and Ockham.[4]

Thomas's approach clearly contradicts this modern tendency. His description of the act's production focuses on the different causal influences of the intellect and the will. Whereas the will is an efficient cause, the object presented by the intellect is a final cause. The intellect and will play complementary but distinct roles in the act's production. Similarly, the stages of the act are not simply successive acts of the intellect and will that influence each other in the realm of final causality. For instance, the judgment of choice is like the matter for the act of the will. Similarly, although Thomas distinguishes between the interior and exterior acts as natural acts, he does not consider them to be distinct human acts. With respect to the referral of acts, no special act of the will is needed for an act to be meaningfully directed to God as an end. If the agent has charity and performs the right kind of act, then the act is at least virtually ordered and meritorious. For the act to be meritorious, the agent must have actually loved God at some previous time. Nevertheless, the act's merit does not depend on the agent's actual ordering of the act to God or some sort of proximate

4. P. M. S. Hacker, *Mind and Will,* 195–208; Kahn, "Discovering the Will," 235–36.

causal connection to such willing. Thomas does not look for some proximate intellectual efficient cause.

In contrast to Thomas, Scotus describes the known object's causality in such a way that it belongs either to the same order or at least to a similar order as the will's causality. The known object is a subordinate cause, but it is either an efficient cause, which seems to be Scotus's more frequent opinion, or a *sine qua non* cause. In his discussion of the act's stages, Scotus seems to focus on the will's act as distinct from the intellectual acts. Both form distinct and seemingly independent causal stages in the production of an act. The causal sequence is also important for merit. For Scotus, an act is virtually referred to God and meritorious only if the agent's intention can somehow be explicitly traced back to an actual willing of God.

Although Ockham thinks that the intellect and the will are really the same, he paradoxically gives an even starker account of their different causal roles. Like Scotus, he describes the causation of the act of understanding and the will as belonging to the same order, namely that of efficient causality. He also resembles Scotus in his description of the act's stages as distinct causal contributions of the intellect and the will. He goes beyond Scotus in his division of the interior and the exterior acts. For Ockham, the exterior act is a natural act that is caused by an interior act. This separation of the interior from the exterior act foreshadows that of modern thinkers in its reduction of the exterior human act to physical causality, its separation of interior mental acts from natural acts, and its description of interior acts as hidden to outside observers.

Although Thomas, Scotus, and Ockham are all broadly Aristotelian, their different Aristotelian accounts reflect underlying disagreements in these three areas. These trends may represent a shift from an earlier to a later medieval intellectual culture, but they also reflect views that continued to exist in different schools. Thomists continued to exist alongside Scotists through the end of the eighteenth century, and Ockham's views had a more varied but continued influence through the modern period. The different views of Thomas, Scotus, and Ockham are not only in themselves plausible attempts at understanding human action, but they formed the background to late medieval and early modern descriptions of human action.

228

BIBLIOGRAPHY

Primary Sources

Abelard, Peter. *Scio te ipsum.* Edited by Rainer M. Ilgner. Corpus Christianorum, Continuatio Mediaevalis 190. Turnhout: Brepols, 2001.

Albert the Great. *Opera Omnia.* Edited by Auguste Borgnet. 38 vols. Paris: Vivès, 1890–1899.

———. *Opera Omnia.* Edited by Bernhard Geyer and Wilhelm Gubel. Monasterium Westfalorum: Aschendorff, 1951–.

Aristotle. *Ethica Nicomachea.* Translated by Robert Grosseteste. Edited by René Antonin Gauthier. *Aristoteles Latinus,* vol. 25, fasc. 1–3. Corpus Philosophorum Medii Aevi. Leiden: Brill; Brussels: Desclée, 1972–1974.

———. *Nicomachean Ethics.* Translated by Christopher Rowe. Oxford: Oxford University Press, 2002.

Bonaventure of Bagnorea. *Opera Omnia.* 10 vols. Quaracchi: Collegium S. Bonaventurae, 1882–1902.

Capreolus, Johannes. *Defensiones theologiae divi Thomae Aquinatis.* Edited by Ceslaus Paban and Thomas Pègues. 7 vols. Tours: Alfred Cattier, 1900–1907; repr. Frankfurt am Main: Minerva, 1967.

Montefortino, Hieronymus de. *Summa Theologica Ioannis Duns Scoti.* 6 vols. Rome, 1900–1903.

Parisiensis, Iohannes (Quidort). *Le Correctorium Corruptorii "Circa" de Jean Quidort de Paris.* Edited by Jean-Pierre Muller. Studia Anselmiana 12–13. Rome: Pontificium Institutum S. Anselmi, 1941.

Salmanticenses. *Cursus Theologicus.* 20 vols. Paris: Palme, 1870–1883.

Scotus, Johannes Duns. *Cuestiones Cuodlibetales.* Edited and translated by Felix Alluntis. Madrid: Biblioteca de Auctores Cristianos, 1968.

———. *Opera Omnia.* Edited by Luke Wadding. Lyons: Laurentius Durandus, 1639; repr. Hildesheim: Georg Olms, 1968.

———. *Opera Omnia.* Edited by the Scotistic Commission. Vatican City: Typis Polyglottis Vaticanis, 1950–.

———. *Opera Philosophica.* Edited by Girard Etzkorn et al. 5 vols. St. Bonaventure, N.Y.: Franciscan Institute, 1997–2006.

———. *Quodlibet 16.* In Timothy B. Noone and H. Francie Roberts, "John Duns Scotus' Quodlibet: A Brief Study of the Manuscripts and an Edition of Question 16." In *Theological Quodlibeta in the Middle Ages: The Fourteenth Century,* edited by Christopher Schabel, 131–98. Brill's Companions to the Christian Tradition, 7. Boston/Leiden: Brill, 2007.

Thomas Aquinas. *Expositio et Lectura super Epistolas Paul Apostoli.* 2 vols. Edited by Raphael Cai. Turin: Maritetti, 1953.

———. *Opera Omnia.* Rome: Commisio Leonina, 1884–.

———. *Quaestiones Disputatae.* Edited by P. Bazzi et al. 2 vols. Turin: Marietti, 1953.

———. *Scriptum super libros sententiarum.* Edited by Pierre Mandonnet and M. F. Moos. 4 vols. Paris: Lethielleux, 1927–1947.

———. *Super Librum de causis exposition.* Edited by G. D. Saffrey. Texts Philosophici Friburgenses. Fribour: Société Philosophique; Louvain: Nauwelaerts, 1954.

William of Ockham. *Guillelmi de Ockham opera philosophica et theologica.* Edited by Gedeon Gál et al. St. Bonaventure, N.Y.: Franciscan Institute. *Opera philosophica,* 7 vols. (1974–1986). *Opera theologica,* 10 vols. (1967–1986).

Secondary Sources

Adams, Marilyn McCord. "The Structure of Ockham's Moral Theory." *Franciscan Studies* 46 (1986): 1–35.

———. *William Ockham.* 2 vols. Notre Dame, Ind.: University of Notre Dame Press, 1987.

———. "William of Ockham: Voluntarist or Naturalist?" In *Studies in Medieval Philosophy,* edited by John F. Wippel, 219–47. Studies in Philosophy and the History of Philosophy 1. Washington, D.C.: The Catholic University of America Press, 1987.

———. "Duns Scotus on the Will as Rational Power." In *Via Scoti: Methodologica ad mentem Joannis Duns Scoti 1993, Atti del Congresso Scotistico Internationale Roma 9–11 Marzo 1993,* edited by Leonardo Sileo, 839–54. Studia scholastico-Scotistica 5. Rome: Edizioni Antonianum, 1995.

———. "Scotus and Ockham on the Connection of the Virtues." In *John Duns Scotus: Metaphysics and Ethics,* edited by Ludger Honnefelder, Rega Wood, and Mechtild Dreyer, 499–522. Leiden: Brill, 1996.

———. "Ockham on Final Causality: Muddying the Waters." *Franciscan Studies* 56 (1998): 1–46.

———. "Ockham on Will, Nature, Morality." In *The Cambridge Companion to Ockham,* edited by Paul Vincent Spade, 245–72. Cambridge: Cambridge University Press, 1999.

Anscombe, G. E. M. "Thought and Action in Aristotle." In *New Essays on Plato and Aristotle,* edited by R. Bambrough, 143–58. London: Routledge & Kegan Paul, 1965.

———. *Intention.* 2nd ed. Cambridge, Mass.: Harvard University Press, 2000.

———. *Human Life, Action, and Ethics.* Edited by Mary Geach and Luke Gormally. Exeter, U.K.: Imprint Academic, 2005.

———. *Faith in a Hard Ground: Essays on Religion, Philosophy, and Ethics.* Edited by Mary Geach and Luke Gormally. Exeter, U.K.: Imprint Academic, 2008.

Baker, Richard Russell. *The Thomistic Theory of the Passions and Their Influence upon the Will.* Notre Dame, Ind.: University of Notre Dame Press, 1941.

Balic, Carlo. *Les commentaires de Jean Duns Scot sur les quatres libres de Sentences: Étude Historique et Critique.* Louvain: Bureaux de la Revue, 1927.

Bannach, Klaus. *Die Lehre von der Doppelten Macht Gottes bei Wilhelm von Ockham: Problemgeschichtliche Voraussetzungen und Bedeutung.* Wiesbaden: Franz Steiner, 1975.

Barnwell, Michael. *The Problem of Negligent Omissions: Medieval Action Theories to the Rescue.* Leiden/Boston: Brill, 2010.

Beck, Andreas J., and Antonie Vos. "Conceptual Patterns Related to Reformed Scholasticism." *Tijdschrift* 57 (2003): 224–33.

Belmans, Theo G. *Le sens objectif de l'agir humain: Pour relire la morale conjugale de Saint Thomas.* Studi Thomistica 8. Vatican City: Libreria Editrice Vaticana, 1980.

Boler, John. "Transcending the Natural: Duns Scotus on the Two Affections of the Will." *American Catholic Philosophical Quarterly* 69 (1995): 109–26.

Boulnois, Olivier. *Être et représentation: Une généalogie de la métaphysique moderne à l'époque de Duns Scot (XIIIᵉ–XIVᵉ siècle).* Paris: Presses Universitaires de France, 1999.

Bourke, Vernon. *St. Thomas and the Greek Moralists.* Milwaukee, Wis.: Marquette University Press, 1947.

———. *Ethics: A Textbook in Moral Philosophy.* New York: Macmillan, 1951.

Brock, Stephen L. "What Is the Use of *Usus* in Aquinas' Philosophy of Action?" In *Moral and Political Philosophies of the Middle Ages,* 3 vols., Proceedings of the Ninth International Congress of Medieval Philosophy, Ottowa, 17–22 August 1992, edited by B. Carlos Bazán, Eduardo Andujár, and Léonard G. Sbrocchi, 654–64. New York/Ottowa: Legas, 1995.

———. *Action and Conduct: Thomas Aquinas and the Theory of Action.* Edinburgh: T & T Clark, 1998.

———. "Causality and Necessity in Thomas Aquinas." *Quaestio* 2 (2002): 217–40.

———. "*Veritatis Splendor* #78: St. Thomas and (Not Merely) Physical Objects of Moral Acts." *Nova et Vetera*, English Edition, 6 (2008): 1–62.

Brown, Stephen F. "Ockham and Final Causality." In *Studies in Medieval Philosophy*, edited by Johm F. Wippel, 249–72. Studies in Philosophy and the History of Philosophy 17. Washington, D.C.: The Catholic University of America Press, 1987.

Butera, Guissepe. "The Moral Status of the First Principle of Practical Reason in Thomas's Natural Law Theory." *The Thomist* 71 (2007): 609–31.

Byers, Sarah. "The Meaning of *Voluntas* in Augustine." *Augustinian Studies* 37 (2006): 171–89.

Cessario, Romanus. *A Short History of Thomism*. Washington, D.C.: The Catholic University of America Press, 2005.

Clark, David W. "William of Ockham on Right Reason." *Speculum* 48 (1973): 13–36.

Colish, Marcia L. *Peter Lombard*. 2 vols. Brill's Studies in Intellectual History 41. Leiden: Brill, 1994.

Courtenay, William J. "The Dialectic of Omnipotence in the High and Late Middle Ages." In *Divine Omniscience and Omnipotence in Medieval Philosophy: Islamic, Jewish, and Christian Perspectives*, edited by Tamar Rudavsky, 243–69. Dordrecht: Kluwer, 1985.

———. *Capacity and Volition: A History of the Distinction of Absolute and Ordained Power*. Quodlibet 8. Bergamo: Pierluigi Lubrina, 1990.

———. "The Academic and Intellectual Worlds of Ockham." In *The Cambridge Companion to Ockham*, edited by Paul Vincent Spade, 17–30. Cambridge: Cambridge University Press, 1999.

———. *Ockham and Ockhamism: Studies in the Dissemination and Impact of His Thought*. Studien und Texte zur Geistesgeschichte des Mittelalters 99. Leiden/Boston: Brill, 2008.

Cross, Richard. "Duns Scotus on Goodness, Justice and What God Can Do." *Journal of Theological Studies* 48 (1997): 48–76.

———. *Duns Scotus*. Oxford: Oxford University Press, 1999.

———. "Philosophy of Mind." In *The Cambridge Companion to Scotus*, edited by Thomas Williams, 263–84. Cambridge: Cambridge University Press, 2003.

Cunningham, Stanley. *Reclaiming Moral Agency: The Moral Philosophy of Albert the Great*. Washington, D.C.: The Catholic University of America Press, 2008.

Dedek, John. "Intrinsically Evil Acts: An Historical Study of the Mind of St. Thomas." *The Thomist* 43 (1979): 385–413.

———. "Intrinsically Evil Acts: The Emergence of a Doctrine." *Recherches de théologie ancienne et médiévale* 50 (1983): 191–226.

Deman, Th. "Péché." In *Dictionnaire de théologie catholique*, 15 vols. in 23, 12.1., cols. 139–275. Paris: Letourzey et Ané, 1899–1950.

Detloff, Werner. *Die Entwicklung der Akzepatations- un Verdienstlehre von Duns Scotus bis Luther: Mit Besonderer Berucksichtigung der Franziskanertheologen.* Beiträge zur Geschichte der Philosophie und Theologie des Mittelalters 40.1 Münster: Aschendorff, 1963.

Dewan, Lawrence. "The Real Distinction between Intellect and Will." *Angelicum* 57 (1980): 557–93. Repr. in *Wisdom, Law, and Virtue,* 125–50.

———. "'Obiectum': Notes on the Invention of a Word." *Archives d'histoire doctrinale et littéraire du moyen âge* 58 (1981): 37–96. Repr. in *Wisdom, Law, and Virtue,* 403–43.

———. "St. Thomas, James Keenan, and the Will." *Science et Ésprit* 47 (1995): 153–76. Repr. in *Wisdom, Law, and Virtue,* 151–74.

———. "St. Thomas and the Causes of Free Choice." *Acta Philosophica* 8 (1999): 87–96. Repr. in *Wisdom, Law, and Virtue,* 175–85.

———. "St. Thomas, Rhonheimer, and the Object of the Human Act." *Nova et Vetera,* English Edition, 6 (2008): 63–112.

———. *Wisdom, Law, and Virtue: Essays in Thomistic Ethics.* New York: Fordham University Press, 2008.

Dihle, Albrecht. *The Theory of the Will in Classical Antiquity.* Berkeley and Los Angeles: University of California Press, 1982.

Dobler, Emil. *Zwei Syriche Quellen der Theologischen Summa des Thomas von Aquin: Nemesios von Emese und Johannes von Damaskus. Ihr Einfluss auf die anthropologischen Grundlagen der Moraltheologie.* Freiburger Zeitschrift für Philosophie und Theologie 25. Freiburg: Universitätsverlag Freiburg, 2000.

Donagan, Alan. "Thomas Aquinas on Human Action." In *The Cambridge History of Later Medieval Philosophy: From the Rediscovery of Aristotle to the Disintegration of Scholasticism: 1100–1600,* edited by Norman Kretzmann, Anthony Kenny, and Jan Pinborg, 642–54. Cambridge: Cambridge University Press, 1982.

Dreyer, Mechtild, and Mary Beth Ingham. *The Philosophical Vision of John Duns Scotus.* Washington, D.C.: The Catholic University of America Press, 2004.

Dumont, Stephen D. "The Necessary Connection of Moral Virtue to Prudence According to John Duns Scotus—Revisited." *Recherches de théologie ancienne et médiévale* 55 (1988): 184–206.

———. "Time, Contradiction, and the Freedom of the Will in the Late Thirteenth Century." *Documente e studi sulla tradizione filosofica medievale* 3 (1992): 561–97.

———. "The Origin of Scotus's Theory of Synchronic Contingency." *The Modern Schoolman* 72 (1995): 149–67.

———. "Did Duns Scotus Change His Mind on the Will?" In *Nach der Verurteilung von 1277: Philosophie und Tehologie an der Universität von Paris im letzten Viertel des 13. Jahrhunderts,* edited by Jan Aertsen, Kent Emery, and

Andreas Speer, 719–94. Miscellanea Mediaevalia 28. Berlin/New York: de Gruyter, 2001.

Durand, Guy. "Les notions de fin intermédiaire et de fin secondaire dans la Tradition thomiste." *Science et ésprit* 21 (1969): 371–402.

Eardley, Peter. "Thomas Aquinas and Giles of Rome on the Will." *Review of Metaphysics* 56 (2003): 836–62.

————. "The Foundations of Freedom in Later Medieval Philosophy: Giles of Rome and His Contemporaries." *Journal of the History of Philosophy* 44 (2006): 353–76.

————. "The Problem of Moral Weakness, the *Propositio Magistralis*, and the Condemnation of 1277." *Mediaeval Studies* 68 (2006): 161–203

Ebbesen, Sten. "Is Logic Theoretical or Practical Knowledge?" In *Itinéraires d'Alberte de Saxe: Paris:Vienne au xive siècle, Actes du Colloque organisé le 18–22 juin 1990 dans le cadre des activités de l'URA 1085 du CRNSà l'occasion du 600e anniversaire de la mort d'Albert de Saxe*, edited by Joël Biard, 267–76. Études de Philosophie Médiévale 69. Paris: Vrin, 1991.

Effler, Roy R. *John Duns Scotus and the Principle "Omne quod movetur ab alio movetur."* St. Bonaventure, N.Y.: Franciscan Institute, 1962.

Elders, Leo. "La théorie Scotiste de l'acte indifférant et sa critique par Cajetan." In *Regnum Hominis et Regnum Dei, Acta Quarti Congressus Scotistici Intenationalis Patavii 24–29 septembris 1976*, edited by Camille Bérubé, 2.207–14. Studia Scholastico-Scotistica 7. Rome: Societas Internationalis Scotistica, 1978.

————. "La doctrine de la conscience de saint Thomas d'Aquin." *Revue Thomiste* 83 (1983): 533–57.

Emery, Kent, and Andreas Speer. "After the Condemnation of 1277: New Evidence, New Perspectives, and Grounds for New Interpretations." In *Nach der Verurteilung von 1277: Philosophie und Theologie an der Universität von Paris im letzten Viertel des 13. Jahrhunderts*, edited by Jan Aertsen, Kent Emery, and Andreas Speer, 3–19. Miscellanea Mediaevalia 28. Berlin/New York: de Gruyter, 2001.

Finnis, John. *Aquinas: Moral, Political and Legal Theory*. Oxford: Oxford University Press, 1998.

Finnis, John, and Germain Grisez. "The Basic Principles of Natural Law: A Reply to Ralph McInerny." *American Journal of Jurisprudence* 26 (1981): 21–31.

Finnis, John, Germain Grisez, and Joseph Boyle. "'Direct' and 'Indirect': A Reply to Critics of Our Action Theory." *The Thomist* 65 (2001): 1–44.

Flannery, Kevin. *Acts Amid Precepts: The Aristotelian Structure of Thomas Aquinas's Moral Theory*. Washington, D.C.: The Catholic University of America Press, 2001.

Foot, Philippa. *Moral Dilemmas*. Oxford: Clarendon Press, 2002.

Freppert, Lucan. *The Basis of Morality according to William of Ockham*. Chicago: Franciscan Herald Press, 1988.

Gaine, Simon Francis. *Will There Be Free Will in Heaven?: Freedom, Impeccability and Beatitude*. London/New York: T & T Clark, 2003.

Gallagher, David. "Aquinas on Moral Action: Interior and Exterior Acts." *Proceedings of the American Catholic Philosophical Association* 64 (1990): 118–29.

———. "Thomas Aquinas on the Will as Rational Appetite." *Journal of the History of Philosophy* 29 (1991): 559–84.

———. "Free Choice and Free Judgment in Aquinas." *Archive für Geschichte der Philosophie* 76 (1994): 247–77.

———. "The Will and Its Acts (IaIIae, qq. 6–17)." In *The Ethics of Aquinas*, edited by Stephen Pope, 69–89. Washington, D.C.: Georgetown University Press, 2002.

Garrigou-Lagrange, Réginald. "La fin ultime du péché venial: Et celle de l'acte imparfait, dit 'imperfection.'" *Revue Thomiste* 7 (1924): 314–17.

———. *Christian Perfection and Contemplation: According to St. Thomas Aquinas and St. John of the Cross*. Translated by M. Timothea Doyle. St. Louis, Mo./London: Herder, 1946.

———. *De Beatitudine: Commentarium in Summam Theologicam St. Thomae I-II qq. 1–54*. Turin: Berruti, 1951.

Gauthier, René Antonin. "Saint Maxime le Confesseur et la psychologie de l'acte humain." *Recherches de Théologie Ancienne et Médiévale* 21 (1954): 51–100.

Gidziunas, Viktoras. "Scotism and Scotists in Lithuania." In *De doctrina Ioannis Duns Scoti*, Acta Congressus Scotistici Internationalis 11–17 sept. 1966, Studia Scholastico-Scotistica 4, vol. 4: *Scotismus decursu saeculorum*, 239–48. Rome, 1968.

Goris, Harm J. M. J. *Free Creatures of an Eternal God: Thomas Aquinas on God's Infallible Foreknowledge and Irresistible Will*. Publications of the Thomas Instituut te Utrecht, New Series 4. Nifmegen: Stichtung Thomasfonds, 1996.

Grajewski, Maurice J. *The Formal Distinction of Duns Scotus: A Study in Metaphysics*. Washington, D.C.: The Catholic University of America Press, 1944.

Grisez, Germain. "The Structure of Practical Reason: Some Comments and Clarifications." *The Thomist* 52 (1988): 269–91.

Gründel, Johannes. *Die Lehre von der menschlichen Handlung im Mittelalter*. Beiträge zur Geschichte der Philosophie und Theologie des Mittelalters 39.5. Münster: Aschendorff, 1963.

Hacker, P. M. S. *Mind and Will*, vol. 4 of *An Analytic Commentary on the Philosophical Investigations*, part 1. Oxford: Blackwell, 1996.

Hause, Jeffrey. "Thomas Aquinas and the Voluntarists." *Medieval Philosophy and Theology* 6 (1997): 167–82.

Hechich, Barnaba. "Il Problema delle 'Reportationes' nell' Eredità Dottrina del B. Giovanni Duns Scotus, OFM." In *Giovani Duns Scoto: Studi e ricerche nel VII Centenario della sua morte,* edited by Marin Carbajo Nunez, 59–129. Rome: Antonianum, 2008.

Hedwig, Klaus. "Actus indifferens: Über die Theorie des indifferenten Handelns bei Thomas von Aquin und Duns Scotus." *Philosophisches Jahrbuch* 95 (1988): 120–31.

———. "Das Isaak-Opfer: Über den Status des Naturgesetzes bei Thomas von Aquin, Duns Scotus, and Ockham." In *Mensch und Natur im Mittelalter,* edited by Andreas Speer and Albert Zimmerman, 2..645–61, Miscellanea Mediaevalia 21.2. Berlin: de Gruyter, 1992.

Heynck, Valens. "Der Einfluss des Skotismus auf dem Konzil von Trient (Bonaventura Pio da Constacciaro, OFM Conv., Der Führer der Skotischen Gruppe in der Ersten Tagungsperiode, 1535–1547)." In *De doctrina Ioannis Duns Scoti,* Acta Congressus Scotistici Internationalis 11–17 sept. 1966, Studia Scholastico-Scotistica 4, vol. 4: *Scotismus decursu saeculorum,* 259–90. Rome, 1968.

Hirvonen, Vesa. *Passions in William of Ockham's Philosophical Psychology.* Studies in the History and Philosophy of Mind 2. Dordrecht/Boston/London: Kluwer, 2004.

Hittinger, Russell. *A Critique of the New Natural Law Theory.* Notre Dame, Ind.: University of Notre Dame Press, 1987.

Hoenen, Maarten J. F. M. "Late Medieval Schools of Thought in the Mirror of University Textbooks: The *Promptuarium Argumentorum* (Cologne 1492)." In *Philosophy and Learning: Universities in the Middle Ages,* edited by Martin J. F. M. Hoenen, J. H. Josef Schneider, and Georg Wieland, 329–69. Education and Society in the Middle Ages and Renaissance 6. Leiden: Brill, 1995.

———. "Scotus and the Scotist School: The Tradition of Scotist Thought in the Medieval and Early Modern Period." In *John Duns Scotus: Renewal of Philosophy,* Acts of the Third Symposium Organized by the Dutch Society for Medieval Philosophy Medium Aevum, May 23 and 24, 1996, edited by E. P. Bos, *Elementa* 72 (1998): 197–210.

Hoeres, Walter. *Der Wille als Reine Volkommenheit nach Duns Scotus.* Salzburger Studient zur Philosophie 1. München: Pustet, 1962.

Hoffmann, Tobias. "The Distinction between Nature and Will in Duns Scotus." *Archives d'histoire doctrinale et littéraire du moyen âge* 66 (1999): 184–224.

———. "Moral Action as Human Action: End and Object in Aquinas in Comparison with Abelard, Lombrard, Albert, and Duns Scotus." *The Thomist* 67 (2003): 73–94.

———. "L''akrasia' selon Duns Scot." In *Duns Scot à Paris: Actes du colloque de Paris, 2–4 septembre 2002*, edited by Olivier Boulnois et. al., 487–518. Turnhout: Brepols, 2004.

———. "Aquinas on the Moral Problem of the Weak-Willed." In *The Problem of Weakness of Will in Moral Philosophy*, edited by Tobias Hoffmann, Jörn Müller and Matthias Perkams, 221–47. Leuven: Peeters, 2006.

———. "Aquinas and Intellectual Determinism: The Test Case of Angelic Sin." *Archiv für der Geschichte der Philosophie* 89 (2007): 122–56.

Holopainen, Taina. *William of Ockham's Theory of the Foundations of Ethics.* Helsinki: Luther-Agricola-Society, 1991.

Honnefelder, Ludger. "Ansätze zu einer Theorie der praktischen Wahrheit bei Thomas von Aquin und Johannes Duns Scotus." In *Was ist für den Menschen Gute?: Menschliche Natur und Güterlehre*, edited by Jan Szaif and Matthias Lutz-Bachmann, 246–62. Berlin: De Gruyter, 2004.

Hursthouse, Rosalind. "Intention." In *Logic, Cause and Action: Essays in Honour of Elizabeth Anscombe*, edited by Roger Teichmann, 83–105. Cambridge: Cambridge University Press, 2000.

Ingham, Mary Beth. "Duns Scotus, Morality, and Happiness: A Reply to Thomas Williams." *American Catholic Philosophical Quarterly* 74 (2000): 173–95.

———. "Did Scotus Modify His Position on the Relationship of Intellect and Will?" *Recherches de théologie et philosophie médiévales* 69 (2002): 88–116.

Inglis, John. *Spheres of Philosophical Inquiry and the Historiography of Medieval Philosophy.* Brill's Studies in Intellectual History 81. Boston/Leiden: Brill, 1998.

Inwood, Brad. *Ethics and Human Action in Early Stoicism.* Oxford: Clarendon Press, 1985.

Irwin, Terence. "The Scope of Deliberation: A Conflict in Aquinas." *Review of Metaphysics* 44 (1990): 21–42.

———. "Who Discovered the Will?" *Ethics, Philosophical Perspectives* 6 (1992): 453–73.

———. *The Development of Ethics: A Historical and Critical Study*, vol. 1: *From Socrates to the Reformation.* Oxford: Oxford University Press, 2007.

Iserloh, Erwin. *Gnade und Eucharistie in der Philosphischen Theologie des Wilhelm von Ockham.* Wiesbaden: Franz Steiner, 1956.

Jensen, Steven J. "A Defence of Physicalism." *The Thomist* 61 (1997): 377–404.

———. "Do Circumstances Give Species?" *The Thomist* 70 (2006): 1–26.

———. "When Evil Actions Become Good." *Nova et Vetera*, English Edition, 5 (2007): 747–64.

———. "The Error of the Passions." *The Thomist* 73 (2009): 349–79.

———. *Good and Evil Actions: A Journey through Saint Thomas Aquinas.* Washington, D.C.: The Catholic University of America Press, 2010.

Kahn, Charles. "Discovering the Will: From Aristotle to Augustine." In *The Question of Eclecticism: Studies in Later Greek Philosophy,* edited by John M. Dillon and A. A. Long, 234–59. Berkeley and Los Angeles: University of California Press, 1988.

Kaluza, Zenon. *Les querelles doctrinales à Paris: Nominalistes et réalistes aux confins du xive et du xve siècles.* Bergamo: Lubrina, 1988.

Kenny, Anthony. *The Anatomy of the Soul: Historical Essays in the Philosophy of Mind.* Oxford: Blackwell, 1973.

———. *Aquinas on Mind.* London/New York: Routledge, 1993.

Kent, Bonnie. *Virtues of the Will: The Transformation of Ethics in the Late Thirteenth Century.* Washington, D.C.: The Catholic University of America Press, 1995.

———. "Aquinas and Weakness of Will." *Philosophy and Phenomenological Research* 75 (2007): 70–91.

———. "Evil in Later Medieval Philosophy." *Journal of the History of Philosophy* 45 (2007): 177–205.

Kim, Yul. "A Change to Thomas Aquinas's Theory of the Will: Solutions to a Long-Standing Problem." *American Catholic Philosophical Quarterly* 82 (2008): 221–36.

King, Peter. "Ockham's Ethical Theory." In *The Cambridge Companion to Ockham,* edited by Paul Vincent Spade, 227–44. Cambridge: Cambridge University Press, 1999.

Koch, Josef. *Kleine Schriften.* 2 vols. Raccolta di Studi e Testi 128. Rome: Edizioni di Storia e Letteratura, 1973.

Künzle, Pius. *Das Verhältnis der Seele zu ihren Potenzen: Problemgeschichtliche Untersuchungen von Augustin bis und mit Thomas von Aquin.* Freiburg: Universitätsverlag Freiburg, 1956.

Labourdette, M.-Michel. "Connaissance practique et savoir moral." *Revue Thomiste* 48 (1948): 142–90.

Langston, Douglas C. *God's Willing Knowledge: The Influence of Scotus' Analysis of Omniscience.* University Park: Pennsylvania State University Press, 1986.

———. "Did Scotus Embrace Anselm's Notion of Freedom?" *Medieval Philosophy and Theology* 5 (1996): 145–59.

———. *Conscience and Other Virtues: From Bonaventure to MacIntyre.* University Park: Pennsylvania University Press, 2001.

Lee, Patrick. "The Relationship between Intellect and Will in Free Choice according to Aquinas and Scotus." *The Thomist* 49 (1985): 322–42.

Lee, Sukjae. "Scotus on the Will: The Rational Power and the Dual Affections." *Vivarium* 36 (1998): 40–54.

Llano Cifuentes, Alejandro. "Aquinas and the Principle of Plenitude." In *Thomas Aquinas and His Legacy,* edited by David Gallagher, 131–48. Studies in Philosophy and the History of Philosophy 28. Washington, D.C.: The Catholic University of America Press, 1994.

Long, Steven. "A Brief Disquisition Regarding the Nature of the Object of the Moral Act according to Thomas Aquinas." *The Thomist* 67 (2003): 45–71.

Lottin, Odon. *Psychologie et morale aux xiie et xiiie siècles.* 6 vols. Louvain: Abbaye du Mont César; Gembloux: Ducolot, 1942–1960.

Luscombe, D. E. *The School of Peter Abelard.* Cambridge Studies in Medieval Life and Thought, Second Series 14. Cambridge: Cambridge University Press, 1969.

MacDonald, Scott. "Synchronic Contingency, Instants of Nature, and Libertarian Freedom: Comments on 'The Background to Scotus's Theory of the Will.'" *The Modern Schoolman* 72 (1995): 169–75.

———. "Aquinas's Libertarian Account of Free Choice." *Revue Internationale de Philosophie* 2 (1998): 309–428.

MacIntosh, J. J. "Aquinas on Necessity." *American Catholic Philosophical Quarterly* 78 (2004): 371–403.

MacIntyre, Alasdair. Review of *The Theory of the Will in Classical Antiquity,* by Albrecht Dihle. *Ancient Philosophy* 6 (1986): 242–45.

Mahoney, Edward P. "Sense, Intellect, and Imagination in Albert, Thomas, and Siger." In *The Cambridge History of Later Medieval Philosophy: From the Rediscovery of Aristotle to the Disintegration of Scholasticism: 1100–1600,* edited by Norman Kretzmann, Anthony Kenny, and Jan Pinborg, 602–22. Cambridge: Cambridge University Press, 1982.

Mahoney, John. *The Making of Moral Theology: A Study in the Roman Catholic Tradition.* Oxford: Clarendon Press, 1987.

———. "Reverberations of the Condemnation of 1277 in Later Medieval and Renaissance Philosophy." In *Nach der Verurteilung von 1277: Philosophie und Tehologie an der Universität von Paris im letzten Viertel des 13. Jahrhunderts,* edited by Jan Aertsen, Kent Emery, and Andreas Speer, 902–30. Miscellanea Mediaevalia 28. Berlin/New York: de Gruyter, 2001.

Mann, William E. "Ethics." In *The Cambridge Companion to Abelard,* edited by Jeffrey Brouwer and Kevin Guilfoy, 279–304. Cambridge: Cambridge University Press, 2004.

Marenbon, John. *The Philosophy of Peter Abelard.* Cambridge: Cambridge University Press, 1997.

Maurer, Armand. "Ockham's Conception of the Unity of a Science." *Medieaeval Studies* 20 (1958): 98–112.

————. "The Unity of a Science: St. Thomas and the Nominalists." In *St. Thomas Aquinas, 1274–1974: Commemorative Studies*, 2 vols., edited by Armand Maurer, 2.269–91. Toronto: Pontifical Institute of Mediaeval Studies, 1974.

————. *The Philosophy of William of Ockham in Light of Its Principles*. Studies and Texts 133. Toronto: Pontifical Institute of Mediaeval Studies, 1999.

McCluskey, Colleen. "Happiness and Freedom in Aquinas's Theory of Action." *Medieval Philosophy and Theology* 9 (2000): 69–90.

————. "The Roots of Ethical Voluntarism." *Vivarium* 39 (2001): 185–208.

————. "Intellective Appetite and the Freedom of Human Action." *The Thomist* 66 (2002): 434–42.

McDonnell, Kevin. "Does Ockham Have a Theory of Natural Law?" *Franciscan Studies* 34 (1974): 383–92.

McGrade, A. S. "Natural Law and Omnipotence." In *The Cambridge Companion to Ockham*, edited by Paul Vincent Spade, 273–301. Cambridge: Cambridge University Press, 1999.

McInerny, Ralph. "The Principles of Natural Law." *American Journal of Jurisprudence* 25 (1980): 1–15.

————. *Aquinas on Human Action: A Theory of Practice*. Washington, D.C.: The Catholic University of America Press, 1992.

————. *Ethica Thomistica*. Rev. ed. Washington, D.C.: The Catholic University of America Press, 1997.

McNicholl, A. J. "The Ultimate End of Venial Sin." *The Thomist* 2 (1940): 373–410.

Millett, Benignus. "Irish Scotists at St. Isidore's College, Rome, in the Seventeenth Century." In *Scotismus decursu saeculorum*, vol. 4 of *De doctrina Ioannis Duns Scoti*, Acta Congressus Scotistici Internationalis 11–17 sept. 1966, Studia Scholastico-Scotistica 4, 365–472. Rome, 1968.

Minges, Parthenius. "Bedeutung von Objekt, Umständen und Zweck für die Sittlichkeit eines Aktes nach Duns Scotus." *Philosophisches Jahrbuch* 19 (1906): 338–47.

————. *Ioannis Dus Scoti doctrina philosophica et theologica*. 2 vols. Ad claras aquas: Collegium S. Bonaventurae, 1930.

Möhle, Hannes. *Ethica als Scientia Practica nach Johannes Duns Scotus: Eine philosophische Grundlegung*. Beiträge zur Geschichte der Philosophie des Mittelalters, n. f. 44. Münster: Aschendorff, 1995.

————. "Scotus's Theory of Natural Law." In *The Cambridge Companion to Scotus*, edited by Thomas Williams, 312–31. Cambridge: Cambridge University Press, 2003.

Morisset, Paul. "Le syllogisme prudentiel." *Laval théologique et philosophique* 19 (1963): 62–92.

————. "Prudence et fin selon saint Thomas." *Sciences ecclésiastiques* 15 (1963): 73–98, 439–58.

Muller, Richard. "The 'Reception of Calvin' in Later Reformed Theology: Concluding Thoughts." *Church History and Religious Culture* 91 (2011): 255–74.

Müller, Sigrid. *Handeln in einer kontingenten Welt: Zu Begriff und Bedeutung der rechten Vernunft (recta ratio) bei Wilhelm von Ockham.* Tübinger Studien zur Theologie und Philosophie 18. Tübingen: Francke, 2000.

Naus, John. *The Nature of the Practical Intellect.* Rome: Libreria Editirice dell'Universita Gregoriana, 1959.

Nisters, Thomas. *Akzidenentien der Praxis: Thomas von Aquins Lehre von dem Umständen menschlichen Handelns.* Freiburg/München: Karl Abler, 1992.

Noone, Timothy B. "Duns Scotus on *Incontinentia.*" In *The Problem of Weakness of Will in Moral Philosophy,* edited by Tobias Hoffmann, Jörn Müller and Matthias Perkams, 285–305. Leuven: Peeters, 2006.

———. "Nature, Freedom, and Will: Sources for Philosophical Reflection." *Proceedings of the American Catholic Philosophical Association* 81 (2008): 1–23.

Noone, Timothy B., and H. Francie Roberts. "John Duns Scotus' Quodlibet: A Brief Study of the Manuscripts and an Edition of Question 16." In *Theological Quodlibeta in the Middle Ages: The Fourteenth Century,* edited by Christopher Schabel, 131–98. Brill's Companions to the Christian Tradition 7. Boston/ Leiden: Brill, 2007.

Normore, Calvin. "Ockham, Self-Motion and the Will." In *Self-Motion: From Aristotle to Newton,* edited by Mary Louise Gill and James G. Lennox. Princeton, N.J.: Princeton University Press, 1994.

———. "John Duns Scotus' Moral Theory." In *The Cambridge Companion to Scotus,* edited by Thomas Williams, 129–60. Cambridge: Cambridge University Press, 2003.

Nussbaum, Martha. *Aristotle's De Motu Animalium.* Princeton, N.J.: Princeton University Press, 1978.

Oberman, Heiko Augustinus. *The Harvest of Medieval Theology: Gabriel Biel and Late Medieval Nominalism.* Cambridge, Mass.: Harvard University Press, 1963.

———. "Duns Scotus, Nominalism, and the Council of Trent." In *John Duns Scotus, 1265–1965,* edited by John K. Ryan and Bernardine M. Bonansea, 311–44. Studies in Philosophy and the History of Philosophy 3. Washington, D.C.: The Catholic University of America Press, 1965.

Osborne, Thomas M. "Faith, Philosophy, and Nominalism in Luther's Defense of the Real Presence." *Journal of the History of Ideas* 64 (2002): 63–82.

———. *Love of God and Love of Self in Thirteenth-Century Ethics.* Notre Dame, Ind.: University of Notre Dame Press, 2005.

———. "William of Ockham as a Divine-Command Theorist." *Religious Studies* 41 (2005): 1–22.

———. "Premotion and Contemporary Philosophy of Religion." *Nova et Vetera,* English Edition, 4 (2006): 607–32.

BIBLIOGRAPHY

———. "Perfect and Imperfect Virtues in Aquinas." *The Thomist* 71 (2007): 39–64.

———. "Rethinking Anscombe on Causation." *American Catholic Philosophical Quarterly* 81 (2007): 89–107.

———. "Augustine and Aquinas on Foreknowledge through Causes." *Nova et Vetera*, English Edition, 6 (2008): 219–32.

———. "The Separation of the Interior and Exterior Acts in Scotus and Ockham." *Mediaeval Studies* 69 (2008): 111–39.

———. "The Threefold Referral of Acts to the Ultimate End in Thomas Aquinas and His Commentators." *Angelicum* 85 (2008): 715–36.

———. "Thomas and Scotus on Prudence without All the Major Virtues: Imperfect or Merely Partial?" *The Thomist* 74 (2010): 1–24.

———. "Unbelief and Sin in Thomas Aquinas and the Thomistic Tradition." *Nova et Vetera*, English Edition, 8 (2010): 613–26.

———. "Thomas Aquinas and John Duns Scotus on Individual Acts and the Ultimate End." In *Philosophy and Theology in the Long Middle Ages: A Tribute to Stephen F. Brown*, edited by Kent Emery Jr., Russell L. Friedman, and Andreas Speer, 351–74. Studien und Texte zur Geistesgeschichte des Mittelalters. Leiden: Brill, 2011.

———. "William of Ockham on the Freedom of the Will and Happiness." *American Catholic Philosophical Quarterly* 86 (2012): 435–56.

Pasnau, Robert. *Thomas Aquinas on Human Nature: A Philosophical Study of Summa theologiae Ia 75–89*. Cambridge: Cambridge University Press, 2002.

Pernoud, Mary Ann. "The Theory of *Potentia Dei* according to Aquinas, Scotus and Ockham." *Antonianum* 47 (1972): 69–95.

Pesch, Otto Hermann. *Theologie der Rechtfertigung bei Martin Luther und Thomas von Aquin*. Mainz: Matthias-Grünewald, 1967.

Pilsner, Joseph. *The Specification of Human Actions in St. Thomas Aquinas*. Oxford: Oxford University Press, 2006.

Pinckaers, Servais. "La structure de l'acte humaine suivant saint Thomas." *Revue Thomiste* 55 (1955): 393–412.

———. "Le rôle de la fin dans l'action morale selon saint Thomas." *Revue des sciences philosophiques et théologiques* 45 (1961): 393–412.

———. *Ce qu'on ne peut jamais faire: La question des actes intrinsèquement mauvais: Historie et discussion. Étude d'éthique Chrétienne* 19. Fribourg: Éditions universitaires; Paris: Cerf, 1986.

———. *The Sources of Christian Ethics*, translated by Mary Thomas Noble. Washington, D.C.: The Catholic University of America Press, 1995.

Potts, Timothy C. "Conscience." In *The Cambridge History of Later Medieval Philosophy: From the Rediscovery of Aristotle to the Disintegration of Scholas-*

ticism: 1100–1600, edited by Norman Kretzmann, Anthony Kenny, and Jan Pinborg, 687–704. Cambridge: Cambridge University Press, 1982.

Prentice, Robert. "The Degree and Mode of Liberty in the Beatitude of the Blessed." In *Deus et Homo ad mentem I. Duns Scoti. Acta tertii Congressus Scotistici internationalis Vindebonae 28 sept.–2 oct. 1970*, 327–42. Studia scholastico Scotistica 5. Rome: Societas internationalis Scotistica, 1972.

Putallaz, François-Xavier. *Insolente liberté: Controverses et condamnations au xiiiᵉ siècle*. Fribourg: Éditions Universitaires; Paris: Cerf, 1995.

Ramirez, Iacobus. *De hominis beatitudine*. 5 vols. Madrid, 1942.

———. *De actibus humanis: In I-II Summa Theologiae Divi Thomae Expositio (QQ. VI–XXI)*. Edicion de las Obras Compeltas de Santiago Ramirez 4. Edited by Victorino Rodriguez. Madrid: Instituto de Filosofia "Luis Vives," 1972.

———. *De vitiis et peccatis: In I-II Summae Theologiae Divi Thomae Expositio (QQ. LXXI–LXXXV)*. 2 vols. Edicion de las Obras Completas de Santiago Ramirez 8. Edited by Victor Rodriguez. Madrid: Instiuto de Filosofia "Luis Vives," 1990.

Rhonheimer, Martin. "Intentional Actions and the Meaning of Object: A Reply to Richard McCormick." *The Thomist* 59 (1995): 279–311.

———. "The Perspective of the Acting Person and the Nature of Practical Reason: The 'Object of the Human Act' in the Thomistic Anthropology of Action." *Nova et Vetera*, English Edition, 6 (2008): 63–112.

Rist, John. *Augustine: Ancient Thought Baptized*. Cambridge: Cambridge University Press, 1994.

Robert, Aurélien. "L'explication causale selon Guillaume d'Ockham." *Quaestio* 2 (2002): 241–65.

Roberts, D. W., Jr. "A Note on the Classical Origin of 'Circumstances' in the Medieval Confessional." *Studies in Philology* 43 (1946): 6–14.

Schmutz, Jakob. "L'héritage des subtils cartographie du Scotisme du l'Âge Classique." *Les Études philosophiques* 1 (2002): 51–81.

———. "Du péché de l'ange à la liberté d'indifférance: Les sources angélogiques de l'anthropologie moderne." *Le Études philosophiques* 2 (2002): 179–86

———. "Le petit scotisme du Grand Siècle: Étude doctrinale et documentaire sur la philosophie au Grand Couvent des Cordeliers de Paris, 1517–1771." *Quaestio* 8 (2008): 365–472.

Seel, G. "Der antike modallogische Determinismus und Ockhams Kritik an Duns Scotus." In *L'homme et son univers au Moyen Âge*, Actes du VIIe Congrès international de philosophie médiévale, 20 août–4 septembre, edited by Charles Wenin, 2.510–20. Louvain-la neuve: Editions de l'Institut supérieur de philosophie, 1996.

Sherwin, Michael. *By Knowledge and by Love: Charity and Knowledge in the*

Moral Theology of St. Thomas Aquinas. Washington, D.C.: The Catholic University of America Press, 2005.

Stadter, Ernst. *Psychologie und Metaphysick der menschlichen Freiheit: Die ideengeschichtliche zwischen Bonaventura und Duns Scotus.* München: Schoningh, 1971.

Stump, Eleanore. "Aquinas's Account of Freedom: Intellect and Will." *The Monist* 80 (1997): 576–97.

———. *Aquinas.* London/New York: Routledge, 2003.

Teske, Roland. "The Will as King over the Powers of the Soul: Uses and Sources of an Image in the Thirteenth Century." *Vivarium* 32 (1994): 62–71.

te Velde, Rude A. "*Natura in se ipsa recurva est*: Duns Scotus and Aquinas on the Relationship between Nature and Will." In *John Duns Scotus: Renewal of Philosophy,* edited by S. P. Bos, 155–69. Acts of the Third Symposium Organized by the Dutch Society for Medieval Philosophy Medium Aevum, May 23 and 24, 1996. Elementa, Schriften zur Philosophie und ihrer Problemgeschichte 72. Amsterdam: Rodopi, 1998.

Torrell, Jean Pierre. *Initiation à saint Thomas d'Aquin: Sa personne et son oeuvre.* Fribourg: Éditions Universitaire de Fribourg, 1993.

Trottmann, Christian. "La vision béatifique dans la seconde école franciscaine: De Mathieu d'Aquasparta à Duns Scot." *Collectanea Franciscana* 64 (1994): 121–80.

Urban, Linwood. "William of Ockham's Theological Ethics." *Franciscan Studies* 33 (1973): 310–50.

van Steenberghen, Fernand. *Aristotle in the West: The Origins of Latin Aristotelianism.* Translated by Leonard Johnston. Louvain: Nauwelaerts, 1955.

Vazquez, Isaac. "La Enseña del Escotismo en España." In *Scotismus decursu saeculorum,* vol. 4 of *De doctrina Ioannis Duns Scoti,* Acta Congressus Scotistici Internationalis 11–17 sept. 1966, Studia Scholastico-Scotistica 4, 191–220. Rome, 1968.

Vignaux, Paul. *Justification et prédestination au xive siècle.* Paris: Leroux, 1934.

Vos, Antonie. *The Philosophy of John Duns Scotus.* Edinburgh: Edinburgh University Press, 2006.

Wallace, William A. *The Role of Demonstration in Moral Science: A Study of Methodology in St. Thomas Aquinas.* Washington, D.C.: The Thomist Press, 1962.

Wawrykow, Joseph P. *God's Grace and Human Action: "Merit" in the Theology of Thomas Aquinas.* Notre Dame, Ind.: University of Notre Dame Press, 1995.

Westberg, Daniel. "Did Aquinas Change His Mind about the Will?" *The Thomist* 58 (1994): 41–60.

———. *Right Practical Reason: Aristotle, Action and Prudence in Aquinas.* Oxford: Clarendon Press, 1994.

White, Graham. *Luther as Nominalist: A Study of the Logical Methods Used in Martin Luther's Disputations in the Light of Their Medieval Background*. Helsinki: Luther-Agricola-Society, 1994.

White, Kevin. "Aquinas on Purpose." *Proceedings of the American Catholic Philosophical Association* 81 (2008):133–47

Wieland, Georg. *Ethica-Scientia Practica: Die Anfänge der philosophischen Ethik im 13. Jahrhundert*. Beiträge zur Geschichte der Philosophie un Theologie des Mittelalters, n. f. 21. Münster: Aschendorff, 1981.

———. "Happiness (IaIIae, qq. 1–5)." Translated by Grant Kaplan. In *The Ethics of Aquinas*, edited by Stephen Pope, 57–68. Washington, D.C.: Georgetown University Press, 2002.

Williams, Thomas. "How Scotus Separates Morality from Happiness." *American Catholic Philosophical Quarterly* 69 (1995): 425–46.

———. "The Libertarian Foundations of Scotus's Moral Philosophy." *The Thomist* 62 (1998): 193–215.

———. "The Unmitigated Scotus." *Archiv für Geschichte der Philosophie* 80 (1998): 162–81.

———. "A Most Methodical Lover? On Scotus's Arbitrary Creator." *Journal of the History of Philosophy* 38 (2000): 169–202.

———. "From Metaethics to Action Theory." In *The Cambridge Companion to Scotus*, edited by Thomas Williams, 332–51. Cambridge: Cambridge University Press, 1999.

Wippel, John F. *The Metaphysical Thought of Godfrey of Fontaines: A Study in Late Thirteenth-Century Philosophy*. Washington, D.C.: The Catholic University of America Press, 1981.

———. *The Metaphysical Thought of Thomas Aquinas: From Finite Being to Uncreated Being*. Monographs of the Society for Medieval and Renaissance Philosophy 1. Washington, D.C.: The Catholic University of America Press, 2000.

Wolter, Allan B. *The Philosophical Theology of John Duns Scotus*. Edited by Marilyn McCord Adams. Ithaca, N.Y.: Cornell University Press, 1990.

———. "Reflections on the Life and Work of Scotus." *American Catholic Philosophical Quarterly* 67 (1993): 1–36.

———. "The Unshredded Scotus: A Response to Thomas Williams." *American Catholic Philosophical Quarterly* 77 (2003): 315–56.

Wood, Rega. "Göttliches Gebot und Gutheit Gottes nach Wilhelm von Ockham." *Philosophisches Jahrbuch* 101 (1994): 38–54.

———. *Ockham on the Virtues*. West Lafayette, Ind.: Purdue University Press, 1997.

———. "Ockham's Repudiation of Pelagianism." In *The Cambridge Companion to Ockham*, edited by Paul Vincent Spade, 350–73. Cambridge: Cambridge University Press, 1999.

Index

Abelard, Peter, 151–52
Abraham, 73, 85, 172
active and passive potency, 22–23, 50
adultery, xviii, 73, 84, 98–99, 153–54,
    156–57, 159, 161–62, 164, 172, 173, 180,
    183, 185, 188–89
affectio commodi and *affectio iustitiae*,
    24–26, 45–46, 57, 59, 174
Albert the Great, xiii, 116, 153
angels, 25–26, 37–40, 44, 56–57, 58, 128,
    135
Anselm of Canterbury, 24–25, 37, 39, 45, 56
Aristotle, 21–23, 40, 42, 48, 75, 81, 89, 167,
    217, 223, 228; *Nicomachean Ethics*, xiii,
    xix, 62–64, 77, 91, 96, 98–100, 106,
    110–13, 114, 116–30, 132, 134–35, 150,
    161, 195–96
Arts Faculty, xix, 20
attrition and contrition, 171
Augustine of Hippo, xvii–xviii, 34, 109–11,
    115–16, 131, 222–23
Aureoli, Peter, 213, 217

beatitude. *See* happiness
beatific vision, 10–13, 27–29, 34–35, 41,
    54–55, 174, 176
Biel, Gabriel, xv
Boethius, 149
Bonaventure, 120–21, 153–54, 192
boulesis, 110–12, 118–20, 134
Brock, Stephen L., 130–31
Byers, Sarah, 110–11

Cajetan, Thomas de Vio, 15
certitude in moral reasoning, 102,
    127–28

charity, xxiii, 159, 168, 171, 174, 176, 186,
    200–18, 226–8
choice *(electio)*, 10, 68–69, 72, 102, 107–8,
    115, 120–21, 122–30, 134–40, 141–48;
    and *prohairesis*, 110–12, 135–36
Cicero, 149, 165
circumstances: 149–84, 187–88; circum-
    stance *"circa quid,"* 155; circumstance
    "cur" (why, of the end), 152, 161–2, 169–
    70, 178–79, 194, 198, 206; "prohibited"
    and "not prohibited" as circumstances,
    172–73; right reason as a circumstance,
    178–79; evil circumstances, 98, 160,
    168–73, 181–82
cithara player, 75, 89–90, 102
command *(imperium)*, 92–93, 102, 104–5,
    137–39, 144; commanded acts, 153,
    164–65, 187–88, 190–91, 199–200; rela-
    tion to *praeceptum* of prudence, 72;
    stage of act, 114–16, 121, 130–32, 187
condemnation of *1277*, xix, 20, 59
conditional and efficacious willing, 119,
    133–36, 139–40. *See also velleitas*
connatural goods, 204
conscience, 71–73, 87, 104, 123, 129
consent, xxi, 114–15, 121, 129–30, 132, 136,
    144–45
continence and incontinence, 72, 77–78,
    179–80
contingency, 2–3, 18–19, 39, 43–44, 45,
    49–53, 55, 65, 69, 74–75, 80, 81–82, 97,
    106; contingently virtuous, 179–84,
    198; diachronic and synchronic, xxi,
    29–31; and merit, 201, 215–17, 226. *See
    also* necessity
Correctorium fratris Thomae, 20–21, 23

Decalogue, 173. *See also* divine commands
divine commands, 74, 84–85, 99, 171–73,
    180–81, 183, 215, 220
deliberatio (thinking over), 125–128,
    142–143
deliberation (*consilium*), xxii–xxiii,
    72, 78–79, 109–114, 132, 141–47; and
    choice (*electio*), 88–90, 102, 121–30,
    136, 139–40, 142–43; and the practical
    syllogism, 74–75, 78, 88–90, 124, 129,
    135–36, 140, 143, 145–47; and "think-
    ing over" (*deliberatio*), 125–28, 142–43;
    under the will's control, 15, 63
determinism, 19–20, 30–31, 36, 59
dictamen, 141–42, 146–47
dictative knowledge, 100–02, 105, 179
Dominicans, xv, 20–21
Donagan, Alan, 116, 130

efficient cause of action, xxii, 2, 12–8,
    32–45, 50–51, 56–57, 108, 121, 146–47,
    167, 223, 227–28.
end: *finis operis* and *finis operantis*; 152,
    162, 164; and means (*ea quae sunt ad fi-
    nem*), 8–10, 15, 37, 62, 69, 75, 78–79, 87,
    89, 97, 109, 112–14, 188–21, 123–31, 134,
    137–44, 146, 163–64, 187, 225; proxi-
    mate end and remote end, 160–66,
    182–83, 206; proximate end as object,
    160–66, 187; ultimate end, 8, 28, 72,
    119, 123–24, 136, 144, 202–10. *See also*
    circumstances; happiness
evil and freedom, 10, 12, 37–38, 52–53
evil objects, 48–49, 59, 133–34, 180–81
execution, 72, 113, 116, 130–32, 138–39,
    141, 143–44, 163, 188

faith, 55, 70, 159–60, 165, 174, 176, 211
final cause of action, xxii, 13–17, 40–42,
    91–92
fornication, xviii, 27, 62, 73–74, 76–78, 123,
    134–35, 140, 152, 164
formal and material object, 158–60, 184
formal cause of action, xxiv, 14–17, 146
formality / nature of the good (*ratio boni*),
    8, 10, 53, 76, 123, 133

Fourth Lateran Council, 150
Franciscans, xviii–xix, 19–23, 32. 44–45,
    169, 190, 224
free choice (*liberum arbitrium*), 8, 13,
    16–18, 26, 34, 56–58, 110–11, 117, 137,
    145–48

Gauthier, René Antonin, 116, 130
Godfrey of Fontaines, 21, 32, 36, 39–40,
    gnome, 72, 115
good, threefold, upright (*honestum*), 52,
    97, 119; pleasant (*delectabile*), 52, 62,
    76–77, 119, 179–80, 196–97, 226; useful
    (*utile*), 9, 52, 119
good in common or universal good, 8, 13,
    19, 27–28, 118
good in itself and good for the agent, 26
goods, particular, 7–12, 17, 19, 27, 38, 103,
    125, 224
grace and charity, 206–207, 211–12, 214–15
grace, created, 201, 204, 206, 211
grace, sanctifying (*gratia gratum faciens*),
    203, 206–08, 211
grace, uncreated (Holy Spirit), 203
Gregory of Nyssa, 115

habit, 4–5, 78, 86, 94, 102, 110, 112, 164,
    180, 195, 197, 202, 206–208, 211–215
habitual reasoning and habits of knowl-
    edge, 67, 78, 84, 86, 90–91, 104
happiness, xxi–xxiv, 8–13, 27–28, 37–38,
    45, 53–54, 56, 59, 118, 124–25, 128, 133,
    146, 176, 206, 222, 224–225. *See also*
    beatific vision
Henry of Ghent, xviii–xix, 32–35, 39–43,
    56, 91
hope, 159–60, 174, 176, 211

ignorance, 15, 88–89, 134–35, 158
image (sense) or phantasm, 19, 36, 39–40
instant of nature, 30, 40
instant of time, 29–30, 143
intention, xxi, 67, 114, 117–23, 125, 130, 132,
    137–39, 144, 145, 151–52, 163, 178, 188,
    191, 200, 221, 228
Isaac, 73–74, 85, 172

Jensen, Steven, 74
John Damascene, xviii, 115, 222
judgment of choice (*iudicium electionis*), xxii, 72, 103, 123–25, 129, 132, 145–48, 227

liberty of exercise and liberty of specification, 10–17, 37, 58, 65, 68, 108, 147
love, 34–35, 50, 98, 143, 199,
love of God, 13, 34–35, 85, 116, 136–37, 165, 168, 204, 208, 213; love of God and love of neighbor, 70, 136–37; precept to love God, 70, 74, 106, 143, 171, 215
Lychetus, Francis, 196
lying, xviii, 172

material cause, 2–3, 167
matter of act, xxiii, 131, 145–46, 150–51, 155–56, 165, 167, 182–84, 219, 227; matter *circa quam*, 155–56, 163–64
matter of virtue, 76, 207
Maximus the Confessor, 115
merit, 46, 88–89, 98, 126, 134, 136, 140, 142–43, 172, 176, 200–218, 224–28; condign (*de condigno*) and congruous (*de congruo*), 203, 214; forensic account of, xxiii, 216–217, 220
moral evil, 193–200, 217
moral science, 61, 80, 91, 98–100, 216; and prudence, xxii, 79, 83, 86–88, 90, 94–97, 102–6
moral virtues, 72, 181, 193–97, 221, 223. *See also* habit
mortal sin, 53, 59, 128, 190, 211
murder, xviii, 65, 73–74, 84–85, 157, 171–72, 180, 186

natural inclination, 75, 26, 69, 84, 86, 106–7; and will, xxi, xxv, 10, 13, 18–19, 23–28, 39, 45, 48, 52–53, 59, 107, 117–19, 146, 224–26
natural goodness, 185–92
natural law, 69–71, 73, 84–85, 94, 173, 222, 224
natural species of act, 153–54, 163, 172–73, 177–81, 184, 185, 220, 227–28

natural vs. supernatural, 24, 28, 49, 168, 185–86, 200–218, 220
necessity and freedom, 10–11, 28, 30–31, 49, 54, 59, 90, 124, 195
necessity of the end, 54, 59
necessity of the present, 31
Nemesius, 114–15, 122, 129, 150
nolle, 27, 53, 133–34
Nominalism, xiii, xv–xvi

object of act. *See* formal and material object
Old Law (Mosaic Law), 70, 208
omission, 158
ostensive knowledge, 100–102, 105

Pasnau, Robert, 16–7
passion, xvii, xxv, 4–5, 17, 19, 77, 112, 135, 194–95
Peter Lombard, 152
practical knowledge, degrees of, xxii, 66–67, 79, 87, 103–04, 106, 222
pactical syllogism, xxii, 61–63, 67–69, 71–75, 78–81, 88–90, 103, 106–8, 122–24, 129, 135–36, 139–40, 143, 145–47
praxis, 81–83, 88, 91–93, 101, 140–41, 144
precepts, affirmative and negative, 74–75
precepts, exceptionless, 74–75, 100. *See also* evil objects
principle of parsimony, 47, 49
principles, 70–71, 83–86, 96–100, 107, 117, 171, 225
propositio magistralis, 20
prudence, xxii, 63–64, 71–72, 75–76, 78–79, 83–84, 86–88, 90, 94–97, 100–107, 179

referral of acts, 205–206, 210–211
responsibility, 111, 135–36, 158,
revelation, xvii, 70, 98, 100, 173, 176, 216–217. *See also* faith
right reason (*recta ratio*), 46, 81, 87, 92–93, 97, 102, 169–70, 178–81, 183–85, 189–92, 196, 198–99, 219

INDEX

Scotism, xiv–xv, 15, 228

self-motion, 13, 17–19, 23, 52, 59, 163

sensation, 3–7, 19, 23, 36, 39–40, 46–50, 53–54, 57, 152, 159

sensitive appetite, 3–4, 17, 23, 36, 46–50, 55

sententia, 115, 123, 141, 146–47

simplex velle, xxii, 110, 116–21, 130, 132, 145, 224. *See also boulesis*

sine qua non causality, 32–35, 39–43, 56,

skill (*techne, ars*), 63–64, 70, 75–76, 83, 86, 89, 100–102, 104–6

Stoicism, 110–13, 115–16, 131, 144

synderesis, 71, 84, 122–23, 129

synesis, 72

theological virtues, 174, 176, 184, 211; acquired, 176. *See also* faith; hope; charity

theft, 73, 98–99, 152, 155–57, 160–64, 170, 172–73, 187–88, 193

thinking over. *See deliberatio*

use (*uti*), 131, 136–37, 144, 187

velleitas, 119

venial sin, 205–06, 211

virtual intention, 138

virtual referral. *See* referral of acts

voluntarism, 13, 58–59, 223–224

voluntary and involuntary, 3, 75, 113, 150, 158, 189, 219–20

Westberg, Daniel, 79, 117, 130–31

William de la Mare. *See Correctorium fratris Thomae*

William of Alnwick, xx

Human Action in Thomas Aquinas, John Duns Scotus & William of Ockham was designed in Meta Serif with Copperplate Gothic display and typeset by Kachergis Book Design of Pittsboro, North Carolina. It was printed on 60-pound Sebago Cream and bound by Maple Press of York, Pennsylvania.

CPSIA information can be obtained at www.ICGtesting.com
Printed in the USA
BVOW06s1442280116

434005BV00005B/10/P